MARGINS OF DESIRE

MANCHESTER
1824

Manchester University Press

'distinctively one's own and undistinctively like everyone else's'
Golders Green (Hendon and Finchley): A place of delightful prospects (1908)

Margins of desire

THE SUBURBS
IN FICTION AND CULTURE
1880–1925

Lynne Hapgood

Manchester University Press
Manchester and New York

distributed exclusively in the USA by Palgrave

Published by Manchester University Press
Oxford Road, Manchester M13 9NR, UK
and Room 400, 175 Fifth Avenue, New York, NY 10010, USA
www.manchesteruniversitypress.co.uk

Distributed exclusively in the USA by
Palgrave, 175 Fifth Avenue, New York, NY 10010, USA

Distributed exclusively in Canada by
UBC Press, University of British Columbia, 2029 West Mall,
Vancouver, BC, Canada V6T 1Z2

British Library Cataloguing-in-Publication Data
A catalogue record for this book is available from the British Library

Library of Congress Cataloging-in-Publication Data applied for

ISBN 0 7190 5970 4 *hardback*
EAN 978 0 7190 5970 4

First published 2005

13 12 11 10 09 08 07 06 05   10 9 8 7 6 5 4 3 2 1

FOR SAM AND JACOB

Typeset in Goudy Old Style with Della Robbia display
by Graphicraft Limited, Hong Kong
Printed in Great Britain
by CPI, Bath

CONTENTS

ILLUSTRATIONS

ACKNOWLEDGMENTS

I WANT to thank John Lucas, whose early interest in my ideas about the literary suburb encouraged me to pursue my research, and to give special thanks to John Stokes and Michael Bell for the personal and intellectual support and encouragement they have consistently given me over a number of years. I am grateful to Michael Luck for introducing me to the work of his grandmother, Mary Hamilton. The suburbs are a topic that cuts across disciplines and personal histories: it was an unexpected bonus to find that American colleagues were interested in the idea of the suburban in British fiction. Thanks to Nancy L. Paxton and Robert L. Caserio, in particular, for comments on my discussion of John Galsworthy, and again to Nancy, whose academic integrity has been an inspiring model for me. I also want to thank my colleagues at The Nottingham Trent University for supporting my request for study leave to work on this project, and Sharon Ouditt and Peter Smith who assumed my responsibilities during my period of leave. The final stages of archival research were completed with the welcome help of a research leave award from the Arts and Humanities Research Board. Sam Griffiths has generously engaged with my ideas in many challenging conversations and given me unfailing support throughout this project. I cannot thank him enough.

Earlier versions of material in chapters 2 and 8 appeared under the following titles: 'The Unwritten Suburb: Defining spaces in John Galsworthy's *The Man of Property*' in Lynne Hapgood and Nancy L. Paxton (eds), *Outside Modernism: In pursuit of the British novel 1900–1930* (Basingstoke: Macmillan, 2000), and 'Literature of the Suburbs: Versions of repression in the novels of A. Conan Doyle, W. Pett Ridge and George Gissing', *Journal of Victorian Culture* (Autumn 2000), 287–322. For permission to reproduce the revised material here, I would like to thank Palgrave Macmillan and Edinburgh University Press.

INTRODUCTION
The defining suburb

'THEY suggest so much they mean nothing at all', Edward Thomas wrote about the streets and houses of a south London suburb in 1906. He continued:

> The eye strains at them as at Russian characters which are known to stand for something beautiful or terrible; but there is no translator: it sees a thousand things that at the moment of seeing are significant, but they obliterate one another. They propose themselves as a problem to the mind.[1]

There are a number of interesting elements in Thomas's description of his bafflement in the face of what was perceived at the beginning of the twentieth century as a remarkable social phenomenon – the spread of the London suburbs.[2] He remarks on the strange contrast between the human-scale functionality of the suburb and its suggestion of a hinterland of inaccessible meanings, and he evokes the disturbing effect of the apparently knowable abdicating responsibility for significance. The meaning of the suburb, he implies, is beyond an individual's apprehension and can only be recuperated through a synthesis of a multiplicity of perceptions.

The unfolding of this strange phenomenon was first recognised in the mid-nineteenth century, although it was not until the 1880s and 1890s that it became a positive social fact: an entirely new kind of society was evolving on the very doorstep of Britain's capital city. During these years, and until the outbreak of war in 1914, London's margins continued to be redrawn as new communities colonised

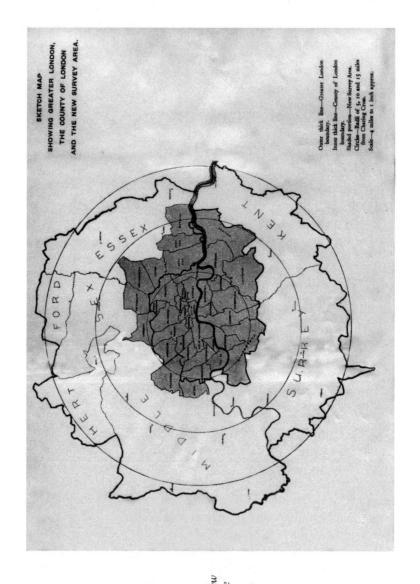

SKETCH MAP

SHOWING GREATER LONDON,
THE COUNTY OF LONDON
AND THE NEW SURVEY AREA.

Outer thick line—Greater London
  boundary.
Inner thick line—County of London
  boundary.
Shaded portion—New Survey Area.
Circles—Radii of 5, 10 and 15 miles
  from Charing Cross.
Scale—4 miles to 1 inch approx.

HERTFORD

ESSEX

MIDDLESEX

KENT

SURREY

1

'the spreading of a
great coral reef'
Diagram from *The New
Survey of London Life
and Labour, vol. 1:
Forty years of change*

them, redesignating what was marginal as integral. Social commentators, so recently exercised by the struggle to define the horrors
of inner city conditions, were faced with the task of defining the
enigma of a new kind of landscape which seemed single-mindedly
intent on evading definition. Lists of figures and tables are some help
in conveying to us today the scale of the changes that threatened
to overwhelm people's capacity to understand, but it is still easy to
underestimate the speed and scale of this expansion, and its impact
on the public imagination.[3] In 1889 the *Builder* was prompted to ask,
'who could say when that extension [to London] was going to end?'[4]
In 1900 *Building News* called it 'one of the social revolutions of the
time'; the sense of its organic inevitability is captured by Patrick
Geddes's comparison of London's suburbs in 1915 to 'the spreadings
of a great coral reef'.[5]

My argument is grounded in the history of the suburbs at the
turn of the twentieth century, but my intention is to explore the
ways in which the literary suburb was constructed in response to
what was perceived as a fundamental and irreversible social change.
My focus is those novels and commentaries which were concerned
directly with the suburbs and suburban life, or with the social and
cultural agendas which were pushed to the forefront of public consciousness by suburban expansion. This book examines how the suburbs generated new themes and genres in the contemporary novel as
the triple identity that they came to assume – a potent fusion of
material reality, individual dreams and social futures – opened up
new literary territories. In this body of work we can see social categories being refashioned in relative rather than absolute terms,
and social formations being re-imagined in a suburban landscape.
Suddenly, it seemed, the poor and the slums had lost their charm
as literary subject matter as authors turned their attention to the
suburbs and to the growing audience of readers who lived in them.
The hopes and fears that played around the idea of a suburb simultaneously displaced both the long cherished but jaded potency of the
rural idyll and the dangerous dynamic of urban modernity in the
public imagination. The subsequent updating of literary landscapes
was to prove nothing less than a cultural revolution. Yet the striking
late nineteenth-century shift of literary location from city to suburb,
and its implications for the understanding of profound changes in
the late Victorian and Edwardian world-view, have gone almost
unnoticed or, at least, almost without comment.[6] How could the

suburbs, that familiar symbol of conformity and uniformity, be at the heart of such a revolution? I hope to reveal that the suburban trick, whether in a social or a literary context, was to look ordinary and to be extraordinary.

Edward Thomas's account of the suburbs is emblematic of the literary argument I make in this book. It recognises the resistance of the suburbs to a totalising definition, and the location of their meaning in a community of many minds. It makes explicit the relationship of the actual suburbs (the undiminished visual impact of the concrete) with the possibility of a suburban imaginary (an apprehension of their meaning that can breach the contingencies of reality). In so doing, he proposes the suburb as a nexus of diverse perceptions, of a series of 'small' narratives that share the burden of meaning and combine to produce the potential for interpretation. My argument uses this idea of the suburb as an entry point to a wide range of literary texts and their readership; to an exploration of the new themes and forms that the suburbs inspired and, importantly, to their provision of an alternative context for understanding late Victorian and early twentieth-century responses to the enigmas of the modern.

Important to an understanding of the distinctive nature of suburban fictions is a recognition of the subversively egalitarian nature of the suburban project. For the first time in the history of English society, land was being redistributed for the benefit of the majority. The small plots and the recurring patterns of house and garden transformed the use of space so that 'where one large house existed ten or a hundred or more have been built, absorbing the acres of gardens and private park lands'.[7] For the most part, of course, this was undertaken reluctantly and, in a political sense, haphazardly, and the process was usually driven by market forces. Even so, London's environs saw a wave of suburban expansion from 1890 to the first years of the First World War, which began to reflect the value of the individual, rather than the anonymity of the masses, as the overcrowding of the inner city had done. By offering 'a piece of property and a piece of land that was distinctively one's own and undistinctively like everyone else's', the suburbs manifested outward integration and inward subversion.[8] This process of individuation became a formidable barrier to the vertical strategies of class hierarchy, social engineering and political grouping. Thomas's perception of the suburbs helps us to understand how suburban narratives followed a centrifugal trajectory, spreading outwards like the suburbs themselves, drawing on the plenitude and energy of new social units for subject matter and audiences.

The way in which the horizontal expansion of the suburbs challenged vertical social hierarchies is mirrored in the challenge an expanding suburban culture posed to established literary values. My approach to the fiction of the suburbs is, therefore, necessarily one of critical egalitarianism. It cuts across familiar critical boundaries to bring texts and writers into unfamiliar associations, helping to create a more inclusive picture of literary production in the period. Canonical and non-canonical texts, forgotten, neglected and well known; novels and magazine stories; formally realised narratives and informal memoirs; utopias and dystopias; high seriousness and high humour; realism and romance, and more, are all found in the suburban medley. The majority of the texts I discuss, although very popular when they were published, are now long out of print or exist in a critical limbo. In addition, as I have already indicated, the fictional suburb, its credit possibly undermined by a modern association with mediocrity, has attracted little critical attention. My aim is to reverse that neglect by giving more just consideration to the eclectic texts which contributed to a realist and conceptual construction of the suburb.

My argument, then, suggests a framework for identifying what constitutes a suburban fiction. Previously, in their scale and diversity these newly defined suburban writings have evaded all but the most general of critical taxonomies, so grouping them together requires a critical repositioning. However, the fact that we cannot expect a single mode or hierarchy of understanding (no 'translator', in Thomas's terms, of the questions raised by the existence of the suburbs) poses a problem of evaluation. What I hope to establish is a critical perspective that makes possible a claim for the intrinsic individual value and interest of suburban fictions but, equally, for the validity of evaluating them as a coherent body of work. While individual novels retain their distinctive political, moral and formal responses to the suburbs, they conjoin productively to imply an overarching suburban narrative. The connections of meaning across texts are produced within the triangulated geography of the suburban imaginary. Each text is positioned on a map, which charts, with varying emphases, the literal topography of the new suburbs (realistic location), their political, social and cultural associations (fictional themes) and their relation to individual, private desire (multiple narratives). This is not intended to convey a symbolic relationship. It is a point worth emphasising, that suburban texts are synthetic rather than symbolic. What brings these texts together as a body of fiction is a series of overlaps between locations, suburban types and shared material. More importantly, they share a recognition of, and an engagement with, the version of the modern that the suburbs embodied. The material suburb always insists on its ordinariness: its mysteries lie in the possibility that it offers to novelists, and suburb-dwellers, for self-invention and for new futures.

The realisation of this geography in fiction collapses the familiar genres of realism, utopianism and romance into one another and reconstitutes them as a distinctive suburban literary mode of genre hybridity. Its readiness to play with literary form is one indicator of the perceived light-hearted or casualness of the suburban mode. Sandra Kemp's use of the phrase 'generic promiscuity' seems a doubtful way of capturing this experimental and responsive spirit.[9] P. J. Keating more helpfully notes a 'relaxation of mood' and a 'more light-hearted portrayal of working-class life' at the turn of the century.[10] Writers who focused on suburban realities and social critique, such as George Gissing, Arnold Bennett, Shan Bullock, H. G. Wells and others, continued to work within the formal expectations of the realist novel. Others reworked realism, assuming the material world as a context rather than striving to represent it. In these fictions, realism is merely a fictional shorthand used to suggest the background against which the narrative takes place. In yet another version of the suburban novel, the present that is desired completely usurps the real present on which it is predicated. A similarly cavalier approach characterises the treatment of utopia. William Morris's *News from Nowhere* (1891), which draws on the literary heritage of utopianism, helps us to appreciate how the utopian idea is reworked in other suburban fictions. In Jerome K. Jerome's *Three Men in a Boat* (1889), the utopian future is reclaimed for the immediate present and the imagined 'nowhere' is located in the imagined 'here'; while in the suburban fictions of Keble Howard and Arthur Conan Doyle, utopia is domesticated, reducing its visionary scale from whole societies to particular roads, homes and families. Utopianism in Edward Thomas's and Richard Jefferies' essays, and in E. M. Forster's short stories and early novels, seems divorced from social realities altogether, internalised and privatised in psychological, sexual and/or spiritual landscapes.

Romance is the most pervasive element of the suburban literary mode. Romantic fiction was the staple of popular novels and stories, and the most popular choice at libraries, bookshops and magazine stands. By the turn of the twentieth century, romantic fiction, particularly for women, had become identified with suburban culture. Romance served the suburban project in two ways: in its familiar role as a source of pleasure and relaxation but also, more distinctively, as a means of investing the most ordinary everyday objects and experiences – streets, houses, shopping, meals, outings, flirtations, even the exchanging of library books – with significance. The combination of a romance narrative and a realist framework had been a familiar element in the social problem novel from Elizabeth Gaskell's *Mary Barton* (1848) to late nineteenth-century slum novels such as Walter Besant's *The Children of Gibeon* (1886). What happened in suburban fiction was rather different. Here we see a deliberate fusion of romance and realism; the realistic is the site where romance is embedded. The leisure and daily activities of suburban life have the potential to offer glimpses of a present utopia.[11] These are the epiphanies of suburb-dwellers, as romance and realism negotiate to find a momentary synonymity in the experience of the individual. As Cicely, in William Pett Ridge's novel *A Clever Wife*, declares, 'I had no idea that the suburbs could contain joy.'[12]

The fictional matter of the narratives is brought within the scope of the suburban imaginary by its insistence on those social concerns which were identified most closely with suburban life, and over which suburban growth was thought to exercise most influence. The state of suburbanism was an in-betweenness of country and city, of class categories, and of gender identities, which was struggling for definition and, in so doing, helping to define society's future. Aspects of this state are dominant themes of all suburban writings from 1880 onwards, their pervasiveness and the range of responses they inspire indicating a growing awareness of the instability of deep social structures. Even so, within fiction, these concerns are structured by a chronology based on desire, either for the stability of the past or for the promise of the future – a chronology in which the suburbs remain intermediate, in between.

Rural England belonged in the past. For Edwardians, caught between a 'lurking grief at the memory of the lost domain' and a recognition that 'change was inevitable and in many respects desirable', the suburb was a site of reconciliation, where the rural could be re-imagined and reinterpreted.[13] Class relations, however, were always imagined in the present. Class divisions, sharply delineated and conflictual in the city, were, as I have argued elsewhere, reconfigured in the suburbs.[14] Within the broad and broadening church of the middle classes, individuals increasingly defined their own social position in relation to those above or below them, rather than using the absolute categories borrowed from feudalism and consolidated by industrialisation. Looking back towards the beginning of the century from the vantage point of 1940, *The New Survey* claimed that 'the dividing lines between . . . classes are indistinct . . . each class has, so to speak, the fringe of those who are placed with the next division above or below'.[15]

New gender identities belonged to the future: they were still being talked about more than tested out. Suburban streets laid out in rows of domestic housing, whether small working class developments or more spacious villas with gardens, were manifestations of the traditional middle-class belief in home and family, which was being inflected in new ways by suburban domestic aspirations, especially in relation to masculinity. Perhaps surprisingly, however, images of the New Woman and later, of the flapper, were particularly popular in the suburbs.[16] For many young women the New Woman was a model of rebellion, although they were frequently mocked because their 'rebellious' behaviour owed little to considered principle – 'her chief tokens of advancement [being] that she does not live with her mamma, and that she professed not to be afraid of walking home from the station at night alone'.[17] A familiar motif, seen, for example, in Keble Howard's *The Bachelor Girls and their Adventures in Search of Independence* (1907) and H. G. Wells's *Ann Veronica* (1909), is that of the suburban girl transgressing suburban boundaries, going to London to be a 'New Woman' and returning to the suburbs when her adventures were over. However, the suburbs themselves were certainly seen as feminising and feminised territory, the site of a cultural regendering: as Roger Silverstone argues, 'the suburbanization of culture has often been equated . . . with a feminization of culture'.[18]

In the physical, literary and cultural geographies of the suburbs, then, the triangulated suburban narrative subsumes city and country as distinct locations, refashions literary genres and, through its interrogation of new social concerns, signals the passing of the old world. It is a narrative about change and, specifically, about an emerging democracy defining and positioning itself in relation to new cultural forms. Whether democracy is perceived as the menace that stalks the streets (as Soames Forsyte sees it in *The Forsyte Saga*), or as a tableau of harmonious humanity (in the view of William Guest in *News from Nowhere*), the possibility of social and political equality frames the significance of suburban literary themes.[19]

P. J. Keating and David Trotter have both identified suburban fiction as part of the literature of social realism. Together with Sandra Kemp and Charlotte Mitchell, Trotter later narrowed that generic definition to identify it with Edwardian fiction in particular.[20] Valuable as their work is, their focus is confined to representations of the suburbs or of suburban life. If we expand our understanding of suburban fiction, as I suggest, to include those writings shaped more generally by suburban meanings, whether in endorsement or rejection, how, then, might it be positioned in the literary-critical picture of the period?

There is a growing body of recent scholarship that has begun to frame a more inclusive and interrogative version of literary history which will be helpful in answering this question. Maria DiBattista and Lucy MacDiarmid, in *High and Low Moderns: Literature and culture 1889–1939*, and Carola M. Kaplan and Anne B. Simpson, in *Seeing Double: Revisioning Edwardian and modernist fiction*, argue for a horizontal critical approach which draws popular fictions and literary modernisms together in a way that recognises their cultural connections as well as their differences. Nancy L. Paxton considers how the use of the term 'modernism' has 'eclipsed' a sense of literary difference in this period; Ann L. Ardis aims to '"recover" a turn-of-the-twentieth century cultural landscape in which modernism did not (yet) throw gigantic shadows'.[21] These critics provide opportunities to discuss texts that fall outside modernism in a way that is clearly differentiated from the critical positions that marginalised those texts.

The opening up of critical horizons makes it possible to assess the particular contribution of suburban fiction to thematic and generic diversity, and to recognise the emergence of what might be termed the suburbanisation of the literary imagination as the widespread response of writers to suburban themes and to a suburban readership transformed aspects of the literary and cultural tradition. The change of narrative location from city to suburb, as I have indicated, suggests a profounder change from a collective, public set of meanings (which was effectively the value-system of the culturally powerful), to a privatised one (in which each individual constructed his or her version of meaning). If we follow Malcolm Bradbury and James McFarlane in considering literary divisions in spatial terms, and accept that 'London increasingly comes to typify the great city of modernity' and that 'Modernism was *of course* [my italics] very much an urban phenomenon', the shifting of literary locations to the suburbs can also represent the desire to forge a different kind of modernity, an alternative to High Modernism, through more co-operative and popular literary forms.[22]

The Romantic impulse was suburbanised just as the modern urban impulse was. The experiences of nature and the sublime were domesticated in garden romances, or mediated through the words of the Romantic poets in pocket editions that were the companions of suburban walks.[23] Such excursions were made interesting by their literary associations rather than by their natural splendour, as Glen Cavaliero explains:

> The fact that the rural experience had come to be essentially alien from that of the majority of readers led inevitably . . . to a feeling for it as something 'vague, primitive, poetic'. The emasculating of the last-mentioned term is another symptom of the same estrangement; for 'poetic' has taken on the sense of 'fanciful' or 'decorative', much as the country comes to be thought of in conventional tourist terms as 'picturesque', 'refreshing', and so on.[24]

Suburban nature was the culmination of a long social and cultural process, and the new sensibility engendered by its relationship with the rural idea reflected its construction of an aestheticised and com-modified holiday landscape. Literary interest moved from the excite-ment of extremes, both of the rural (wildness/nature/heightened sensibility/the sublime) and of the urban (density/intensity/drama), to an appreciation of the equilibrium of the ordinary.

There were corresponding shifts in the relationship between writers and readers. So-called 'low' culture and 'high' culture were linked together by an extensive intermediate ground at whose per-meable boundaries writing and reading were shaping a new literary paradigm. This was a period of intense interest in the form and func-tion of the novel, as writers sought to define its future and also to formulate a system of values that would differentiate kinds of fictional writing, particularly those aimed exclusively at the mass market. H. G. Wells is one writer who consciously inhabited this intermedi-ate literary territory and his attempt to define it constitutes a rare articulation of the suburban. In his 1914 essay, 'The Contemporary

Novel', he sets out the case for the future of the novel as a part of an irregular but long-running debate on the art of fiction and the role of the novel in the modern world.[25] In a distinctly suburban mode, he argues that the modern novel 'must steer its way between the rocks of trivial and degrading standards and the whirlpool of arbitrary and irrational criticism'. His emphasis is on the immediacy of a novel to its cultural context, and he celebrates the importance of the most minor activity, arguing that 'nothing is irrelevant if the author's mood is happy, and the tapping of the thrush on the garden path, or the petal of apple-blossom that floats down into my coffee, is as relevant as the egg I open or the bread and butter I bite'.[26] Further, he evokes the idea of the text as a conversation between author and reader, and implies that the successful novelist is the one who is most clearly in touch with the world of his readers. Wells may have been looking to the future but he was actually describing what was already happening. The apparent informality of suburban fiction, the emphasis on what interested or delighted the reader, the desire for immediacy and engagement with the present, were a catalyst for the proliferation of genres that is associated with the suburban imagination.

I have organised my discussion of the texts that inhabit the suburban imaginary into three sections: suburban visions, suburban dreams and suburban realities. I hope to convey the breadth of the available material, but this book is not a survey of suburban fictions. My selection of texts has been guided by two principles. My first aim is to illustrate the idea of multi-narratives – the variety of narrative responses, both thematic and formal, to the physical and cultural facts of the rapidly changing suburb during this period. The second, complementary aim is to show how very different texts, drawn from both sides of past and present critical divides, work together to open out the 'intermediate' territory that is suburban culture. In order to do this, I have moved away from an author-centred approach, subordinating the idea of an author's body of work to the examination of particular novels or writings that are illustrative of my larger argument or make a significant contribution to it.

I begin my discussion with suburban visions – with those brave leaps of the intellect and imagination that offer a new perspective on the present by fostering an optimistic sense of the future. Jerome K. Jerome in *Three Men in a Boat* (1889), and William Morris in *News from Nowhere* (1891), translate their hopes for the human

environment into utopias, evoking the happiness that an ideal society would experience and relocating the new spirit of London to
London's heart – the river Thames. Both writers were socialists but
both opted out of social realism, arguably the literary form most
closely concerned with the material world. Morris worked within the
utopian tradition, while Jerome jettisoned straightforward narrative
in favour of a collage of overlapping chronologies.

Other visions take other forms. In chapter 2, I focus on the evocations of suburban idylls by popular novelists such as Arthur Conan
Doyle and Keble Howard, and the microcosmic domestic utopias that
they create. They carve out self-contained worlds, safe from London's
dangers, where the sanctity of family life and the pre-eminence of
love flourish in *rus in urbe* surroundings. *The Man of Property* (1906)
concludes this discussion, as John Galsworthy exposes the flaws of
the suburban idyll in his depiction of Robin Hill and the mystery of
its ownership. Chapter 3 considers the work of Richard Jefferies,
Edward Thomas and E. M. Forster, focusing on the lost domain of the
rural past and the human experience it symbolised, and the way in
which the existence of the suburbs interrogated their aestheticised
landscapes. These writings envision a countryside beyond the suburbs, resonant with history, mediated by a past literary and national
culture, and characterised by a metaphysical or sexual sublime that is
gendered as masculine.

Fiction by and for women is the focus of discussion in Part II,
'Suburban dreams'. Women's suburban writing is characterised by
the capacity to 'dream', to evoke other worlds within the material
suburb. Chapter 4 considers how the idea of a garden as a personal
rural domain inspired garden romances such as Elizabeth von
Arnim's *Elizabeth and Her German Garden* (1898) and Barbara
Campbell's *The Garden of a Commuter's Wife* (1901). Both make use
of a feminine, quasi-autobiographical form involving letters, memoirs, journals and scrapbooks to reveal the simultaneous identity of
every garden as the secret garden of its female owner. Chapters 5 and
6 move from writers to readers to address a vital aspect of suburban
fiction, that is, the fiction that was read *in* the suburbs by suburb-
dwellers, rather than fiction *about* the suburbs. In these chapters I
want to acknowledge the part played by women's romance fiction
in opening up imaginative territories. I begin with stories published
in *Forget-Me-Not*, *Home Notes*, *Hearth and Home*, *Gentlewoman* and
Woman, magazines which were all launched during the 1890s; and

I continue with the novels of writers popular in the early twentieth century – Sophie Cole, Alice Askew, Louise Gerard and Mary Hamilton – whose imaginative territories span the British Empire from London to Africa and India.

I conclude my exploration of the range of suburban fictions in Part III, 'Suburban realities', with three chapters that consider versions of realism in representations of the suburbs. Even within this shared genre, there is considerable variety of tone and approach. Some novels focus on the failure of imagination in the suburbs, their reductive environment of repression, intellectual sterility and conformity, and most acknowledge these situations as possibilities. Even so, to include George Gissing's savage critique of modern culture, the social comedy of W. Pett Ridge and H. G. Wells, G. K. Chesterton's bizarre games with genre, the working-class sympathies of Edwin Pugh and Shan Bullock, and Arnold Bennett's broad humanism all in the same category reveals their differences rather than their similarities.

Diversity across the range of suburban fictions is not a virtue in itself but it contributed to the breaking down of a monolithic literary culture and to the emergence of the kaleidoscope of individual perspectives that was a feature of *fin-de-siècle* innovation. I hope this discussion will contribute to the larger picture of such innovation, and give some sense of the energy that was released into culture by the changing social formations of the suburbs. I also hope that my discussion of texts which explored the suburbs' possibilities, or exposed their limitations, will help to explain why material features as apparently banal as housing developments should accumulate such significance that they appeared to defy definition and to 'propose themselves as a problem to the mind'. My conviction is that an understanding of the mystery of the suburbs is most likely to be found through the work of novelists whose imagined territories offer a panorama of possibilities for reading the suburban narrative.

Notes

1 Edward Thomas, [1906] *The Heart of England* (Oxford: Oxford University Press, 1982), 5.
2 Contemporary commentary on the suburbs can be found in chapter 3 of C. F. G. Masterman, [1901] *The Condition of England*, edited and with an introduction by J. T. Boulton (London: Methuen, 1960), and Patrick Geddes, [1915] *Cities in Evolution: An introduction to the Town Planning*

Movement and to the study of cities (London: Ernest Benn, 1968). *The New Survey of London Life and Labour, vol. 1: Forty years of change*, convened and with an introduction by H. Llewellyn Smith (London: P. S. King and Son, 1930), contains valuable information in table form about population growth in the new suburbs, transport development and use of libraries during the period 1890–1930. The work done at Leicester University has set the standard for analysis of urban development in the Victorian age. See H. J. Dyos, *Victorian Suburb: A study of the growth of Camberwell* (Leicester: Leicester University Press, 1961); D. D. Reeder 'A Theatre of Suburbs: Some patterns of development in West London, 1801–1911' in H. J. Dyos (ed.), *The Study of Urban History* (London: Edward Arnold, 1968); and F. M. L. Thompson (ed.), *The Rise of Suburbia* (Leicester: Leicester University Press, 1982).

The brief, but very important, period of development from 1880–1900 is rarely addressed in any detail in histories of the suburbs: they tend to deal with actual growth rather than contemporary perceptions of that growth. However, in 'Slums and Suburbs' (in H. J. Dyos and Michael Wolff (eds), *The Victorian City: Images and realities*, vol. 1, (London: Routledge and Kegan Paul, 1973), 359–388), H. J. Dyos and D. D. Reeder write with insight about urban form and personal meaning.

3   See Asa Briggs, 'The Human Aggregate' in Dyos and Wolff (eds), *The Victorian City*, vol. 1, 83–104, for a discussion of the question of scale in describing London at this time, and the development of statistical surveys.

4   J. Macvicar Anderson in the *Builder* (11 November 1899), 437.

5   *Building News* (1900), cited in Donald J. Olsen, *The Growth of Victorian London* (London: Batsford, 1976), 201; Geddes, *Cities in Evolution*, 26.

6   With the notable exceptions of Kate Flint, 'Fictional Suburbia', *Literature and History*, 8:1 (Spring 1982), 67–81; P. J. Keating, *The Haunted Study: A social history of the English novel, 1875–1914* (London: Fontana, 1991), 319–327 (although the bulk of his discussion covers early twentieth century novels); and David Trotter, *The English Novel in History 1895–1920* (London: Routledge, 1993). S. Kemp, C. Mitchell and D. Trotter (eds), *Edwardian Fiction: An Oxford companion* (Oxford: Oxford University Press, 1997) includes a brief entry under 'suburban fiction', but the focus is again on the early twentieth century.

7   'The Villa and the New Suburb' in Olsen, *The Growth of Victorian London*, 187–264 (201).

8   Jane Brown, *The Pursuit of Paradise: A social history of gardens and gardening* (London: Harper Collins, 2000), 157.

9   Kemp et al. (eds), *Edwardian Fiction*, xvii.

10 Keating, *The Haunted Study*, 319.

11 *The New Survey* traces a steady rise in the purchasing power of workers' wages from 1890 to 1930, as well as a shorter working week and increased holiday (9). See also José Harris, *Private Lives, Public Spirit: Britain 1870–1914* (Harmondsworth: Penguin, 1993): 'For the first time in British (and perhaps human) history, the sheer fact of scarcity receded' (33).

12 William Pett Ridge, *A Clever Wife* (London: Richard Bentley and Son, 1895), 393.

13 Harris, *Private Lives*, 36.

14 For a detailed discussion of class in the suburbs see Lynne Hapgood,
    '"The New Suburbanites" and Contested Class Identities in the London
    Suburbs, 1880–1900' in Roger Webster (ed.), *Expanding Suburbia:
    Reviewing suburban narratives* (New York and Oxford: Berghahn Books,
    2000), 31–50.
15 *The New Survey*, 61.
16 *Gentlewoman* (27 January 1917), 85: 'the flapper is purely a suburban
    invention, unknown to Mayfair or real country life'.
17 'Studies in the Suburbs III – Our Advanced Woman', *Hearth and Home*
    (21 February 1895), 528.
18 Roger Silverstone (ed.), *Visions of Suburbia* (London and New York:
    Routledge, 1997), 7.
19 John Galsworthy, *The Forsyte Saga*, vol. 1 (Harmondsworth: Penguin,
    2001), 604; William Morris, [1891] *News from Nowhere, or, An epoch of
    rest: being some chapters from a utopian romance*, edited by James Redmond
    (London: Routledge and Kegan Paul, 1970), e.g. 180.
20 For Keating and Trotter, see note 6. Kemp et al. (eds), *Edwardian Fiction*,
    xiii.
21 Nancy L. Paxton, 'Eclipsed by Modernism' in Lynne Hapgood and
    Nancy L. Paxton (eds), *Outside Modernism: In pursuit of the British novel
    1900–1930* (Basingstoke: Macmillan, 2000), 3–21; Ann L. Ardis,
    Modernism and Cultural Conflict, 1880–1922 (Cambridge: Cambridge
    University Press, 2002), 4.
22 Malcolm Bradbury and James McFarlane, *Modernism 1890–1930*
    (Harmondsworth: Penguin, 1976), 182, 183.
23 See Barbara T. Gates for an interesting account of the 'female sublime'
    and the experience of women travellers in *Kindred Nature: Victorian and
    Edwardian women embrace the living world* (Chicago and London: Chicago
    University Press, 1998).
24 Glen Cavaliero, *The Rural Tradition in the English Novel 1900–1939*
    (Basingstoke: Macmillan, 1977), 201. Michael Waters, *The Garden in
    Victorian Literature* (Aldershot: Scolar Press, 1988), 153 ff., argues
    that terms such as land, landscape, wild, country and countryside had
    become unstable and had all but lost their meanings as early as
    the mid-nineteenth century. See also the introductory essay in
    U. C. Knoepflmacher and G. B. Tennyson, *Nature and the Victorian
    Imagination* (Berkeley and Los Angeles: California University Press, 1977).
25 H. G. Wells, [1914] 'The Contemporary Novel' in Patrick Parrinder
    and Robert Philmus (eds), *H. G. Wells's Literary Criticism* (Brighton:
    Harvester Press, 1980), 192–206. This essay is thought to have been
    triggered in part by Wells's exchanges with Henry James. Walter Besant,
    Henry James, D. H. Lawrence, Rebecca West, Arnold Bennett and
    Virginia Woolf were all engaged in what was later termed the Art of
    Fiction debate, developing their theories in letters, reviews and essays,
    often in response to one another's work.
26 Wells, 'The Contemporary Novel', 193, 197.

Part I

SUBURBAN VISIONS

1

✳

THE UTOPIAN SUBURB

Jerome K. Jerome
William Morris and the 'logical dream'

HE suburban imaginary as utopia finds its most complete expression in two of the earliest examples of suburban fiction in the period under discussion, Jerome K. Jerome's *Three Men in a Boat* (1889) and William Morris's *News from Nowhere* (1891).[1] These novels both create a transformed London, reorganised as a ruralised landscape for human-scale communities on the margins of the city. The location of this new world is the river Thames, whose meandering flow connects the countryside of Gloucestershire with the docks and harbours of industrial and imperialist London. The people of London inhabit the length of the riverbanks in small communities, and the river itself in numerous boats, in a way that reconciles the fixity of the built environment with the fluidity of human experience. Crucially, the idea of community in these novels is founded on a spirit of equality that challenges social hierarchies and asserts the value of the individual as a member of the social whole.

Critical opinion has always placed William Morris and Jerome K. Jerome on different sides of the low/high culture divide so that even the obvious similarity of their fictional material – accounts of friends' boating trips on the Thames – has been ignored. Identifying their position within the geography of the suburban imaginary enables profounder similarities to be recognised. Both novels present radical opposition to the late nineteenth-century cultural milieu: to the impact of urbanisation, to the pervasive intellectual pessimism, to contemporary notions of high and low culture and to literary realism. *Three Men in a Boat* celebrates the joys of egalitarianism at a time when society was shaken by fears of class conflict, and within an imperialist and hierarchical social structure which was only just beginning to take on the implications of the 'masses' as a political and cultural entity. *News from Nowhere* also concerns itself with the masses in a vision of the future inspired by Morris's faith in a materialist Marxist ideology which places as much emphasis on a revolutionised emotional environment as it does on social revolution. The radical possibilities of both of these novels lie in their recognition of the connection between a reorganised London, the restructuring of social relations and the possibility of personal happiness within the suburban imaginary.

The critical history of both novels has established literary categories that it has been hard for them to escape and has hindered the perception of their connections. William Morris, already an established literary and cultural figure when *News from Nowhere* was published, has consistently inspired serious critical interest. Originally serialised in the *Commonwealth* (the journal of the Socialist League) for a committed audience, it was published in book form soon afterwards. It has never won a wide general readership, and has, in fact, created bemusement and irritation among many socialist readers wary of a fictional realisation of materialist socialist politics. There is a consensus of critical opinion among the readers of *News from Nowhere* (who are, by and large, those who analyse it), that it is a difficult and uncomfortable experience. Patrick Parrinder argues that Morris's political naivety makes readers experience 'discomfiture when asked seriously to imagine a world in which enjoyment and leisure are not paid for in the coin of other people's oppression and suffering'.[2] ('Seriously' is the key word here – a point to which I shall return). James Buzard contends that *News from Nowhere* is 'seen as quintessentially, quaintly Victorian in the nostalgia for pre-industrial civilisation'.[3] It can be difficult, too, for readers who are essentially sympathetic to Morris's Marxist aims: Raymond Williams notes the 'uneasiness' of readers before 'the scale and nature of his [Morris's] social criticism', while Roger Lewis interrogates a communist society that is imagined in a 'political pastoral' traditionally identified with 'the pastoral of Toryism'.[4] These approaches have served to categorise *News from Nowhere* as a socialist novel and to delimit its critical reception.[5]

The case with Jerome is very different, but the result is the same: a failure to allow the text freedom to find its appropriate literary position and connections. The critical reception of *Three Men in a Boat* is an interesting case study in cultural snobbery. The class and culture war sparked by its publication is a measure of its radicalism. What the critics found almost impossible to deal with (and what readers clearly responded to) was the unabashed gaiety of the book's mood and, more specifically, the idea of the lower classes enjoying themselves. While readers inundated Jerome with letters of appreciation,[6] the critics rejected its 'weak imitations of American fun',[7] its 'Yankee humour' and 'forced and vulgar manner',[8] and condemned Jerome as a 'new humorist'.[9] If we read the critical terminology from another, more egalitarian, perspective, we see embedded in the insults the fear of irreverent and overconfident breakaway cultures ('Yankee'), contempt for what is associated with the common people ('vulgar') and fear of change ('new'). Jerome's humorous text, with 'its new atmosphere of good-fellowship', provided a catalyst for discussions of taste, mass culture and class, and exposed entrenched cultural fears about the future.

The reaction of the literary reviewers was not simple snobbishness. We are talking here about a conscious fight to maintain the divisions of class and culture. They felt that it was important to make clear that Jerome's 'new' humour was 'beneath contempt' because they could not define or delimit it according to the moral and conventional framework of existing literary culture and social behaviour. They realised that the art of *Three Men in a Boat*, which so cleverly realises the irrepressible high spirits of three men engaged in the current craze for boating, was not simply a mirror held up to one aspect of social activity, nor as innocent as it may at first look. Jerome's book was an insouciant snub to authority, to deference, to class boundaries and to sacrosanct notions of taste and culture. In 1889 it was dangerously original. It was a piece of writing in the public domain which realised the establishment's second worst nightmare. The worst was the rise of the masses in riots of the starving and unemployed, who would bring about the degeneration of the race. But the second worst was the rise of the masses who would debase, trivialise and fail to appreciate the gifts of their masters; who would make manifest 'the sad results to be expected from the over-education of the lower orders' by producing a vulgarised version of middle-class culture.[10]

If we pursue a critical approach suggested by the suburban imaginary of the river Thames, that is, by Morris's and Jerome's shared vision of topographical and related psychological transformations, then the perceived difficulties of *News from Nowhere*, and the common triviality of *Three Men in a Boat*, can be reassessed. A reading of *Three Men in a Boat* is 'thickened' and politicised by its association with the specifically socialist framework of Morris's narrative, and the recuperation of the medieval as a way of envisaging the future in *News from Nowhere* is likewise 'thickened' and modernised by association with the contemporary context of *Three Men in a Boat*.[11] The echoes which resonate across these two novels creates an impression of textual association. However, before we can trace the richness and suggestiveness of their associations through their common choice of location in the river Thames, it is important to understand the Thames's peculiar appropriateness to both writers and to the suburban idea.

For both Morris and Jerome the river Thames was a personal passion and therefore probably an instinctive choice for the site of their fictions. Before his literary success, Jerome 'had only ever known happiness on the river. He called it "fairy-land" and believed it.'[12] Morris chose to build the house of his dreams, Kelmscott, on the banks of the upper Thames. The intimate familiarity of both men with the river through their own boating experiences informs their novels. Morris argued that 'The only safe way to read a utopia is to consider it as the expression of the temperament of its author', and the mood of his and Jerome's evocations of the Thames is generated as much by shared 'temperament' (that is, by a shared capacity for optimistically envisioning social and human potential) as by any late nineteenth-century sense of literary or political identity.[13] This mood also suggests the influence of the personal on the formation of their literary aesthetic, which, together with their subject matter, locates their fictions in the larger context of suburbanisation of the imagination. The Victorian era may well have celebrated the Thames as the greatest river in the world, leading to London, the world's greatest city; but for Jerome and Morris access to the river meant journeying up river and away from London to rediscover an unspoilt landscape and a sense of community that they both felt were being threatened by the tendencies of nineteenth-century life. The river – a different element where different rules apply – provided both writers with the perfect playground for discovery and rediscovery without the imperialist connotations of exploration. It allowed for invention, for new identities, for the reconfiguration of human relations and for a new version of the London landscape.

The Thames, of course, already had an identity freighted with significance. In both novels, the Thames also functions as an archetypal English text inscribed with certain notions of beauty, freedom, reflection and humanity. During the nineteenth century, there was a growing interest in the history and culture of the Thames which amounted to a cult. In the many guide books and history books written during this period, such as the Halls' *Book of the Thames*, a discursive and reflective account which inspired many imitations, the river is an embodiment and a reminder of the simultaneity of past and present, an infallible source of happiness and recuperation, and a symbol of a gentle, strong and purposeful English culture. These books were part of the literary context of Morris's and Jerome's novels, one that Jerome acknowledges but Morris dismisses. In *News from Nowhere*, Guest says, 'Besides, I have not read any books about the Thames: it was one of the minor stupidities of our time that no one thought fit to write a decent book about what might fairly be called our only English river'.[14] Both writers draw on the familiar associations of the Thames in their use of it as a fictional anchor but it is the 'emotional forces' associated with the Thames which Jerome and Morris evoke in their novels and which provide the shared historical, political, cultural and topographical meanings resonating across both texts.[15]

The relevance of the Thames to the construction of the suburban idea is historically specific. Even before Morris and Jerome began writing their novels, the Thames valley was rapidly being laid out as a suburb. Architect-designed riverbank villas joined the long-established country houses. Speculative developments opened up new plots and in-filled others, until the new domestic style, 'homely, like colloquial talk', spread patchily down the Thames from Chiswick to Richmond and beyond.[16] In *Arcadia for All*, Dennis Hardy and Colin Ward tell the fascinating story of the suburbanisation of the Thames, as those with little money but the desire to escape from the city added improvised housing and semi-permanent camp sites to the numbers of dwellings legitimately lining the river bank. All classes flocked to the river, and people of all incomes strove to find a foothold in this most accessible part of London's rural outskirts.[17] Hotels, guesthouses, pubs and boat yards spread up the river in response to the growing demands of leisure trippers who could only snatch days or weekends away from the city. As Christopher

Matthew and Benny Green point out, 'the river had suddenly become democratized'.[18] The association of the Thames with democracy is embedded in the experience of J, George and Harris, the three friends in *Three Men in a Boat*, and William Guest, the visitor to Nowhere from the nineteenth century in *News from Nowhere*. For the writers of both novels, the primary and proper function of the Thames was as the site of their suburban utopias.

Jerome's utopia is an exuberant gamble. Located in the here-and-now of Victorian London, it merges past, present and future in a seamless text whose vision of class harmony, holiday and community on the river Thames is the realisation of a futuristic alternative to the familiar, conflict-torn, ugly and unhappy city. The spirit of democracy is embodied in the youthful health and energy of J, Harris and George, in the trust and pleasure of their friendship, and in the optimism of youth which, given congenial conditions, easily believes in its own permanence and its right to a place in the world. It is most closely associated with the ordinary. The reader's impression of the egalitarian 'now' is one of infectious laughter and easy badinage inspired by the adventures of daily life – peeling potatoes, pitching camp, opening tins, reading maps and negotiating river obstacles – all of which are described in loving detail as though such activities had never been attempted before.

Nothing is sacred to the three young men, who are set on discovering the world at first hand and reinventing it for themselves. 'Throw the lumber over, man', J exhorts as he packs for his journey, in a mock-philosophical polemic against possessions and wealth.[19] J, Harris and George determinedly refuse to know their place: they picnic on the banks of the Thames and calmly sidestep the attempts of landowners to eject them; they pull down notices and fencing erected by the landowners to enclose their property; they block the river so that steam launches cannot get through. They turn social values on their heads, shunning Maidenhead because it is 'too snobby to be pleasant'; and they stop going to Henley regatta because the King's patronage has 'spoiled [it] . . . Before that, it had been a happy, gay affair, simple and quiet.'[20] Happiness for them, indeed, means simplicity, sincerity and, above all, inclusiveness. It means enjoying to the full whatever comes to hand, whether it be George's banjo and his teach-yourself-to-play book, the beauty of the river, a good joke or a quiet moment of private reflection.

Three Men in a Boat affirms the special distinctiveness of the ordinary by its humorous deflation of pomposity and pretension. Many, if not most, of the boating incidents are comic inversions of material from Henry Taunt's *A New Map of the River Thames*, which represented an ideal view of the river, of camping and of the outdoor life that would have seemed to Jerome absurdly out of touch with the ordinary person's experience of a few hours or days on the river.[21] In the spirit of secularism, the three men compare the comforting qualities of hymns unfavourably with those of the popular song 'He's Got 'Em On'.[22] During a wet and miserable night, in a parody of Shakespeare's *The Merchant of Venice* ('On such a night', the 'music of the spheres'), they tell stories of death and disaster and sing 'Two Lovely Black Eyes', still the rage of lower-class London in 1888. While the deference that makes Mr Pooter the fall guy of many incidents in the equally famous 'suburban', *The Diary of a Nobody* (1888–89), set the upper classes laughing; it is J's, Harris's and George's rejection of deference in *Three Men in a Boat* that set the lower classes laughing.

At the here-and-now level of *Three Men in a Boat*, the perfect day is made possible by a plan hatched between friends for a river holiday. But over the longer time span suggested by the text, Jerome's perfect day appears as a vision of a society in which the happiness of the individual is collectivised and politicised in an egalitarian social structure. This happiness is realised in a passage which occurs on the second day of their journey:

> On a fine Sunday it [Boulter's Lock on the Thames] presents this appearance nearly all day long, while, up the stream and down the stream, lie, waiting their turn, outside the gates, long lines of still more boats; and boats are drawing near and passing away, so that the sunny river, from the palace up to Hampton church is dotted and decked with yellow, and blue, and orange, and white, and red, and pink. All the inhabitants of Hampton and Moulsey dress themselves up in boating costume, and come and mouch around the lock with their dogs, and flirt, and smoke, and watch the boats, and, altogether, what with the caps and jackets of the men, the pretty coloured dresses of the women, the excited dogs, the moving boats, the white sails, the pleasant landscape, and the sparkling water, it is one of the gayest sights I know of near this dull old London town.[23]

This passage is surely one of the warmest and most spontaneous expressions of a love of humanity in fiction. It creates a tableau in

2

'one of the gayest sights I know of near this dull old London town'
Boulter's Lock (1897) by John Edward Gregory

which personal and public happiness converge and personal satisfaction and public good coincide; and it offers a vision of unity to a divided society.[24] 'Happiness in seeing others happy' is the state of mind that J reveals at the moment when he describes the Bank Holiday crowds – a profoundly political response that transforms the 'masses' from depersonalised numbers into an active and colourful community.[25]

The Thames of Nowhere at the heart of Morris's future communist utopia is strikingly similar to the playground of Jerome's nineteenth-century, brave new rising classes. Whereas Jerome constructs the Thames as a social space in which the past, the immediate present and the assumed future merge, however, the Thames in News from Nowhere is used to juxtapose those time frames. The images that Guest has of nineteenth-century London, the grimy Thames with its ugly bridges on the banks of the shabby suburb where he lives, are influenced by his mood of pessimism after a quarrelsome Socialist meeting As he contemplates the future, he has the sudden inspiration for 'an amusing story', and when he enters Nowhere, the first thing he sees is the Thames transformed. The beauty of the river is brought to life as a space thronged with men and women – a space for both work and pleasure. The protected beauty of a river fenced off and appropriated for the use of landowners and aristocracy was as offensive to Morris as to Jerome when set against the ugliness and misery of the cities. In News from Nowhere, there are no sentimental or prettified rural retreats because there is no urban squalor to escape from. Along the banks throughout Guest's journey he sees the houses and farms of the diffused suburb, with people working and waving. He notes with pleasure that:

> Both on this day and yesterday we had, as you may think, met and passed and been passed by many craft of one kind of another. The most part of these were being rowed like ourselves, or were sailing, in the sort of way that sailing is managed on the upper reaches of the river; but every now and then we came on barges, laden with hay and other country produce, or carrying bricks, lime and timber, and the like.[26]

Just as J, Harris and George negotiate their route in and out between numerous small craft and spend their evening leisure time in companionable pubs, Guest and his guides encounter people in homes and communes on their way. Morris's emphasis on the unity between people, their activities and their emotions is realised in the harmoniously proportioned tableaux of human activity throughout Nowhere. The laying of the meal in the Guest House, the haymakers near Oxford, the Obstinate Refusers, all reflect the happiness of physical and mental self-determination, much as Jerome's picture of the boaters does. And human beings, again as in Jerome, are always at the centre of the picture – as we see in Morris's description of the harvest festival whose 'best ornament was the crowd of handsome, happy-looking men and women that were sat down to table, and who, with their bright faces and rich hair over their gay holiday rainment, looked, as the Persian poet puts it, like a bed of tulips in the sun'.[27] The movement of people through their environment – in the gardens, fields and houses of Nowhere – always occurs in a poetic symbiosis with that environment, corresponding to drifts of fragrance, gleams of light, the flow of the river, the drawing in of dusk and the opening out of dawn. There is the same easy relationship between people and nature, and between desire and activity, that I have already noted in *Three Men in a Boat*. The river provides a frame for a spontaneity of action and feeling which transforms the conventions of daily working life and social intercourse into holiday – the holiday that encompasses the whole of life in Nowhere, and maybe even in the nineteenth-century London of *Three Men in a Boat*. The river journeys in both these novels are the very opposite of the solitary journeys of the medieval quest, the Romantic search for the sublime or the *fin-de-siècle* escape from the repugnant masses. They are the immediately shared experiences of people bound together by friendship – by what Geoffrey Harvey calls in relation to Jerome – 'a shared landscape'.[28]

Morris's and Jerome's shared faith in a future egalitarian society is underlined by their view of history, contained in and charted by the route of the Thames. Although, as a utopia, the Thames is outside time, it is also demonstrably of time, in that it flows through the past and the present towards the point of its utopian transformation. Guest's four-day journey follows hard on the heels of J's, George's and Harris's two-week jaunt. Topographically they take exactly the same journey, up to the higher reaches of the Thames, and they are all witness to the history that the Thames embodies. In *Three Men in a Boat*, this is an evolutionary history which contextualises the daily activities of the friends and their place in the nineteenth century. In *News from Nowhere*, by contrast, we see a revolutionary history which comments on itself and its own transformations.

In the earlier text, as the friends journey up river the Thames's meandering route is a reminder of England's history, of events, of people, of invasions and battles, of the rise and fall of the powerful, and of the activities and labours of the peasants and the poor. The incidents that Jerome chose to emphasise tell a political story about the struggle for democracy, justice and equality. When he describes Kingston, for example, the brilliant focus is Harris 'in a red and orange blazer', set in relief by 'the distant glimpses of the old grey palace of the Tudors'. It is always the present which is coloured and animated; but it is the past which constantly reminds him to value it. In *News from Nowhere*, Guest can only begin his journey up the Thames, as it flows beyond history, once the conversations with Hammond as to how the revolution happened (the contemporary context of *Three Men in a Boat*) have ended. Freedom of access to the banks, the removal of ugly locks and bridges and the changed agricultural and domestic landscape of the river banks all attest to different social formations and different structures of feeling, but these transformations are necessarily measured against the river of Guest's memory.

A significant moment of textual congruence occurs in the two novels' accounts of the signing of the Magna Carta at Runnymede. J's account is a vision of a movement through history towards the freedom of the working man. This long section begins with J's identification of himself and his friends, from their perspective on the river, with the yeomen of 1215 (and, in an arresting example of textual association, with the people of Nowhere's river banks): 'We could almost fancy that the centuries between us and the ever-to-be-famous morning of 1215 had been drawn aside, and that we, English yeomen's sons in homespun cloth, with dirk at belt, were waiting to witness the writing of that stupendous page of history.'[29] The section concludes by fusing the optimism of those who lived in the past ('We wait') with the appreciation and understanding of those alive in the present ('now we know'). In *News from Nowhere*, when William Guest reaches Runnymede, he shares J's vision of equality. Although the inhabitants of Nowhere no longer classify themselves in hierarchies, those whom Guest meets in the chapter 'Early Morning at Runnymede', those 'young women clad in light woollen most gaily embroidered; the men being clad in white flannel in bright colours', are the descendants of Jerome's yeomen who witnessed the signing of the Magna Carta.[30]

It is helpful in understanding the nature of Jerome's and Morris's utopian vision of a suburbanised future to see it as anticipating an evolving debate within a small but influential group of sociologists and urban planners who were beginning to see the urban future in suburban terms during the 1890s. 'The logical dream', Patrick Geddes's inspired paradox, which he argued was necessary in order to envision the cities of the future, reveals the productive tension that fuelled their work, just as material realities and aesthetic landscapes interacted to produce the utopias envisioned in *Three Men in a Boat* and *News from Nowhere*.[31] Morris's and Jerome's vision, in which city and countryside could be reorganised and the industrial and agricultural worlds could be reconciled in a socialised and humanised landscape, was shared by town planners such as Ebenezer Howard, writers and thinkers such as H. G. Wells and sociologists such as Charles Booth, among others.

The elements of their dream were essentially suburban and remarkably consistent, whatever the political or religious perspective of the thinker. They were defined in reaction to what were perceived as the 'evils' of the city and reworked in terms of what was seen as the 'lost' countryside. Practical issues of suburban design were important, but they were always subordinated to how that design would deliver a new mode of civilised living. The key words – health, housing, community and happiness – were underpinned by a deeply held belief in the possibility of change and progress, even of perfectibility. Visions of the new urban living were more likely to be expressed in the positive terms of a way of life than simply as an escape from current urban conditions; the word 'happiness' echoes through writings from town planning documents to novels. In 1883, the *Bedford Park Gazette* referred to the distinctive quality of life in the suburb as 'corporate happiness'.[32] This was not an abstract idea and the word 'corporate' did not carry the connotations of big business and anonymous workers that it does today. It was an idea tuned specifically against the prevailing misery of the urban condition, and against the parallel cultural despair which cultivated 'unhappiness as a fine art' in the way so deplored by William Morris.[33] (It is ironic that some years later G. K. Chesterton, in *The Man Who Was Thursday* (1908), used Bedford Park as an example of just that self-conscious and self-indulgent nurturing of the negative.) To the modern reader, the pervasiveness of the word 'happiness' throughout this literature suggests an optimism and a hope that would give inspiration and energy in the face of opposition or lack of progress.

The word itself – suburb – comes and goes in these writings, changing and adapting according to context, co-opted because no other word existed to describe the particular forms of 'intermediate and new kinds of social and physical organisation'.[34] In struggling to imagine a new London, these urban commentators not only evolved new forms of organisation but also set linguistic change in motion. Phrases such as 'Garden Suburb', 'Garden City', 'rural suburbs', *'rus in urbe'*, 'Town-country' and later 'New Town' came into use. Acutely aware of the transitional state of their society and of the imminence of even greater changes and possibilities, these social visionaries faced what H. G. Wells called a 'dissolving and changing human landscape'.[35] What emerges clearly is a vision of London reorganised, either as a city that has become country, or as a city dispersed across a resettled countryside; it is a human landscape of houses grouped in relation to work and leisure with access to open spaces. The brilliant answer to urban misery and rural depopulation was, whatever the nomenclature, the suburb.

Charles Booth's survey assessing the extent of poverty in London, begun early in the 1880s, followed the centrifugal movement of urban populations and concluded with a summary of suburban districts as part of his projection of the city's future. In the *Final Volume* (1902), Booth acknowledged that people who had the freedom to move out of the city would do so, and he welcomed the evidence that he had collected of a developing suburban environment. Characteristic of Booth's thinking is his gradual movement from recorded data to a holistic vision of its meaning. The reader has a sense of the pieces coming together as Booth realises what 'great possibilities clearly lie before us in the reorganization of urban life within itself, as well as in its relation with the surrounding country and with the (still) wide world beyond'.[36] Claiming inspiration from H. G. Wells, and underlining the material basis of Jerome's and Morris's utopias, he finally lays out his vision of a future suburbanised countryside: 'We want to see London spreading itself over the Home Counties, not as an escape from the evil left behind but as a development of energy which will react for good over the whole area as it now exists'.[37]

Ebenezer Howard's roots, like Charles Booth's, were also essentially practical; but while Booth recorded change, Howard initiated it. Howard was a planner whose *To-Morrow, A peaceful path to real reform* (1898) was to become the founding document of the Garden City movement.[38] In his short book, Howard gave a shape, an objective and a vocabulary to the desires of the time. He designed a revolutionary landscape which he called 'Town-country', a productive 'marriage' generating 'new hope, new life, a new civilisation'.[39] This Town-country would, he argued, transform the casual suburban development driven by speculators on the one hand and individual desire on the other, into an organised process in which 'the country must invade the town'.[40] The spirit of this new civilisation would be that it was tailored to human needs. Walking distance was intended to mark the limits of a 'social city', which would then link up with other cities to form clusters. In this way Howard wished to draw the powers of nature into alliance with the technological advances of the late nineteenth century to lay out England in dispersed 'suburbs'. His diagram of the Three Magnets plots out the triangulation of the suburban imaginary. His 'third alternative', in which 'all the advantages of the most energetic and active town life, with all the beauty and delight of the country may be secured in perfect combination' was a vision of rationality and affectivity, of materialism and spirituality, of personal independence and benign social planning not unlike the futures envisioned in *News from Nowhere* and *Three Men in a Boat*.[41]

In 1901, with *Anticipations*, and in 1905, with *A Modern Utopia*, H. G. Wells formally joined the debate.[42] As a successful science-fiction writer, he had been a participant for some time but, unlike Morris and Jerome, he had begun to lose faith in the power of the novel to inform and change society.[43] Wells's vision aligned most closely with his contemporaries over the issue of what he called urban 'diffusion'. Like Booth and Howard (and Morris), he deplored the unplanned suburbs that had spread out from London as a missed opportunity for fundamental reorganisation. Ideally, he suggested, the suburbs should the best of all worlds, morally enhancing, and offering in microcosm an Englishman's model of his ideal nation: 'Indeed', he claimed in *Anticipations*, 'the London citizen of the year 2000 A.D. may have a choice of nearly all England . . . as his suburb'.[44] Later in the discussion, he describes a future suburb in detail:

> It will certainly be a curious and varied region, far less monotonous than our present English world . . . perhaps rather more abundantly wooded, breaking continually into park and garden, and with everywhere a

scattering of houses. These will not . . . follow the fashion of the vulgar
ready-built villas of the existing suburb; because the freedom people will
be able to exercise in the choice of a site will rob the 'building estate'
promoter of his local advantage . . . Each district, I am inclined to think,
will develop its own differences of type and style. As one travels through
the urban region, one will traverse open, breezy, 'horsey'/suburbs, smart
white gates and palings everywhere . . . gardening districts all set with
gables and roses, holly hedges, and emerald lawns . . . and river districts
with gaily painted boat-houses peeping from the osiers. Then presently
a gathering of houses closer together, and a promenade and a whiff of
band and dresses, and then, perhaps, a little island of agriculture.[45]

Wells criticised William Morris's suburban vision in *News from
Nowhere* as attractive but impractical. However, he shared Morris's
desire to bring together man's artistic, social and material achievements and, in *A Modern Utopia*, he paints a picture in his characteristically conversational mode (which is probably why T. W. H.
Crosland called it 'a classically suburban book')[46] of a suburbanised
world that is strongly reminiscent of Morris's and Jerome's.

The work of turn-of-the-century urban planners, sociologists and
thinkers substantiates the material feasibility of Morris's and Jerome's
hopes for a better society. However, despite their considerable
influence, the optimism that defined their work and their shared
belief in the possibility of a 'logical dream' has been largely forgotten
in the inevitable compromises, conflicting interests and practical
considerations that have shaped the urban development of the twentieth century.[47] The distinctiveness of *News from Nowhere* and *Three
Men in a Boat* has been enduring because they are clearly differentiated from other contemporary fiction that interrogated the structures
and conditions of urban living in the late 1880s. Both novels are
examples of a formal resistance to social realism and, while this has
been partly responsible for these novels' mixed critical history, it is
also one of their claims to serious critical consideration. I have
already noted one critic's discomfiture with the idea of reading *News
from Nowhere*'s utopia 'seriously'. John Goode's question ('[when]
reading Morris do we overlook the literariness which makes for distance and ambiguity in order to extract useful ideas?') is an apposite
corrective here.[48] By way of contrast, it is the comedy of *Three Men
in a Boat* that has always been a barrier to critical open-mindedness.
Jerome later commented that word 'humour' seemed to be used as a
term of 'reproach'.[49] In their attempt to find an appropriate literary

form for their 'dream' of a future society, both novels pursue what I argue are suburban priorities. They reject the forms and language that would associate them with the urban literary tradition, and employ a vestigial narrative structure that subordinates events to state of mind, and action to feeling. Both novels distract attention from their dominant characters, either to suggest their ordinariness or to draw attention to the identity of a group. Both novels rework literary language with a readily accessible simplicity and directness.

It is easy for the reader to assume that the narrative of *Three Men in a Boat* tells the story of the beginning, middle and end of a holiday jaunt on the Thames. However, the apparent 'nowness' of a holiday period is a clever illusion: there is very little in the text that constructs a continuous narrative present. While history (as embodied in the Thames) moves slowly towards the fulfilment of society's aspirations, the moment in time that we share as readers is taken out of time: a holiday can ignore days of the week and hours of the morning, and is dedicated to the full realisation of selfhood. On closer examination we can see that the laughter, jokes and escapades Jerome describes are representative rather than specific, a catalyst for the sharing of experience rather than events that play some part in a plot. Many of J's stories are reminiscences of earlier trips, some with Harris and George and some with other friends. Some are retellings of stories told to him by friends and acquaintances. Some are rehearsals of tried and tested jokes. Even those activities that appear to be taking place in the present are already being exaggerated in the telling and mythologised for future reminiscences. The present is often diffused into meditations on the past or reflections about the future. The text does not draw the reader into a narrative so much as into a conversation between friends, full of interruptions, verbal shorthand, silences and moments of complete engagement. By dispersing a dominant narrative into a collage of past, present and anticipated experiences, Jerome celebrates not just the immediacy of holiday fun but also happiness as state of being.

The centrality of the Thames to Jerome's text makes an important formal contribution to the non-narrative shape of *Three Men in a Boat*, and in so doing, it provides a possible structure for an imagined culture and consciousness fundamentally at odds with the late nineteenth century. Because of its unusually slow-flowing, meandering route the Thames is famously a river that encourages reflection and philosophy. The assumed narrative, the narratives-within-the-narrative,

the reminiscences, daydreams and fairy tales, the historical commentaries and tourist travelogue, the anecdotes, jokes and conversations – the chameleon diversity of Jerome's text complements and is
complemented by the movement of the Thames in its idiosyncratic
determination to *be* somewhere rather than *go* somewhere.

The Thames has an important function, too, in *News from
Nowhere*. Morris's formal originality has often been acknowledged,
but critical discomfort has once again been created by the attempt
to reconcile the stasis of the subtitle (*An epoch of rest: being some
chapters from a utopian romance*), which suggests a state of being, with
the dynamism of revolutionary politics, which suggests a purposeful
narrative. The novel opens and closes as a nineteenth-century realistic
narrative and – inasmuch as Guest enters Nowhere as a nineteenth-
century man with a vision of a better society, goes through certain
experiences and leaves it with his capacity to maintain the pursuit
of happiness deepened – Morris writes a conventional narrative of
character development. Yet the protean Thames of Morris's text suggests many interrelated and overlapping possibilities for self- and
social invention (not least in the relationship between a nineteenth-
century river and a post-revolutionary society, a stream of time and a
pool of calm) that bring into fundamental connection a whole series
of affective elements which the reader experiences as the rightness of
Marxist ideology in a living landscape.

Jerome's and Morris's use of language is fundamental to their
vision but, again, it has given their critics some difficulty. Jerome
sought an effect of counterpoint, using the demotic 'colloquial clerk's
English' of *Three Men in a Boat* to parody J's poetic and philosophical
musings and to endorse the energy and interest of everyday social
intercourse; but 'conversations garnished with such phrases as "bally
idiot", . . . "doing a mouche" . . . "who the thunder" and so forth'
were guaranteed to arouse outrage or contempt.[50] The popularity of
such a novel inspired fears about the perceived appropriation and
adaptation of the English language by the lower classes, fears that still
fuel modern debates about 'dumbing-down' and American cultural
imperialism.[51]

Morris's simplicity is seen as disorientating, with a childlike
insistence and archaisms which are subversive of his futuristic
vision.[52] Yet such reactions are odd for, in many ways, the discourse
of Nowhere is its most radical feature. Morris was well aware that the
language of the late nineteenth century carried associations of class,

of urbanisation, of *laissez-faire* economics and of labour which were dangerous reminders of the misery that these things produced. He stripped the language of *News from Nowhere* of the connotations of contemporary urbanisation and industrial history as far as possible. Instead, he deployed a concentrated and closely focused language of the senses and emotions which promises the possibility of collective understanding.

In his attempt to evoke an 'atmosphere' of future happiness, Morris distanced the language of Nowhere not only from the literary language of realism, but also from the artful language of rhetoric and the subtleties of psychological ambiguity.[53] He remade the intellectual, the logical and the ideological in the image of the human and natural world (experience, sensation), and simplified them in the mathematical sense, making meaning single. Because of this *News from Nowhere* has been described as a picture, a trance, and, of course, the dream that it says it is.[54] Each of these images responds to the reader's sense of verbal patterns, and the shift from narrative to verbal texture is similar in effect to Jerome's time-displacing collage. The reiteration of 'happy', 'pretty', 'sunny', 'healthy', 'blush' etc. evokes a continuous state of being, not time-related action, a public mood to be witnessed and enjoyed, not a private pleasure to be satisfied by narrative closure.

In their different ways, Jerome K. Jerome's *Three Men in a Boat* and William Morris's *News from Nowhere* formulated an aesthetic 'capable of creating ideal constructs of reality and inducing an aesthetic appreciation of political thought' for the late nineteenth century.[55] Jerome seizes the 'now' and demonstrates the value of the individuals who make up the 'masses' and the delights of a new egalitarianism through a generous-spirited humour. Morris projects his vision forward into the future, bringing the apparently conflicting ideologies of scientific materialism and affective humanism together in a vision of a happy society. For both, a dream of the diffused city, of the difference but interaction between the best of the rural and the urban, of the fluidity of change, is captured in the site of their suburban imaginary, the river Thames. Other utopias were less expansive and less generous than those of *News from Nowhere* and *Three Men in a Boat*. Deeply embedded in Morris's and Jerome's grand visions of social transformation and collective happiness were suburban tropes which, with differing degrees of emphasis, made the crucial connections between space, power and knowledge that characterise the fiction of the suburbs: the location of personal and social reinvention; the need for harmony between individual, culture and place; and the intrinsic value of the ordinary.

Notes

1 Jerome K. Jerome, [1889] *Three Men in a Boat (to say nothing of the dog)* (Stroud: Alan Sutton, 1989), and Morris, *News from Nowhere*.

2 Patrick Parrinder, 'News from Nowhere, The Time Machine and the Break-Up of Classical Realism', *Science Fiction Studies*, 3 (1976), 265–274 (267).

3 James Buzard, 'Ethnography as Interruption: *News from Nowhere*, narrative, and the modern romance of authority', *Victorian Studies* (Spring 1997), 445–474 (446).

4 Raymond Williams, *Culture and Society* (Harmondsworth: Penguin, 1961), 159; Roger C. Lewis, '*News from Nowhere*: Arcadia or utopia?', *Journal of the William Morris Society*, 7: 2 (Spring 1987), 15–25 (18).

5 John Goode, 'Now from Nowhere: William Morris today' in *Collected Essays of John Goode*, edited by Charles Swann (Staffordshire: Keele University Press, 1995), 321–335 (321). Michelle Weinroth, *Reclaiming William Morris: Englishness, sublimity, and the rhetoric of dissent* (Montreal and Kingston, London, Buffalo: McGill-Queen's University Press, 1996) is also interesting on how critics have tried to co-opt Morris for a range of political and nationalist positions.

6 See 'Author's Advertisement' in Jerome K. Jerome, [1889] *Three Men in a Boat* (Ware: Wordsworth Classics, 1992).

7 *Punch* (1 February 1890), 57.

8 *Punch* (3 January 1891), 4.

9 Cited in Jerome K. Jerome, *My Life and Times* (New York and London: Harper Brothers, 1926), 114.

10 H. G. Wells in *The Saturday Review* (26 September 1896). Wells's comment arises from a sense of disappointment, shared by many in the literate classes, that the Education Act of 1870 had failed to educate the working classes. See Keating, *The Haunted Study*, 450.

11 See the discussion of the relationship between narrative strategies and the writing of history in Peter Burke, 'History of Events and the Revival of Narrative' in Burke (ed.), *New Perspectives on Historical Writing* (Cambridge: Polity Press, 1991), 233–248 (in particular 240 ff.).

12 Christopher Matthew and Benny Green, 'Introduction' in Jerome K. Jerome, [1889] *Three Men in a Boat* (London: Michael Joseph, 1982), 7.

13 'Temperament' was Morris's word for differentiating his private and imaginative apprehension of socialism from its ideology. See William Morris, 'Looking Backward', cited in E. P. Thompson, *William Morris: Romantic to revolutionary* (New York: Pantheon Books, 1976), 693.

14 *News from Nowhere*, 159.

15 Maud Bodkin, 'Archetypes in "The Ancient Mariner"' in David Lodge (ed.), *Twentieth Century Literary Criticism* (London: Longman, 1972), 190–200 (192).

16 J. J. Stevenson in *Building News* (26 February 1875), cited in Dennis
    Hardy and Colin Ward, *Arcadia for All: The legacy of a makeshift landscape*
    (London and New York: Mansell, 1984), 165.
17 Hardy and Ward, *Arcadia for All*. See chapter 5, 'Arcadia on the River'.
18 Matthew and Green, 'Introduction', 7.
19 *Three Men in a Boat*, 35.
20 *Three Men in a Boat*, 143.
21 Henry Taunt, [1872] *The Thames of Henry Taunt*, facsimile of 5th edition
    (1886–87), edited by Sue Read (Gloucester and Wolfeborough Falls:
    Alan Sutton, 1989), e.g. 232–235, 223–235, 232, 233. This was one
    of the best and the most popular of the guides to the Thames.
22 In his autobiography, Jerome recalls an incident from his youth that
    equates boating with godlessness. In his description of how he first
    began to go boating, he comments: 'England in those days was still a
    Sabbath-keeping land. Often people would hiss us as we passed, carrying
    our hamper and clad in fancy "blazers"' (Jerome, *My Life*, 111).
23 *Three Men in a Boat*, 70.
24 George Gissing's portrayal of the masses on a Bank Holiday in the
    chapter, 'Io, Saturnalia!' in *The Nether World* [1889], in which he creates
    a Bosch-like Garden of Earthly Delights, is very different. A comparison
    would make even clearer the imaginative optimism of Jerome's social
    vision, and the possibilities offered by the rejection of realism.
25 Herbert Spencer, *Social Statics: Or the conditions essential to human
    happiness specified and the first of them developed* (London: John Chapman,
    1851), 69.
26 *News from Nowhere*, 140.
27 *News from Nowhere*, 180.
28 Geoffrey Harvey, 'Introduction' in [1889] *Three Men in a Boat* (Oxford:
    Oxford University Press, 1998), xviii.
29 *Three Men in a Boat*, 125.
30 *News from Nowhere*, 132.
31 Geddes, *Cities in Evolution*, 86.
32 Cited in M. J. Bolsterli, *The Early Community at Bedford Park: 'corporate
    happiness' in the first garden suburb* (London: Routledge and Kegan Paul,
    1977), 76.
33 William Morris, *The Political Writings of William Morris*, edited by
    A. L. Morton (London: Lawrence and Wishart, 1984), 73.
34 Raymond Williams, *The Country and the City* (London: Chatto and
    Windus, 1973), 289.
35 H. G. Wells, *The Work, Wealth and Happiness of Mankind* (London:
    William Heinemann, 1932), 204; see also H. G. Wells, [1905] *A Modern
    Utopia* (London: Everyman, 1994), 5 ff.
36 Charles Booth, *Life and Labour of the People in London: Final volume*
    (London: Macmillan, 1902), 180.
37 Booth, *Final Volume*, 204–205.
38 Ebenezer Howard, *To-Morrow, A peaceful path to real reform* (London:
    Swan Sonnenschein and Co. Ltd, 1898).
39 Howard, *To-Morrow*, 10.
40 Howard, *To-Morrow*, 148.

41 Howard, *To-Morrow*, 7.
42 H. G. Wells, *Anticipations of the Reaction of Mechanical and Scientific Progress upon Human Life and Thought*, (London: Methuen, 1902) and Wells, *A Modern Utopia*. H. G. Wells's ideas about the future of society, which later came out in book form as *Anticipations*, were published in *The Fortnightly Review* during 1901. It was these articles and the later collected edition that put him firmly in the public eye as a social prophet.
43 'But from its very nature . . . fiction can never be satisfactory in this application [social forecasts]. Fiction is necessarily concrete and definite; it permits of no open alternatives' (Wells, *Anticipations*, 2, footnote).
44 Wells, *Anticipations*, 46.
45 Wells, *Anticipations*, 61–62.
46 T. W. H. Crosland, [1905] *The Suburbans* cited in Keating, *The Haunted Study*, 324.
47 Charles Booth's was only one of a number of important social surveys at the time, but its scope and his subsequent contributions to planning and transport debates made his work something of a measure for social development. See *The New Survey*, which plots social changes from the those recorded in Booth's survey to 1940. H. G. Wells's reputation now rests on a number of popular novels, but he was highly regarded as a social commentator in the early twentieth century. See Michael Foot, *H. G.: The History of Mr Wells* (London: Doubleday, 1995). Ebenezer Howard was the inspiration for the Garden Cities and their successors the New Towns, but the idea of the need for a human-scale balance between city and country in designing urban areas has profoundly influenced every aspect of urban planning in the twentieth century.
48 Goode, *Collected Essays*, 321.
49 Jerome, *My Life*, 189.
50 Contemporary review cited in John Carey, *The Intellectuals and the Masses: Pride and prejudice among the literary intelligentsia, 1880–1930* (London: Faber and Faber, 1992), 59; *Punch* (1 February 1890), 57.
51 Alfred Moss, *Jerome K. Jerome: His life and work*, with an introduction by Coulson Kernahan (London: Selwyn and Blount, 1928), 138.
52 See Parrinder, '*News From Nowhere*', 270; W. B. Yeats, 'The Happiest of Poets' in Geoffrey Grigson, *A Choice of William Morris's Verse* (London: Faber and Faber, 1969), 123; Fiona MacCarthy, *William Morris: A life for our time* (London: Faber and Faber, 1994), viii. Jack Lindsay argues for the positive nature of Morris's vision of the past in *William Morris: His life and work* (London: Constable, 1975), 378.
53 Krishan Kumar, 'A Pilgrimage of Hope: William Morris's journey to utopia', *Utopian Studies*, 5:1 (1994), 89–107 (89 ff.). See also Goode, *Collected Essays*, 324 ff. where he discusses the rhetorical strategies of *News from Nowhere* in terms of Morris's design work.
54 Marie-Louise Berneri, *Journey to Utopia* (London: Freedom Press, 1982), 259–260; Stephen Coleman and Paddy Sullivan (eds), *William Morris and News from Nowhere: A vision for our time* (Bideford: Green Books, 1990), 55.
55 Weinroth, *Reclaiming William Morris*, 14.

2

THE SUBURBAN IDYLL

Arthur Conan Doyle
Keble Howard
John Galsworthy

I N the 'Author's warning' at the beginning of *The Smiths of
Surbiton: A comedy without a plot* (1906), Keble Howard sets out
his manifesto for suburban fiction:

> In this book, possible patron, I have attempted to tell the story of two
> simple lives. You will observe that I have described it on the title page
> as 'a comedy without a plot'. There are no plots, you will remember, in
> simple lives . . .
>
> For the same reason, there are no people of title in this story; no
> epigrams; no deeds of heroism; no strangely beautiful women; no
> extraordinarily handsome men; no hairbreadth escapes; no theological,
> sociological, or tautological discussions.
>
> The Smiths are neither superior nor fashionable. They are sufficiently
> humdrum, indeed, to take a cheerful view of life, to be fond of each
> other, to have children, read the books they like, visit the theatres they
> like, and whistle the music they like.

Howard tilts here at sensational popular fiction and the serious social
problem novel, as well as briefly gesturing towards the prevalent
cultural snobbery which had identified the suburbs as the home of
low cultural forms and uninformed enthusiasms. He aligns himself
with what he argues is a new body of fiction, taking the suburbs as its
location, directed at a suburban readership and portraying a realistic
picture of suburban life. In fact, many of these fictions are examples
of romantic realism, merging representations of daily life in the suburbs with the promise of happiness and security in a domestic utopia.
Although they may play with issues of modernity, these novels are

essentially reactionary. They subordinate the reality of the city, emphasising instead the suburbs' moral distance from London and claiming them as an inviolable territory of the emotions in which the newly defined middle classes can be heroes and heroines. Keble Howard and Arthur Conan Doyle are representative of novelists who constructed idealised versions of the suburbs in response to clashes of contemporary opinion about the future direction of urban development. Directly or indirectly, they were part of a general attempt during the first years of the twentieth century to re-establish an equilibrium perceived to be have been lost during the turbulent 1880s and in the challenges to social convention of the 1890s.

Superficially, these romantic idylls share many characteristics with the utopias of William Morris and Jerome K. Jerome. They make a particular notion of happiness their concern, mounting a successful challenge (in terms of their considerable popularity) to the contemporary taste for social problem novels, to the grim realities of French naturalism that had dominated the 1880s, and to the ironic mode of the 1890s. In an attempt to 'take a cheerful view of life' – to create what we would call today a 'feel-good factor' – they offer their readers serene and circumscribed worlds that directly counterbalance a perception of the city as atomistic, unhealthy and corrupt. By moving from the slums to the suburbs, they present a city whose structures and processes appear to be initiated, implemented and managed for social improvement, and which is purpose-built for the convenience and pleasure of ordinary men and women. Ostensibly, these fictional suburbs are free from the moral and political contradictions of the inner city, promising a new civilisation of physical and economic liberation and of moral and physical health.

Romancing the contemporary suburb, however, was not without its artistic problems. However much they may have wished to, those writers who coupled their romances with realistic representations of London's suburbs could not pretend that the city did not exist. The interdependence of city and suburb was too close and too familiar to be totally disentangled while still offering an apparently authentic picture of suburban life. At the same time, none of these novels appears to suggest (or to feel that it was possible to suggest) that the values learned and lived in the suburb could inform or transform urban values, or even that such an interaction might be desirable. To evoke a mood of happiness within a modern context, it was important to create a sufficient sense of distance for readers to feel released from personal responsibility for urban problems. The shrinking of the social whole to the happiness of the individual and the consolidation of the city-suburb divide which we observe in these novels, clearly differentiate their domestic utopias from the holistic and transforming visions of William Morris and Jerome K. Jerome.

A conventionally realistic depiction of modern life also presented problems. A number of strategies were deployed to maintain a recognisable world while simultaneously creating an idyll which could absorb and neutralise the threatening complexity and change with which that world was associated. For instance, the imperative for housing which drove the expansion of the suburbs is mediated through a Christian perspective, to affirm the sanctity of home and family life. At a time when traditional religious practices were being questioned, it was not difficult to go from seeing family life as an expression of Christianity to seeing it as a form of religion in its own right. The home offered an appropriately modern secular religion in which individual interests and Christian ethics could be merged. Ernest Newton, a respected architect writing in the *Builder* in 1891, claimed that:

> Nowadays, when all religions are assailed, and we believe in nothing very strongly, it is almost impossible to make our churches express anything more than a sort of galvanised enthusiasm . . . Belief in the sacredness of home-life, however, is still left to us, and is itself a religion, pure and easy to believe.

His concluding statement, that 'love of home . . . is perhaps the only sentiment which a reticent Englishman is not ashamed to confess to; indeed it is his boast that the English language alone possesses the word "home" in its fullest sense', goes to the very heart of the values of the suburban romances.[1] Home life is a refuge for individuals who feel that institutionalised values have failed them, while the house itself, however small, becomes the signifier of a larger realm of personal meaning. Of course, this idea is not new in fiction. In the mid-nineteenth century, Charles Dickens, Bulwer Lytton and Wilkie Collins had all used the suburbs as a means of delineating the private and the public. However, in late nineteenth-century fiction, the idea had become more pervasive and more specifically a response to contemporary political and sociological debates.

Traditional gender roles were treated in a similar way. If authenticity was to be maintained without undermining suburban integrity, it was important to acknowledge women's changing aspirations but to subsume them in a traditional (if secularised) emphasis on the domestic sphere. In Doyle's and Howard's novels, newly independent young women, despite benefiting from changes in their social, political and legal positions and enjoying the social cachet the 'New Woman', are shown to choose the private sphere rather than being forced into it. These educated and energetic young women voluntarily opt for a domestic way of life which is offered as an ahistorical ideal of moral excellence (a version of the suburban imaginary) in preference to a public existence which functions as the testing ground of the particular historical moment (identified with the realistic context of the novel) through which the individual struggles towards timeless values.

The reworking of masculine identity is more complex. It is possible to argue that the traditional male role of actor in the public sphere remains predominant, and is simply subordinated in the suburban romances to the domestic setting. However, I would argue that because the suburban setting marginalises conventional images of masculinity even as it acknowledges them, it releases the possibility of a different masculinity. This indicator of a potential direction for suburban evolution is an issue that I explore in greater depth in a later discussion of the fictional working-class suburb, but it is important to note its emergence here in novels about the middle classes. Detaching the suburb from the economic logic of the city and the male world of work inevitably involved focusing on men's engagement in the feminine domain of the domestic. The masculine identity that is feminised by being located in the suburbs creates a gender problematic (which may be viewed positively or negatively), in that it seems to be completely at odds with the discourse of masculinity constructed by Britain's imperial vision. It exemplifies a cultural tension identified by José Harris, in which masculinity in the public sphere is shaped by what she calls 'a powerful strain of hierarchy, militarism, "frontier mentality", administrative rationality, and masculine civic virtue', while at home men are being drawn 'in the opposite direction, towards egalitarianism, "progressivism", consumerism, popular democracy, feminism and women's rights'.[2] It is difficult to judge from these novels (since the texts never allow the question to be formulated) whether readers accepted that the gentle masculinities of the suburban idyll could be reconciled with the public male role of defender of the realm.[3]

An important aspect of the transformation of urban into suburban consciousness in these novels is the profound repression of
economic realities which is implicit in the moral distancing of the city
and the resurrection of traditional values in modern dress. This is, of
course, the wider context for the decentring of men from the public
to the private sphere. The movement out to the suburbs had created
new populations, and was invariably connected with improved living
conditions and, therefore, with more stable employment and higher
rents or mortgages. To maintain their standard of living, most new
suburb-dwellers lived under the economic necessity of travelling
daily to the city to finance their suburban life. Yet a repression of the
hard economic facts that underpinned suburban society is common
to suburban romances, despite the realistic surface representation of
the daily patterns of commuter life which Howard and Conan Doyle
both carefully acknowledge. Family and marital love, neighbourliness
and individualism replace economics as the dynamic and logic of
their ideal worlds. The personal significance of the suburbs as a complete, coherent and satisfying world is substituted for the public
significance of the city.

These novels, then, repress the realism that they seem to recreate and celebrate. They record observed situations in engaging detail,
but do not attempt to interrogate them. They anchor their image of a
desirable lifestyle by associating it with recognisable work, domestic
and marital patterns which are largely accurate in referential terms.
However, as Kate Flint argues, they reflect back to their readers little
more than the aspirations that they already have. They emphasise
the importance of the ordinary person and everyday events and
claim the right to believe in happiness – but their world is partial. In
general, these texts do not engage with the demands of the present
or the needs of the future, but present themselves as objects of desire,
as fantasies which validate a suburban way of life. For all their apparent modernity, the new geographies of the suburbs appear innocent,
entering popular fiction as a feminised and domesticated site of
personal happiness and fulfilment.

The suburb as the territory of domestic bliss was clearly dear to
Arthur Conan Doyle. In the preface to a late novel, A *Duet* (1899),
he articulated his faith in the power of suburban love in a statement
which echoes Keble Howard's emphasis on the 'simple', the 'commonplace' and the novel as an evocation of 'atmosphere':

My aim has been, in an age of pessimism, to draw marriage as it may be, and as it often is, beautiful and yet simple, the commonplaces of life being all tinged, and softened, and glorified by the light of love. No startling adventures are here, for they do not come to such people as I have portrayed, nor would I have them sparkling and talking in aphorisms, for this is also unusual in suburban villas. It is atmosphere and the subtle, indefinable, golden-tinted atmosphere of love – which I have wished to reproduce.[4]

The world he created in his suburban fictions is the total antithesis of the London of the short stories for which he is best known – the foggy, ill-lit, mysterious London of Sherlock Holmes. Doyle wrote the first of these, and one of the earliest of the suburban romances, *Beyond the City: the idyl of a suburb*, in 1893, soon after moving with his wife and child to their own suburban home. In his biography of Doyle, John Dickson Carr commented that he:

rejoiced in his new house at number 12 Tennison Road, South Norwood. With its window-frames painted white against dark-red brick, its balcony over the front door, its walled garden, the house stood in semi-rural country ... Next year, he decided, he would have a tennis-lawn. Always fascinated by new contraptions, he had bought a tandem tricycle.[5]

This Norwood of pretty houses and open countryside, of physical activity and healthy personal pleasures, is the setting of a story of three families, the Denvers, the Westmacotts and the Walkers. Doyle (perhaps partly influenced by the Norwood delights of *David Copperfield*) confessedly set out to create a utopia, and he makes clear that the move from the city to the suburbs signifies a move towards domestic and moral perfection. The three families are among those who have decided on such a move – the new suburbanites who wished to turn their backs on the dangerous influences of city life.

Doyle carefully relates their decision to the contemporary scene in a lengthy passage which substantiates the world of the novel by locating it in a recognisable reality. I quote an extract here:

Long before there had been a thought of a township there ... old Mr. Williams had inhabited 'The Brambles', as the little house was called, and had owned all the fields about it ... Gradually, however, as the years passed, the City had thrown out a long brick feeler here and there, curving, extending, and coalescing, until at last the little cottages had been gripped round by these red tentacles, and had been absorbed to make room for the modern villa ...

> For years they [his daughters] had clung to the one field which faced
> their windows, and it was only after much argument and many heart-
> burnings that they had at last consented that it should share the fate of
> the others. A broad road was driven through their quiet domain, the
> quarter was re-named 'The Wilderness', and three square, staring,
> uncompromising villas began to sprout up on the other side.[6]

Here Doyle sums up the history of suburban growth using the
pejorative imagery familiar from the writings of hostile commentators.[7] However, the narrative reveals that the implications of
this discourse are misleading: the development is, in fact, a blessing.
The solitude and isolation of the rural turn into the caring community of the suburbs. The apparitions of an unfeeling, monster-like
city are, in fact, manifestations of the rejection of that city by a series
of happy, loving family units, who are private within their own walls
but at the same time bonded with their neighbours through progressive communal gardens.

The naming of the development as 'The Wilderness' is part of a
familiar metaphorical reversal that attempts to suggest that the new
is simply a reconfiguration of the old. The name appears at first to be
simply the builder's attempt to convey a sense of *rus in urbe*, but
Doyle turns this decorative conceit into a more complex ironic figure,
in order to celebrate the moral probity of the suburbs. The word
'wilderness' in 'Dwellers in the wilderness', the title of chapter 4, suggests a land of limbo, a place outside the structures and the security
of the city which is inhabited by a group of outcasts, and its use is
reminiscent of the way that East Enders had been described in the
1880s. The naming of the poor as outcasts had finally called into
question, not their own moral condition, but that of those who had
rejected them. In the same way, Doyle's metaphor raises the question,
'Who really live in the wilderness – the people of the suburbs, whose
lives are rooted in love and harmony, or the city-dwellers, who
are absorbed by the glamour of crowds and the struggle for money?'
The evidence cumulatively put before the reader substantiates the
viewpoint that to live 'Beyond the City' in 'The Wilderness' is to
have preferred freedom from moral contamination and a life of moral
order.

However, by locking suburbs and city into a *doppelgänger* relationship, and by equating the abandonment of problems with the
search for moral strength, Doyle's text suggests an ambiguity in the
fundamental assumptions behind the narrative. This ambiguity is

increased by a narrowing perception as to what actually is evil about the city. The evil of London is not the city as such, but the City, the modern manifestation of Mammon. The City is represented as powerful and important: nevertheless, it is fraught with moral dangers. This idea is explored through the hero of the novel, Harold Denver, whose parents are delighted when he is offered a job as a stockbroker, but who is tempted by money, falls, and is redeemed by the power of his domestic stronghold in the suburbs. The focus of the novel rarely leaves the suburbs. It is here that Harold is supported when, before his marriage, the evils of the City temporarily overwhelm him. His fiancée, Clara, refuses to accept his offer to release her from their engagement, and she gives Harold the strength he needs to recoup his loss both of money and morality through the special virtue of the suburbs – hard work, that neat link between Christian ethics and capitalism. The concluding paragraph of the novel relates his struggle to the broader theme:

> With his sweet and refined home atmosphere he is able to realise his wish, and to keep free from the sordid aims and base ambitions which drag down the man whose business lies too exclusively in the money market of the vast Babylon. As he goes back every evening from the crowds of Throgmorton Street to the tree lined peaceful avenues of Norwood, so he has found it possible in spirit also to do one's duties amidst the Babel of the City and yet to live beyond it.[8]

The adoption of a suburban life, then, is seen as a conscious decision to balance the demands (or 'duties') of capitalism which shape the outer world with the demands of conscience that shape the inner world. In these terms, Doyle can present moving beyond the city as dynamic rather than escapist – a positive move intended to consolidate the ethics of Christianity and reconnect the individual with a morality that had begun to be unbalanced by sociologically perceived and politically implemented visions of economic and social justice.

It was important to Conan Doyle that the values he endorsed were seen as traditional, and that the reader recognised that suburban growth was only new in terms of bricks and mortar. Newness was seen as a positive value, in that it symbolised the possibility of man's moral renewal, but it was in no way desirable when it appeared in the form of new ideas or new modes of thought. The new is represented in *Beyond the City* by Miss Westmacott, a middle-aged but energetic woman who lives in 'The Wilderness'. She storms into the

suburb carrying dumb-bells, breaking time-honoured social conventions, rallying the suburb to the cause of the New Woman, and
almost overwhelming the emotions of Clara's father, Dr Walker. In a
moment of revelation, Dr Walker comes to his senses and puts Miss
Westmacott firmly in her place; she, in her turn, discovers that she
'liked the doctor better the more masculine and aggressive he
became'. In his life, as in his novels, Doyle valued the chivalric in
relationships between the sexes, and was critical of women, such as
the suffragettes, who broke the conventions of feminine behaviour.[9]

Despite the conflicts and crises, the Norwood of Doyle's novel
is one where the reader can be certain that nothing will go fundamentally wrong. The novel is set during a hot summer, and the daily
activities of tennis, cycling and walking provide the rationale of a
light-hearted community. The surroundings are rural. The air is filled
'with the low drone of insects', and although London is a 'dun cloud
... stretching along the northern skyline', its influence has been
effectively distanced.[10]

By the end of the novel the separate individuals living in the
new houses of 'The Wilderness' have bound themselves together by
marriage and mutual help. Through them suburbia has become
the microcosm of emotional and moral life, 'a common stage' where
'love and humour and fears and lights and shadows were so swiftly
succeeding each other'.[11] Out of the adherence to good moral values
springs personal happiness and laughter – which dominate the tone
of *Beyond the City*.

Doyle's suburban vision is not as far away from his detective
and adventure stories as it may at first seem. He frequently uses the
supposed sanity and moral soundness of the suburbs in these stories
to highlight the strangeness or exoticism of a plot or character. Fear
of invasion – from any number of countries, but notably from France,
Germany or Russia – fuelled a succession of novels during the late
nineteenth and early twentieth centuries and exemplifies an anxiety
about Britain's vulnerability on the world stage. In Doyle's case, this
fear is not one of enemy battalions, but of individuals from countries
colonised by Britain entering the country along the paths pioneered
by the imperialists themselves and threatening the safety of the home
nation.[12] When Holmes and Watson arrive at a 'third-rate suburban
dwelling-house' in London and the door is opened by 'a Hindoo servant, clad in a yellow turban, white loose-fitting clothes, and a yellow
sash', Doyle is announcing danger.[13] Invasions of the suburbs are

frequent. Upper Norwood, the sunny home of the Walker family, is not only the location of *The Sign of Four* (1890) but of the terrible murder in 'The Norwood Builder', while South Brixton is the apparently unexceptionable location of a terrible drama of colonial greed, played out in the humblest of surroundings, in 'The Adventure of the Veiled Lodger'. As Joseph McLaughlin argues, Doyle 'reimagines London as a frontier under threat of invasion from abroad'.[14] In the Sherlock Holmes stories, we see the fears that lay behind his construction of suburban idylls. The suburbs are the last line of resistance. If the extraordinary and/or the evil gain a foothold in the suburbs, then the spirit of England is truly endangered.

It would be easy, but unhelpful, to see Doyle's suburban world as merely an exercise in escapism. As I argued earlier, many contemporary commentators shared his vision of the suburbs' positive contribution to the quality of life. Equally, there is no intrinsic reason why either a contemporary or a modern reader should deny the possibility of personal happiness through love and family. It is the novel itself which questions the authenticity of Doyle's vision, by configuring the imaginary space of the suburbs so absolutely in terms of moral, spiritual and personal distance that it becomes impossible to sustain the logical connection between city and suburb, and to integrate the financial world of the City and its imperatives with the suburban domestic idyll that they make possible. Although Doyle's text implies that the geographies of the heart and of the pocket can safely overlap, the novel creates fault lines at the boundaries between them which undermine its coherence.

Keble Howard's immensely popular suburban novels were published in the early twentieth century and are untroubled by the city/suburb dialectic that haunted Conan Doyle, whose age (he was some twenty years older than Howard) and experience perhaps meant that inner city problems were a more urgent reality for him. Howard's novels also focus on the ordinary and on everyday family life, but they subsume issues of moral probity, financial security, class status and even suburban location into a normative infrastructure for a world of unproblematic happiness. The only acknowledgement of an alternative perspective is expressed in a series of prefaces, such as the one with which I opened this chapter, which affirm the values of suburban life and reject the satirical debunking of them. Howard writes his fictions in deliberate opposition to what he perceived as

3

'London is a dun cloud . . . stretching out along the northern skyline'
Crystal Palace from West Norwood, illustration by John Lukor Jnr from
Percy Fitzgerald, *London City Suburbs as they are Today*

cultural norms, and in his mission to give entertainment to suburban readers he makes an interesting case for a suburban aesthetic. He locates his work, like the suburbs themselves, in the middle ground – at the interstices of contemporary taste, between high and low culture ('there is no scope for artistic work between Mayfair and Whitechapel'), and between modernist plotlessness (modern 'cleverness') and gratuitous satire (which, interestingly, he calls the 'old-fashioned treatment'). His material, he claims, is drawn from 'the middle classes', a claim which is 'a confession of mediocrity' because it does not satisfy the current preference for realist novels about the working classes or romances about the upper classes.[15]

In the three novels that make up the *Smiths* series, *The Smiths of Surbiton* (1906), *The Smiths of Valley View* (1909) and *The Smiths at War* (1917), which were the most popular of his prolific output, Howard presents a sequence of affectionately humorous episodes strung together within a framework of a family – of growing up, marrying and having children.[16] The humour appears as intrinsic to the episodes and not as an authorial style. Readers are invited to understand the episodes as events in the grand narrative of 'Life' – events which revolve around neighbours, reading circles, and supper parties – but the underlying impulse is love, whose most pervasive and treasured images or icons are the garden gate, the front door and the evening fireside. Each episode resolves the conflicts, dangers or disasters that threaten to overwhelm the ordinariness of daily life; and the conventional happy ending is diffused into a general mood, described by one reviewer as 'simplicity and naturalness', and by another as a 'constant shimmer'.[17] Only in the suburbs can the ordinariness envisioned by Keble Howard flourish, because only in the suburbs can the ordinary, the domestic and the personal be recognised as serious. This is a world in which bachelordom is 'a state of barbarity', and a house's perfection is measured by its 'little garden' and its 'admirable situation, two minutes from the river and seven from the station' – the complete embodiment of the *rus in urbe* dream.[18]

Despite his claim that these novels have no plot (a claim made explicit in the subtitle of *The Smiths of Surbiton*), the events in them are part of a sequence that creates two interlocking narratives crucial to his version of the suburban idyll. The first is a realistic narrative, a story of upward mobility in which the rewards of hard work are measured in terms of property. At the end of *The Smiths of Surbiton*, the

Smiths move from Surbiton to a larger house called Valley View, while their newly married daughter moves into a small house just around the corner. The second is less a linear narrative than an evocation of a steadily increasing sense of happiness. The love of Mr and Mrs Smith extends to all of their family and their friends, right down to Aline, the youngest member of the family. The radiating nature of this love is graphically illustrated in the family tree at the beginning of the book. In the suburbs, husbands and wives pass on an emotional inheritance to their families, democratising a dynastic system underpinned by aristocratic or political power.

It is difficult not to feel that Howard cheats in his portrayal of 'simple lives' and their blissful happiness, although there is no overt textual tension of the kind that prompts readers of Doyle's novels to ponder on the equation of money and class with love, happiness and the value of continuity. Money (enough to provide a buffer between the Smiths and disaster) and middle-class upward mobility are the norms, while the useful convention of 'plotlessness' helps Howard's novels to evade the reader's questions. The charity-child taken in by Mrs Smith conveniently disappears later in the novel. Mr Smith's work is lucrative but apparently undemanding. When young George Smith is convalescing, a housekeeper is immediately engaged to look after him. The servants are treated as friends, but they never abuse their privileged position in the family. A carefully itemised list of wedding presents seems entirely unconnected with the hard cash needed to buy them. While slum novels struggle with the dramas of survival, Howard's conservative fictions celebrate what the new middle classes have won for themselves, and locate material success unproblematically in the matrix of family love.

Howard brings the same unquestioning treatment to a number of contemporary themes. *The Bachelor Girls and their Adventures in Search of Independence*, published in 1907, sets itself up as a light-hearted challenge to the 'New Woman' fiction which had made such an impact on the novel market during the 1890s. Howard prefaces a series of amusing incidents, in which two young women try to earn a living in London on their own, with the following observation: 'There is, I know, a tacitly accepted clause in the legislation of fiction which decrees that novels dealing with the struggles for existence of attractive, educated young gentlewomen shall proceed on a level of gloom and end in utter darkness.'[19] In Howard's novel two friends, with little money but high hopes of independence, leave the suburbs to make their way in London. There they are stalked and badly frightened by a man who turns out to be a helpful neighbour living in the same apartment block. The beautiful Billie is enticed to the theatre by another man, who grabs her in the dark; but the incident, which culminates in a loud slap, is comically told. Billie's hard-working flatmate has some success with her illustrations, but none with her writing, and fails to earn enough to support them. Finally, both young women are happy to return to their homes in St John's Wood and concentrate on the love that has entered both their lives during their time in London: only in the suburbs can love find fulfilment. In this novel, the power of the fatally attractive 'Circe' – as Charles Booth called London in the 1880s – is shadowy, vanquished by more substantial suburban pleasures. London is like the Europe of today's student back-packers – a place that is visited as a rite of passage on the way to suburban adulthood. The happy ending, set in a garden in St John's Wood, lies not simply in the restoration of domesticity in marriage, but, Howard claims, in the fact that he chose to finish his novel when he did. The final paragraph tells the reader that in a novel without plot, the ending is, after all, arbitrary:

> Novelists seem afraid to end their books in that way nowadays. It is supposed to be inartistic. I don't know why. If you choose to say good-bye to your characters while the sun is shining, instead of waiting for the clouds to gather, your ending is happy instead of unhappy. That is all the difference.[20]

It is interesting to compare this novel with H. G. Wells's *Ann Veronica*, published two years later, which tells an almost identical tale. The latter novel offered an apparently radical view of a young women's quest for freedom and was instantly condemned for its portrayal of adultery and its anti-marriage views. In *Ann Veronica*, London is portrayed as a dangerous metropolis in which women are particularly vulnerable. As she sets about liberating herself from her suburban background, the difficulties that the heroine encounters are unpleasant and vividly evoked: she is stalked through London by a stranger, nearly raped by a person whom she trusts, and thrown into prison after a suffragette rally. Nevertheless, she still has the courage to defy society and elope with Capes, her tutor, who is a married man. H. G. Wells's radicalism, however, is more apparent than real. After her abandonment to passion, the conclusion of the novel sees

Ann Veronica reconciled with her family, a mother, and head of a beautiful suburban home.

Of course, Howard's attacks on the pessimism of the contemporary novel are disingenuous, because the 'ordinary' that consists in sound finances, unquestioned love and lifelong happiness is as implausible as the content of any monothematic narrative. However, his work is a measure of the rise in social expectations at the turn of the twentieth century, and it demonstrates the powerful desire for stability and personal security that characterised the period, as well as the success of the suburban middle classes in creating a closed world that could fulfil such a desire. The values espoused by Keble Howard were clearly difficult for some to take seriously in his own time – his popularity did not save him from the inevitable ridicule that the alliterative 'Smiths of Surbiton' was bound to provoke. Certainly I would expect some readers today to find a synthetic sentimentality in Howard's novels, although I think that they have something of the enduring fascination of a soap opera, with its daily record of ordinary events in a small community. The common denominator of Howard's and Doyle's suburban novels is that, despite the familiarity of their daily round, such stories are insulated from a wider context of social meaning. It is this that differentiates them so clearly from the utopias of *News from Nowhere* and *Three Men in a Boat* although they share considerable common ground within the suburban genre. The meaning of their ordinariness is dependent on ignoring the existence of the social whole and privatising society's future as personal aspiration.

The images and attitudes encountered in *Beyond the City, Duet* and the *Smiths* series are pervasive in novels of the period. An early example is Florence Warden's mystery novel, *City and Suburban*, published in 1890, in which the newly-married heroine, Cicely, loses her desirable residence in an affluent suburb but finds happiness in a 'little one-brick-thick villa' in a working-class suburb inhabited by clerks.[21] In Shan Bullock's *The Barrys* (1899), Marian's and Frank's flat at Camberwell is the moral base of their lives. When Frank begins to roam the streets of Walworth, it is merely a matter of time before he is unfaithful to his wife. When Marian discovers his infidelity, she rejects him. Simultaneously, she leaves the flat, still furnished and to all appearances unchanged, but devoid now of the spirit of love that gave it meaning. When the couple are reconciled they meet at the old flat, which has been waiting for them. When Frank rounds the corner at the conclusion of the novel, seeing his home again is 'like

sighting heaven from the portals of Purgatory'.[22] Earlier in the novel
the couple had been observed by a friend through their window, in a
sequence which uses the window as a delimiting frame, marking out
the ideal domestic life from the moral chaos of the streets:

> They [Frank and Marian] stood side by side, faces aglow and their eyes
> rapt in admiration of the boy. Now Frank clapped his hands, now shook
> his curls, now turned towards the tall lady and laughed . . . There is a
> hush . . . The child looks from one to another; suddenly stretches its
> arms, and with a cry of 'Father's boy', is carried to Frank's shoulder.[23]

In an earlier novel, *Autobiography and Deliverance* (1881), this
same ideal is achieved by Mark Rutherford after much mental and
emotional pain, while at the end of *Love and Mr Lewisham* (1900) by
H. G. Wells, George Lewisham (in an admittedly ambiguous compromise) sees that the future lies in family life in the suburbs. No
wonder the *Daily Telegraph* felt moved to comment in its review
of that novel that 'a curious wave of what one might call domestic
sentiment seems to be sweeping over the novelist of today'.[24]

In *The Man of Property* (1906), the first novel in *The Forsyte Saga*
series, John Galsworthy offers a penetrating analysis of the popular
suburban idyll, exposing its contradictions while still constructing the
suburbs as the geography of a desired future. *The Man of Property* is
concerned with the rise and fall of the new business classes, and with
the related theme of urban migration, in particular the movement of
population into the city from the country in the early nineteenth
century, and from the city to the suburbs in the mid- to late nineteenth century. Throughout the novel, which opens in the 1880s,
the text is counterpointed with a historical context which provides
diverse perspectives through which the reader can view the actions
and aspirations of Soames Forsyte as he plans to move out of London
into his architect-designed suburban villa.

The Forsytes' relative location on the political map, and their
uncertain direction for the future, are encoded by Soames's centrifugal drive towards a new spatial, cultural and political territory.
Galsworthy is dealing here with pretenders to the upper class, whose
power is threatened by the social changes of the 1880s. Soames has
inherited the Forsytes' entrepreneurial family legacy, but he is dimly
conscious of wanting to define it differently. The title of the novel,
and references to him in the text by several members of his family
as the 'Man of Property', might seem to mark him out as the most

successful of his family. In fact, this title marks out a more equivocal social difference from the older Forsytes. Investing in residential property, the reader is told, is quite different from being a 'man of property'.[25] By choosing to build a house in the country, and in so doing transforming country into suburb, Soames is making a radical change to the location of his family, and is seen by himself and them as constructing a new version of the Forsyte identity.

The countryside around London is foreign territory, which Soames must summon up the courage to conquer. As he explores the site for his new house, he feels he is lost in a 'prairie' and is 'daunted by the loneliness'. He is 'the pioneer leader', 'advancing to the civilization of this wilderness'.[26] Robin Hill, the name of the site that he purchases, is at first quite literally an empty space, a place which can be freshly 'mapped', a cultural location where Soames can situate his future. It is certainly an unwritten textual space. Writing as 'an impressionist working with a realistic technique',[27] Galsworthy encourages the reader to see the social, personal and moral complexities which inform the territorial and cultural transition represented by Robin Hill, and to understand how Soames's desire to relocate the Forsyte future fits into this matrix of ideas.

Soames's first impulse probably derives from a wish to be part of the vanishing world of the pre-1880s suburban aristocracy, a world in which the rising mercantile and business classes appeared to have been acceded the rights of those 'great middle classes' who were 'the wisest, the purest, the strongest in all the land'.[28] At that time, the term 'suburb' was well defined, and denoted the elegant villas and spacious grounds which were perceived as fitting rewards for their achievements. Soames's impulse, then, can be understood as imperial – an attempt to maintain the diminishing empire of the wealthy middle classes – but although this impulse is reactionary, it is not inspired by nostalgia, since he is not recalling his own past. Rather, he is aware of the Forsytes' tentative grip on middle-class status, and the reader knows why. In one sense, Robin Hill is his attempt to locate himself in a more permanent and enduring class hierarchy, but by the end of the 1880s the suburbs had become a class melting-pot. A new, unstable system of relative class positions had emerged, defined in relation to subsequent waves of urban emigrants. Robin Hill, for all its apparent rural seclusion, was likely to be rapidly surrounded by the 'tentacles' of middle-class developments such as 'The Wilderness' in Doyle's novel, *Beyond the City*.

Soames has no grasp of the political and social realities around him because, as Galsworthy stresses, his emotional and sexual imagination is shaped, not by experience and observation, but by contemporary novels.[29] It would be fascinating to know just which novels Galsworthy was thinking of; according to the chronology of the novel, they must have been available from mid-century. However, the echoes of colonial discourse – of migration, of new worlds, of setting up a new community in a better environment and of maintaining traditional values away from the dangers and the corruption of the city – which Galsworthy allows to resonate in Soames's imagination – are more characteristic of the 1890s. His imagination also enshrines a reactionary Christian ideal. The suburban immigrants are spiritual refugees from the Babylon of London. The suburbs have the power to recover a lost Eden where women, unlike Eve, are beyond temptation, and the Tree of Knowledge is rendered harmless in domestic gardens fertilised by domestic love.

There is no doubt that Soames has intimations of artistic, sexual and emotional possibilities beyond his own experience, and that his desire to move to Robin Hill is a way of trying to realise these for himself in the future. However, his aspirations, based on idealised representations or misappropriated artistic visions and rooted in individualistic strategies of escapism and control, are ultimately incapable of realisation. Soames's failure to actualise his suburban site as the locus of the future reveals him as a Forsythian and a human failure, and reveals his view of his world to be an inadequate one. He is a Forsythian failure because he cannot consolidate the investment in which he has sunk his capital. He is a human failure because he cannot understand the nature of his own deepest feelings and thoughts, or how they apply to the evolution of the sexual relationships between men and women.

Galsworthy underlines Soames's failure of understanding in the depiction of his wife, Irene, for whom Robin Hill is ostensibly built. Soames's strongest reason for choosing the Robin Hill site is that it reminds him of his first feelings for Irene, and regenerates in him the freshness of his early responses – responses which he has learned to repress. As his realisation grows that she does not love him and will never respond to him as he had hoped, his expressions of love revert to convention and are translated into terms of property. Robin Hill appears to promise him a second opportunity to engage with her, the new beginning that is encoded in the suburbs. But Soames's limited, self-gratifying imagination works through integration rather than diversification and change. Irene is incorporated into his picture of their suburban future through the fictional images of domestic bliss, which owe much to Ruskin's portrayal of the role of women in *Sesame and Lilies* (1865); but, unlike the wives and daughters of the suburban romances, she does not choose to be a suburban housewife and never lives with Soames at Robin Hill.

Yet Irene seems to hold the key to a different perspective on suburban living. What future did Galsworthy envision for women in his suburban geography of the modern? His portrayal of Irene suggests the complexity of imagining a future identity for women. In the 1880s of the novel Irene exists only for male scrutiny. Interlacing myth with realism, she moves across the undeveloped Robin Hill site as an inhabitant of the Garden of Eden, as Eve alive with the potential for banishment, the female principle and archetype of irresistible but dangerous beauty. Inasmuch as the character of Irene is no more than an unfocused medley of men's perceptions, her identity remains the hermeneutic empty space at the centre of Galsworthy's novel. He had little help from his contemporaries in finding solutions to her mystery. Those visionaries and social planners who wrote about the suburbs at the turn of the twentieth century saw only the broad human picture. In the face of the human distress caused by inner city conditions and the urgency of change, few of them differentiated between the genders or speculated about their individual futures. A possible answer, however, lies in 'Indian summer of a Forsyte', which acts as a second ending to *The Man of Property*. In this interlude, it is to Robin Hill that Irene returns after her divorce from Soames and the sale of the house to Soames's cousin, Young Jolyon. There she befriends Young Jolyon's uncle, who gladly gives her access to the house and gardens, and it is there where she lives before and after marriage to Young Jolyon. It is interesting to speculate as to whether Irene represents the possibility of a suburban ideal within a new gender politics – finding and promoting an independent emotional and sexual identity for women. The ideal future promised by the suburbs is a domestic future. However, Galsworthy seems to be suggesting that such a future could not even be imagined by a man like Soames, for whom ownership is the measure of value, and that it need not be the future envisioned by Doyle and Howard in which intelligent and freethinking women choose suburban home and family as the fullest expression of their femininity. Rather, the suburbs might become a site for the realisation of emotional and sexual equality between men and women.

In *The Man of Property*, Galsworthy refutes the case for the value of suburban life when it is based on the privatisation of utopia and the refusal to engage with the modern. He constructs the failure of Soames from his readiness to read the future in the inadequate models of the past and present: the equation of marriage and property; the pre-lapsarian garden; and the depoliticised rejection of the values represented by London. Galsworthy intended *The Man of Property* to depict the evolution of a society, a dynasty and a class, as well as a history of perceptions, emotions and individuals; perhaps most powerfully, he wanted it to show history in the making.[30] Read in this context, *The Man of Property* is a statement about the failure of human imagination to realise a new kind of social organisation relocated beyond the city in the new world of the suburbs; and it poses a powerful challenge to the suburban idylls of writers such as Howard and Doyle.

Notes

1 Ernest Newton, 'Home-Like Houses', *Builder* (30 May 1891), 60–61 (60).

2 Harris, *Private Lives*, 6.

3 See Sidney J. Low, 'The Rise of the Suburbs', *Contemporary Review*, 60 (October 1891), 545–558. Low's descriptions of the pioneering suburbanites and of outdoor suburban activities and their impact on moral and physical soundness provide an interesting context for Doyle's suburban novels, particularly since Low argues that suburban virtues can be seen as serving the purposes of the Empire.

4 Arthur Conan Doyle, (1899) *A Duet, with an occasional chorus* (London: Smith, Elder and Co., 1903), vii.

5 John Dickson Carr, *The Life of Sir Arthur Conan Doyle* (London: John Murray, 1949), 85.

6 Arthur Conan Doyle, *Beyond the City: The idyl of a suburb* in *The Great Shadow and Beyond the City* (London: Simpkin, Hamilton, Kent and Co., 1893), 157–320 (162–163).

7 Criticism of the ugliness of suburban expansion was widespread: see, for example, 'The Debasement of the London Suburbs', *The Times* (21 April 1892), 14; Percy Fitzgerald, *London City Suburbs as they are Today* (London: Leadenhall Press, 1893), 78, 157, 161; and 'The "Uglification" of London', *Builder* (27 March 1897), 287–289.

8 Doyle, *Beyond the City*, 320.

9 See Paula Krebs's discussion of Doyle's chivalric code in *Gender, Race and the Writing of Empire: Public discourse and the Boer War* (Cambridge: Cambridge University Press, 1999), 89–94.

10 Doyle, *Beyond the City*, 195.

11 Doyle, *Beyond the City*, 30.

12 See Michael Matin, '"The Hun is at the Gate!": Historicizing Kipling's militaristic rhetoric from the imperial periphery to the national center: part II, the French, Russian and German threats to Great Britain', *Studies in the Novel*, 31:4 (Winter 1999), 432–470.

13 Arthur Conan Doyle, [1890] *The Sign of Four* in *The Complete Sherlock Holmes* (Harmondsworth: Penguin, 1984), 89–158 (100).

14 Joseph McLaughlin, *Writing the Urban Jungle: Reading Empire in London from Doyle to Eliot* (Charlottesville and London: Virginia University Press, 2000), 21.

15 Keble Howard, 'An Open Letter to the Smiths (of Surbiton)', preface to *The Smiths of Valley View: Being further adventures of the Smiths of Surbiton*, 2nd impression (London: Cassell and Co., 1909).

16 Keble Howard, *The Smiths of Surbiton: A comedy without a plot* (London: Chapman Hall, 1906); Keble Howard, *The Smiths at War* (London: John Lane, 1917).

17 Excerpts from reviews in the *Daily Mail* and *Punch* of the first edition of Keble Howard, *The Bachelor Girls and their Adventures in Search of Independence* (London: Chapman and Hall, 1907). These quotations are taken from reviews printed in the advertisement pages of the first edition of the novel.

18 Howard, *The Smiths of Surbiton*, 21, 8.

19 Keble Howard, author's note in *The Bachelor Girls*.

20 *The Bachelor Girls*, 324.

21 Florence Warden, *City and Suburban* (London: F. V. White and Co., 1890), 102.

22 Shan Bullock, *The Barrys* (London and New York: Harper and Bros., 1899), 297.

23 *The Barrys*, 274.

24 Unsigned review, *Daily Telegraph* (6 June 1900), 11.

25 John Galsworthy, [1906] *The Man of Property* (Hammondsworth: Penguin, 1967), 25.

26 *The Man of Property*, 66.

27 John Galsworthy, diary entry for 21 December 1910, cited in Harold V. Marrott, *The Life and Letters of John Galsworthy* (New York: Scribner's Sons, 1936), 308.

28 Frederick Greenwood, 'What Has Become of the Middle Classes?', *Blackwood's Magazine*, 138 (August 1885), 175–189 (176).

29 *The Man of Property*, 71.

30 See John Galsworthy, letter to Edward Garnett, 6 June 1905 in Marrott, *Life and Letters*, 174, in which Galsworthy considers the possibility (later abandoned) of tying *The Forsyte Saga* into a coherent scheme of social and political commentary.

3

※

BEYOND THE SUBURBS

Richard Jefferies
Edward Thomas
E. M. Forster

THE suburban idea did not only inspire positive visions of the future such as we have already encountered. Some writers reacted in dismay to the suburbs, seeing them as the heartland of cultural failure, and creating personalised utopias in explicit opposition to the homogeneous future that they appeared to embody. The concluding line of Edward Thomas's poem 'The Glory' – 'I cannot bite the day to the core' – exemplifies a prevalent sense of frustrated alienation from a culture that was perceived as undervaluing the traditional English landscape and English literary ideals, and, by implication, the modes of feeling to which they gave access. It also offers an apt epigraph to a range of writings by Richard Jefferies, E. M. Forster and Edward Thomas himself. The suburban imaginary – whether envisioned in the radical utopias of *News from Nowhere* and *Three Men in a Boat*, the moral idylls of Howard's and Conan Doyle's romances, or the delicate equilibrium of Galsworthy's cautious optimism in *The Man of Property* – could only seem inadequate and inappropriate to those who perceived the suburbs as a symbol of the diminution and dilution of human, cultural and national aspiration. Although, like the suburban writers themselves, they turned to the countryside, that familiar site of resistance to cultural change, in order to address what they experienced as a cultural deficit, they did so in an attempt to recover vanishing traces of the past from the suburban palimpsest. Their hope was that an individual apprehension of the sublime could resolve, through art, what they perceived as the fracturing of culture and the fragmentation of human experience.

The overlaps and connections between Jefferies, Thomas and Forster – writers from very different contemporary contexts and with very different literary reputations – are various and complex, and I do not intend to imply that these writers shared a conscious role in a literary movement or even a congeniality of literary purpose. The writings I discuss comprise an eclectic mix of journalism, essays, short stories, novels and quasi-autobiography, and I will consider the disparities between their authors' literary positions and achievements in an examination of specific texts later in this chapter. However, it is important to recognise the shared impulse that informed their visions. For Jefferies and Thomas, and to a lesser extent for Forster, the countryside was inscribed with personal memories and familiar associations: they drew on happy childhood experiences to recover the landscape as a symbolic home of the heart in their adult writings.[1] The countryside was always a much-loved reality; the ancient landscapes of Wiltshire and Gloucestershire, the South Downs of Sussex and the remote mountains of Wales were loved both for their beauty and as manifestations of a past that had not yet been completely erased. Although Jefferies, Thomas and, in particular, Forster, accepted that the suburbs were an inevitable consequence of urbanisation, their blurring of familiar demarcations, both topographical and cultural, confirmed what these writers did not want to or could not accept – that the countryside as a signifier of cultural and literary values was probably lost forever. As the landscape was overlaid with suburban development, they transformed the countryside into a psychological location; through their love of rural idylls and memories of childhood freedom and innocence, their faith in English continuities was transmuted into a private 'inner myth' through the alchemy of the imagination – a myth that housed their own internal resistance to the mundane external reality of suburban housing.

The aesthetic terrain of the utopias that they created, imagined through a mixture of classical and national myths shaped by a neo-Romantic sensibility, constituted an attempt to reshape the landscape of the modern and to restore or shore up cultural continuity. In their writings, the suburbs become a kind of shadowy borderland of ambiguous meaning or a parallel universe of appearances, beyond or behind which something else, wilder, deeper and truer, can be found by those who desire to discover it. This 'wild space' is a site of masculinity, where adventures, boyish pranks and carefree wanderings can be imagined; more importantly, it promises an encounter with a metaphysical and sexual sublime. When they are considered together, however, these texts put modes of feeling that they have borrowed from the Romantic and classical literary inheritance under stress. They question the privileging of artistic subjectivity and the validity of rural images as expressions of the modern, as well as the power of both to displace the suburbanisation of the imagination that was encroaching on cultural norms as surely as the suburbs were encroaching on the countryside. That the 'wild' was being gradually relegated to the margins of imaginative possibility was confirmed by the co-option of Romantic individualism by mass artistic production.

The aestheticised landscapes imagined by Jefferies, Thomas and Forster were expressions of a powerful and pervasive form of cultural longing. Even so, their 'utopias' seem often oddly inaccessible. They replace the collectivist happiness of the suburban ideal (whether it is desirable or not) with meanings which appear private, even coded, located in a psychosexual context which informs, but never completely coheres with, the narrative or commentary that presents it. This sense of dislocation between personal desire and the public reality of the landscape reflects a larger cultural dichotomy: when the twentieth century dawned, as Glen Cavaliero argues, 'the country and what it stood for were beginning to have an emotional and literary significance at odds with historic facts'.[2] Richard Jefferies' journalism and autobiography, Edward Thomas's essays, and some of E. M. Forster's short stories and early novels can be seen as part of a new and increasing self-consciousness that had made the concept of the countryside more culturally potent that the countryside itself. In these writings, the 'in-betweenness' of the suburbs is stretched so thinly that the past and the present, the country and the city, struggle to find a connection in the present moment.

A number of the writers' attempts to evoke a vision of human experience beyond the suburbs were produced specifically as discourses of resistance to suburbanisation. Nevertheless, the suburbs seem to become a point of reference in these writings, a fact which draws them inexorably back within the frame of the suburban idea, insisting on its cultural presence and demonstrating its shaping influence on literary production. Narratives of escape conjured up in the literary imagination become narratives of integration for their readers, domesticating the wild spaces and bringing all danger and sublimity back to the suburban fireside, whether it is represented by a village pub, a rented cottage or, in Forster's case, a university common room. As a close friend of Jefferies wrote to him about *Wild Life in a Southern County*, 'It is quite a book to take up when you wish to pay a fire-side visit to the country lanes and hedges'.[3] Both Jefferies and Thomas were dependent on London publishing houses to give them a living and so, ironically, economic necessity drove them to democratise their own subjectivities and to contribute to the commodification of the countryside – a fate that Forster escaped.

It is not surprising that many of these writings appealed to a literate, socially conscious readership, reassuring them that the countryside still existed, while simultaneously providing emotional and intellectual maps for their own mental landscapes. When Victorians and Edwardians recoiled from the city that they had created, they turned for relief to the countryside, mediated through popular books and images. As they walked and looked, they could enjoy a sense of adventure and exploration, a medley of cultural experiences from the Garden of Eden, the merging of natural and divine forms in Ovid, the ecstasies of Pan and England's own long pastoral tradition. With their pocket Keatses tucked into their bags, they could also be inspired by Romantic sensibilities and possibilities.

Art had rushed in to fill 'landscapes [that] were either empty ... or inhabited only by the special sensitivity of the poet and essayist'.[4] By the Edwardian period, as Ronald Pearsall comments: 'The countryside was treated as a phenomenon especially laid on by the Almighty for the edification of town-dwellers'.[5] Diarists, watercolourists and amateur photographers systematically set about capturing those elements of the landscape which were thought to epitomise the beauty of the English countryside. Henry Taunt's photographs of the Thames are a perfect example of this nostalgic impulse. The objectification of nature also became an issue of class and taste. Leisure activities and sightseeing in the countryside, celebrated in *Three Men in a Boat*, were for the working classes, while 'Nature, in my opinion', as Rider Haggard wrote in *Rural England*, 'only appears to the truly educated'.[6] The cultural moment that privileged the aesthetic experience of nature over nature itself was caught in Oscar Wilde's provocative essay 'The Decay of Lying', published in 1891. Wilde mocks the hypocrisy of those who wish to recover 'nature', arguing that artifice is the essence of civilised living, and that what we perceive in nature is not intrinsic but culturally constructed. He sees the move away from a natural state as progress: 'If nature had been comfortable, mankind would never have invented architecture, and I prefer houses to the open air'.[7] The logic of his argument, if not its intention, acknowledges the domestication of the Romantic sublime into a series of culturally accessible images.[8]

Two novels, E. M. Forster's *Howards End* (1910) and Edward Thomas's *The Happy-Go-Lucky Morgans* (1913), both of which explicitly address the issue of a suburban future, stand apart from this argument. Neither of these novels colludes with the rural dream, or attempts to establish its validity through the power of personal feeling, although both acknowledge the seductive attractiveness of a vision that can appear to find the resolutions of present problems through the revitalisation of the past. Instead, these texts confront the experience of cultural fracture as a complex moment of change. Neither *Howards End* nor *The Happy-Go-Lucky Morgans* offers an escape to an internalised rural utopia. Their struggle to find an aesthetic articulation of the sense of loss they experienced, which is discussed in more detail later in this chapter, reveals a determination to engage with the modern rather than the nostalgic. The possibility of utopia, whether realised politically and socially or as the creative apprehension of an individual sensibility, is considered and regretfully set aside.

Richard Jefferies is an interesting example of a writer who straddled the fissures of late Victorian culture and society, attempting to earn his living in the London marketplace while writing about the countryside, and simultaneously trying to transform it into a locus of spiritual meaning for a mass readership. Popular in his own day for his bucolic novels and prolific magazine articles, his work might well be dismissed as a curio today, if it did not express so clearly some of the most pressing concerns of his age. His importance to this discussion lies in the facts that he was an early exponent of the urban crisis that manifested itself in a resistance to suburbanisation, and that his thinking was 'symptomatic rather than original'.[9]

Chronologically, Jefferies' work is positioned at the margins of suburban literature. He wrote before the first wave of working-class suburban expansion in the 1890s, at a time when public consciousness was polarised between fears about the future of the countryside, and fears of violent class conflict provoked by the impact of the appalling conditions in London. This dualistic vision of city and country informs his dystopian novel, *After London* (1885), a powerful and disturbing indictment of urbanisation. The first part of the novel describes a London drowned in its own filth and returning to the marshlands from which it had emerged, and an England over-whelmed by a wilderness contaminated almost beyond recovery. However, the novel leaves the problems of the national future unre-solved. The love story of Felix and Aurora, which takes precedence in Part II, is a medieval-style courtly adventure which promises a hopeful new dawn, set in the last surviving area of rural beauty – a Camelot in a rediscovered Garden of Eden. Jefferies' resort to a romance narrative in this context suggests a failure of vision in response to the very fears he depicts. As Felix 'strides on westward' in the final sentence of the novel, there is a strong sense that he is vanishing into the past, rather than heading for the future as Jefferies implies.

Jefferies' vision of a self-destructive urban culture was a common one in the early 1880s. The shock of revelations about urban condi-tions made it difficult to see how an engagement with the present could provide a cultural bridge across the rupture between city and country, or restore what was perceived to have been lost.[10] At the beginning of his writing career, Jefferies still believed that the bound-aries between city and country were clear, claiming in 1879 that 'There is a frontier line to civilization and not far outside the great centres we come quickly even now on the borderline of nature.'[11] He also felt able to claim that the agricultural worker still held the key to power: 'If anything is done socialistically it probably will be through his agency.'[12] In his own time, Jefferies was perceived as a 'Man of the Fields', the title of a biography of him published in 1964. His early essays describing agricultural workers, village life and countryside scenes forged his identity as a writer, and fed the hunger of the Victorian reading public to feel that their connection with nature had not been lost.[13] However, the series of articles he wrote for the *Standard* on 'Nature Near London' in the last year of his life indicates his growing awareness that boundaries between the city and the country were being changed in subtle but far-reaching ways.

Jefferies' response to the London suburbs focused on the 'aristo-cracy, the first families of the suburbs', those successful upper-middle classes whose move out of the city he saw as a contributory factor in the commodification of the countryside as property value and class status.[14] In *Nature Near London*, a collection of these articles pub-lished in 1889, he combines descriptions of the considerable natural beauty to be found within easy walking distance of London, with comments on the way in which the new, successful business class was distorting and damaging a healthy relationship with nature in its affluent suburbs.[15] He was entirely hostile to the suburbs inasmuch as they furnished evidence of society's surrender to mediocrity, of its desire to find reconciliation between town and countryside, and of the individuation of that desire in gardens and suburban villas. He criticised 'semi-country seats, as the modern houses surrounded by their own grounds assume to be', and the attempts of suburban gardens to 'mimic the isolation and retirement of ancient country houses'.[16] The suburbs, he claimed, destroyed nature, since 'sewers carry away the water that used to moisten roots ... Gas-pipes frequently leak so much that the soil for yards is saturated' – an argument that anticipates later critiques of the suburbs such as H. G. Wells's *Tono-Bungay* (1909) and *The New Machiavelli* (1911).[17]

More interestingly, Jefferies felt that the speciousness of suburban man's relationship with the natural world went beyond mere status-seeking. He sensed that the structure of the suburbs was creating a kind of false consciousness and was the surface expression of a deep psychological restlessness. He argued that it was impossible to attempt to divide up one's life, working in the city and seeking rural peace in the suburbs, since, although each world had its own coherence, the power of each of them was unequal. Echoing an experience described in George Gissing's *The Nether World* (1889), and expressed even more powerfully at the end of Mark Rutherford's *Autobiography and Deliverance* (1882), he observed that once 'the unseen influence of mighty London' had been experienced it would always colour the suburb-dweller's perception of his world.[18] People were withdrawing from the dynamic universe of the city, where living and working were bound together, in the search for an ill-founded and ill-defined ideal. His description of a rich commuter reveals that those who adopted the new social patterns did not understand either the old aristocratic way of life or the essentials of a natural, rural one; but they pretended to both, while turning away from their social responsibilities towards the city from which their economic and class power was derived:

> And if the merchant spares an abstracted glance from the morning or evening newspaper out upon the fields from the carriage window, the furrows of the field have but little meaning ... The work in the field is so slow, the passenger by rail sees, as it seems to him, nothing going on ... Thus it happened that, although cornfields and the meadows come so closely up to the offices and warehouses of mighty London, there is a line and mark in the minds of men between them.[19]

Jefferies' 'line and mark' that lies between the country and the city in 'the minds of men' is the emerging suburban space, which is being claimed in denial of both rural and urban realities.

It is not difficult to see the similarities between the mental landscapes of the suburb-dwellers whom Jefferies criticised and his own ambiguous imaginative terrain, although one was shaped by an affluent material situation and the other by a quest for sublimity beyond the suburban 'outpost of bricks and mortar'.[20] Although he was compelled to satisfy the needs of the marketplace with bucolic and courtly novels and with the regular production of over a hundred essays of natural observation, Jefferies' words, as Edward Thomas suggested in his biography, are read through 'a glassy covering of the things described' which encodes his personal narrative of escape.[21] Jefferies borrowed from a tradition which was already culturally embedded, and which fused nature, the sublime, and personal vision in a neo-Romantic artistic transcendence, to bring about a private resolution of the cultural tensions in which he felt caught. Nowhere is this seen so clearly as in *The Story of My Heart*, a book that Jefferies himself called an 'Autobiography of a Soul or of Thought'.[22]

All Jefferies' writings are premised on the intensity and happiness of his unreflective boyhood, and on their objective correlative, the English countryside; but *The Story of My Heart*, published in 1883, most explicitly addresses this theme. It is Jefferies' prose *Prelude*, tracing his development from early experiences with nature and seeking to articulate his individual genius.[23] With Wordsworth, he laments the loss of the 'visionary gleam' and the perceived failure of manhood to fulfil the promise of boyhood's ideal state; but unlike Wordsworth, who wrote at the end of the eighteenth century, Jefferies fails to find a form and a language which could make his vision shareable at the end of the nineteenth. *The Story of My Heart* resonates with echoes not only of Wordsworth, but also of contemporary poets such W. B. Yeats, William Morris and Gerard Manley Hopkins. Jefferies recognised his failure to find his own voice, lamenting that 'One of the great difficulties I have encountered is the lack of words to express ideas'.[24] Critical reception was mixed, but *The Story of My Heart* was never popular.[25] The public who enjoyed his rural novels and countryside and travel essays was not interested in his metaphysical quest. Ultimately, an understanding of nature inhabited by a 'wild spirit', as Jefferies saw himself, was lost in inflated language intended to universalise personal experience into general truth. Grand visions of beauty and liberty appeared to have lost their imaginative power in a world increasingly more comfortable with ordinariness.

Both in his essays and *The Story of My Heart*, Jefferies is the central subjectivity, the sole observing eye offering himself as the conduit of vision for his time. Yet his frequent images of himself prostrate on the grass under the sky in the quest for a visionary connection between man and nature seem a passive, onanistic, version of the Romantic sublime, in which the energy and dynamism of becoming a 'living soul' are embodied in gestures of physical movement and power.[26] Beguiling and sexually charged images of prostration are common in countryside writing of the period. We can find them in Kenneth Grahame's *Pagan Papers* (1893), for instance, and, in their most explicit form, in E. M. Forster's frequently analysed 'The Story of a Panic'. There are many versions in Jefferies' writing, sometimes suggesting sexual energy, but more usually physical lassitude and sometimes casual voyeurism. At these moments, his imaginative landscape seems to be charged with sexual frustration rather than metaphysical and visionary possibilities. An interesting example is found in his essay on the Thames in *The Open Air*, in which (characteristically) he stops rowing to relax and watch the world go by. He observes a commonplace scene – ordinary people enjoying the current craze for boating on the Thames – but his apprehension of it is profoundly different from Jerome K. Jerome's inclusive delight in the everyday world. Jefferies' viewpoint is predominantly a gendered one: strong, athletic males stride along the towpath heaving the boat in which their companions, elegantly dressed ladies, are sitting. Jefferies 'admires' the men, who become 'heroes' (there is more than a hint of homage to the prevalent classical aesthetic here), but he identifies with the passivity of the women and mentally joins them in the stern under the parasols: 'And of such is peace', he says of this androgynous pleasuring of his imagination.[27] His Wordsworthian desire to 'wander' and his Whitmanesque desire to 'loaf' are reduced to a literary ploy for distancing daily life and enjoying perpetual detachment in a personalised utopia: 'I hope succeeding generations will be able to be idle', he wrote in *The Story of My Heart*.[28]

In Jefferies' writings, we can identify clear signs of a cultural separation between popular demand and private desire, between the increasing vigour of the popular culture which supported his work materially and the waning influence of the neo-Romanticism which inspired it. The popularity of his simple descriptive essays, and the failure of what he considered his most important work, *The Story of My Heart*, further point to his essentially suburban literary identity. In the first place, his articles promise an achievable, and therefore democratised, activity. It would not have been conceivable to go out and 'be' a Wordsworth or a Blake (unless you cultivated an artistic persona, like Jefferies himself, or like the young Edward Thomas, reading Shelley's 'Epipsychidion' on a walk to Merton).[29] It was, however, possible to go out and be a Jefferies – to explore the countryside, to notice pleasant sights, to enjoy walking and thinking, and to return home refreshed. Moreover, although it represented a reaction against suburbanisation, his 'countryside' was itself suburbanised. It offered healthy exercise, a familiar Edwardian theme. Jefferies was happy to agree with others commentators, such as Sidney J. Low, that it was 'a sacred duty, incumbent upon every one, man and woman, to add to and encourage their physical life, by exercise, and in every manner. A sacred duty each towards himself, and each towards the whole of the human race.'[30]

Perhaps more significantly, and certainly paradoxically in terms of literary tradition, Jefferies' essays contributed to the democratisation of feeling. They shared in the increasingly secular mode of public thought which was busy diffusing formal religious practice into the activities of daily life. *Three Men in a Boat*, published just after Jefferies' death, refers frequently to Sunday as a time of general relaxation, rather than of church going; and, as I noted earlier, in his autobiography Jerome K. Jerome comments on a generational change of attitude to Sundays.[31] What Jefferies' readers wanted from his writing was artistic consciousness; sensitivity to the world and its beauty; a delight in flowers, weather and landforms; and information about people who lived away from the city. These motifs, mediated through the writing of a 'Man of the Fields', arguably offered them a desirable but unspecific meaningfulness that could fill a spiritual vacuum and provide an apparently traditional and stable framework for thought. Walkers could take their church out of doors and enjoy an undefined and de-institutionalised personal spiritual experience through words about nature.

The problem that Jefferies' own cultural moment posed for him was that his faith in the countryside, and his chosen place in literary tradition, were being overtaken. It was no longer credible to imagine the countryside as England's defining landscape, and it was even more difficult to make it a locus of meaning, as Jefferies tried to do in

The Story of My Heart. Personalised and masculinist, his vision of
utopia resists the shareable and communicative elements which made
his commercial writing so popular. Juxtaposed with the cultural
imperatives of a mass readership and the cultural fact of a com-
modified countryside, his vision shrinks to personal nostalgia and
appears ineffective and reactionary in social and literary terms. In
his writings we see a retreat from the material realities of city and
country and the social issues they raised, which he criticised in
others. There is also a spurious emphasis on the ability of the artist
to offer a transcendent view of life which, in Jefferies' case, seems to
reduce rather than expand the plurality of experience. ·

Jefferies must have come to understand the paucity and ambiguity of his construction of nature. He resisted writing his countryside
pieces, although he was continually forced to fall back on them since
they were his money-earners. Flowers, though capable of inspiring
'Thoughts that do often lie too deep for tears' in 1804, were not
capable of sustaining emotional power nearly eighty years later, or
of easing the tensions in late-Victorian society and belief. There
is certainly evidence in his later notebooks that nature had failed to
live up to the significance he had invested in it. His comment that
'Nature is like a beautiful statue. I must love, must gaze. Yet I cannot
put the life into that I should like to', offers something of an explanation for his own passivity as an observer.[32] He created out of the idea
of nature a mental landscape and a managed physical experience but,
as this quotation shows, he had profound doubts as to whether his art
was adequate, or its material appropriate, to deliver the emotional
and spiritual rewards that he longed for and which he felt that society
needed. The writer who was often linked in the public mind with his
contemporary Thomas Hardy because of their rural locations found
himself in his last days drifting closer to Hardy's very different vision
of nature: 'Nature is very stupid . . . appears to do nothing but make
mistakes and so ultimately arrives at something after continual blot-
ting.'[33] If Jefferies' work draws its own line under the efficacy of the
earlier cultural and literary norms on which it draws, it also reveals how
another cultural space was beginning to open up between the drama
of urban life and its literary articulation in social realism, and nature
and the countryside as the source of the Romantic imagination.

Richard Jefferies' work provided the imaginative stimulus for Edward
Thomas's youthful experiments with material and prose style, and his

influence is plain to see in some of Thomas's own countryside essays.[34] In his biography of Jefferies, published in 1909, he registers both his emotional affinity with Jefferies' work, and his literary debt to it. I am aware that focusing on Thomas as a countryside essayist, and on his link with Jefferies, may give a distorted impression of Thomas's literary achievement; but it is these early writings that first established his reputation and most clearly articulated his response to the suburbs and to his own suburban identity.[35] Born and brought up in the suburbs, for Thomas the countryside was always an enchanted space outside daily experience. Helen Thomas's recollection of her first meeting with her future husband, in one of a row of 'little new villas' with a 'tiny garden, which was kept full of flowers', comes as something of a quaint surprise to those who are familiar with Thomas's poetry.[36] Less of a surprise is the discovery of his childhood contact with the country at the home of relatives in Swindon, a place which swiftly became 'the corner stone of the universe', the source of his love of the countryside and the material for many of his early writings.[37] As a result of his background, Thomas's imaginative impetus was fundamentally different from Jefferies'. For him the suburbs were the known and familiar and the countryside always the other: it was against the backdrop of the suburbs rather than the city that his dream of countryside was defined. This is the context for his only novel, The Happy-Go-Lucky Morgans (1913), a remarkable apprehension of the suburb as a site of cultural reconciliation, to which I will return later. First, I want to focus on Thomas's countryside essays as he seeks to position his imaginative territory beyond the suburbs.

Thomas was deeply conscious of the impact of social change on the rural world he had adopted as his emotional, spiritual and literary home, and of his own role in promoting this change. Like Jefferies before him, he was paid reasonably well for his writings 'from the life and from the hour', which were in demand. Like Jefferies' writings, his essays fed the public appetite for all things rural, however vague and unspecific that term had become, and he often undertook journeyman work which was generated by the commodification of the countryside. Thomas's Pocket Book of Poems and Songs for the Open Air, published in 1907, demonstrates clearly the public preference for an accessible and managed countryside experience to which he was responding. Divided into accessible sections – The Invitation, The Start in the Morning, Wayside Rest, Village and Inn, and Evening – the collection was part of the Jonathan Cape Travellers' Library

Series 'designed for the pocket' and bound flexibly 'against the damage inevitably associated with hasty packing'.[38] Everyone, it seems,
was out and about. If they were not exploring Rome with their
Baedekers, as Miss Bartlett does in E. M. Forster's *A Room with a View*
(1908), they were roaming the countryside accessible from London,
with their books of poetry, provided by Edward Thomas and others,
to suggest appropriate responses and feelings.

But one consequence of the marketing of the countryside as a
panacea for the numerous anxieties of the age was a distancing of the
unique and unified experience of mind, spirit and body that Thomas
was seeking. His writing gradually moved away from an engagement
with the present to descriptions of a quasi-spiritualised, quasi-
mythologised nature found in *Light and Twilight*, a collection of essays
first published in 1911. In its reliance on a fading neo-Romanticism
this writing was typical of the period immediately before the First
World War. Thomas's evocation of an idealised rural landscape offers
a vision of beauty, and a style of writing as insubstantial as the
nymphs and faery-children who inhabit it. Each of the fourteen
essays revolves around an epiphany arising from observing the world
through a heightened, and sometimes morbidly intense, sensibility.
The writing shows glimpses of Thomas's defamiliarising observations
– 'pearly snails, the daisies and the chips of chalk like daisies' – that
in his poetry would later surprise readers with their immediacy.[39]
However, in these essays and others like them, the descriptions have
not shaken themselves free of the tradition of Richard Jefferies,
yearning for a Romanticism that could make 'I and poet and lover
and flowers and cloud and star . . . equals'.[40]

The Heart of England, published in 1906, addresses the difficulty
inherent in trying to leave the totalising environment of the suburbs
behind. It is divided into five parts, and its section headings suggest
a long walk across England, from London, across the evocatively
unspecified Lowlands, Uplands and Mountains to reach, in Part V,
the sea. The journey is one of observation and conversation, mediated
through literary culture and, most powerfully, through Thomas's
inner musings. The opening essay, 'Leaving Town', is located in that
psychological ('line and mark in the minds of men') and topographical ('outposts of bricks and mortar') suburban space which
is designated as marginal by Jefferies, but which Thomas opens up
to accommodate the present as well as the past. It is in this essay
that we find the passage with which I began this book and which so

precisely articulates the suburbs' double meaning. Paradoxically, their very material ordinariness and uniformity comprises everything that men and women are trying to know, and in their potent suggestiveness contains all quests and all symbols. The starting point for reaching the 'Heart of England' is 'the silence of the suburbs' – silent because it is night and everyone is asleep, but 'silent' too because it is not yet possible to understand what they mean, what their history will be and where their humanity lies.[41] Like Masterman, who, in 1901, called the suburbs an untapped 'storehouse of the nation's energies', Thomas sees the suburban street he is describing as a 'great storehouse' whose individuality and significance has not yet been discovered.[42]

The narrator's departure is temporarily delayed by his awareness of two other human beings on the street, an old man and a boy, who act as the ghost of England past and spirit of England future. They also suggest the narrator's divided state of consciousness in the present moment, a defensive literary strategy that Thomas used in a number of his essays.[43] The body and clothes of the old man seem to be created out of nature itself – 'his neglected body seemed to have grown this grey rind that flapped like birch bark' – and his strangeness and implied mobility promise 'the East, the Pole, the Amazon'.[44] His outmoded and impoverished rôle as a watercress seller recalls Wordsworth's leech gatherer, removed by urbanisation from the Lake District to the London suburbs. Yet the watercress seller, apparently a relic from another age, survives by using Thomas's own economic strategies, capitalising on his imagination as material for the pastoral landscapes he paints and then sells in London – towards which he is walking when the narrator first sees him. By contrast, the boy, a resident of the suburb, looks outwards from the suburban street. Excited by the strangeness and promise of freedom he is filled with longing, but falls and weeps as he tries to follow the narrator whose departure is temporarily suspended as he realises that the true mystery of the modern, whether good or bad, is held in the streets in which he stands.

Leaving the suburbs, then, is not easy, even with the aid of the imagination. Departure will not lead to a location where truth and answers may be found, although it might give psychological relief in the face of an overwhelming mystery. At best, leaving town will provide a psychic space in which to construct a landscape imaginary so as to resist the power of suburban suggestion. To bolster that resistance, the countryside must be made into everything that the suburbs are not; but in the face of the suburbs' immensity and complexity, little is left to the countryside except to be simple and contained, and this little is further reduced with every step the narrator takes on his quest. Even as the narrator walks beyond the suburbs, passing an apparently real boundary between suburban and country land, which is marked out by a field full of piles of bricks, his progress only mimics the movement of suburban development itself from the city to the country. His walk away from the suburbs serves to accelerate the centrifugal movement of the city's energy onwards and outwards towards a landscape waiting to be invested with activity and meaning.

The marked difference between Jefferies' objectivity and Thomas's subjectivity in responding to the suburbs can be explained partly by the speed of social change. In the intervening years between Jefferies' death in 1887 and the beginning of Thomas's writing career in the early 1900s, the suburbs had become the desired norm and the accepted (if contested) future of urban living. They could no longer be left behind simply by walking away from them. Not only had the suburbs replaced the city as a focus of public interest: with hindsight, we can see that the dates of Thomas's life – he died in 1917 at Arras – also bracketed the literary attempts to revitalise rural experience as a valid means of resistance to urban and suburban life. The war, as Paul Fussell argues in The Great War and Modern Memory, was to redeploy traditional images of nature in prose and poetry, consigning their former imaginative force to history.[45] Yet, before the war, the English countryside still held a symbolic value for Thomas, as a place in which he, among others, could come to rest or, at least, be productively restless. As Stan Smith incisively puts it, for Thomas the symbol of the countryside 'becomes in the end a momentary place of community and exile together, for those modern men who go nowhere'.[46]

The countryside as a totalising and affective symbol of national culture and worth is a part of a distinctively Edwardian mindset that continues to elude sympathetic scholarly discussion. Alienation and embarrassment often intervene between critics and the texts that celebrate it, but as Smith goes on to explain, the English countryside at this specific moment in history offered what was arguably the last imaginative and cultural common ground.[47] Weakened in its detachment from the agricultural world, aestheticised to satisfy a deep need for the recreations of Arcadia, and constructed as a sub-urbanised park, the English landscape was nevertheless associated strongly enough with national identity for many people, including Edward Thomas, to translate it into a rationale for patriotism. Thomas's early countryside writings act as a powerful *aide-memoire*, not just of a historical period and the literary experiments of a young writer, but of the difficulties that individuals faced at this time in distinguishing between the effects of profound social changes over which they had no influence, and the indelible personal memories that had made them who they were.

Like Richard Jefferies and Edward Thomas, E. M. Forster also looked outwards from the suburbs to the English countryside – to Sussex and Wiltshire, and beyond to Europe – for the expansion of personality and 'view' that could counterbalance the deprivation of beauty and culture which was implicit in the inevitable encroachment of suburban development. One of Forster's deepest fears, it seems to me, was the emerging paradox that the suburbs, whose very rationale was to provide homes and hence stability, in fact exacerbated the modern sense of rootlessness.[48] His anxiety arose directly from his observation of social change, and from his perception that the legitimate mobility of adventure and exploration had been reduced to the restlessness of stasis. The movement of populations triggered by industrialisation from 1840 onwards had aggravated the sense of disconnection from the past and, even within country areas, quasi-feudal relations had broken down so that labourers found themselves returning to the hiring fair looking for a new employer year after year.[49] 'Moving on' in the search for work or for cheaper rents became a characteristic of the urban poor throughout the nineteenth century, as the tragic example of Jo in Charles Dickens's *Bleak House* (1853) shows so clearly. Disturbingly, at the end of the century and beyond, class mobility, for all its advantages, was replicating this effect of physical displacement. Once a decision has been made to move for the sole reason of occupying a particular house, then there is always another house, and another. In *A Room with a View* (1908), Windy Corner exemplifies this point. Bought initially to provide a pleasant *rus in urbe* home for the Honeychurch family, Windy Corner is gradually surrounded by new developments. When the novel opens, more houses are being planned near the church. The winds of change finally blow the house away as the son of the family, unable to

finance such a large home in the new economic climate, sells it on for
development and moves elsewhere.

Forster's response to this situation is much darker than either
Jefferies' or Thomas's. He depicts the suburbs as a site of crushing
repression in their attempt to keep change, drama and adventure at
bay in the name of stability, and he is sceptical about the adequacy
of the rural dream as a cultural sticking plaster. Enforced by the
power of a feminised domesticity, the rigid conventions of the suburb
suffocate the imagination, and repress and distort sexuality. This
sexual repression is shown as limiting for both genders, but, in his
early novels and stories, Forster focuses on issues of masculinity.
Women are depicted as sacrificing their sexuality for economic safety
in marriage. The corollary of women's decision to regulate and
domesticate sexual activity was that men, whether heterosexual or
homosexual, were forced to live their lives in a passionless environment. Forster cannot see a utopian shape for society as a whole, for
the suburbs or for the countryside. Instead, he suggests that sexuality
is a crucial site of surprise and that sex is a route to individual and
social integrity. The opportunities for textual and sexual disruption,
often coded in his novels as a homosexual subtext, point to Forster's
vision of a 'utopia of *différance*'.[50] Despite their uneasy relationship
and their eventual falling-out over what appears to have been a
conflict about sexual honesty, D. H. Lawrence and E. M. Forster were
probably closer on the issue of sexual energy and its importance
to personal and social health than either was prepared to admit to
the other.[51]

The negotiation between the social requirements of a specific
location and the need to discover the extent of human potential is
variously explored in Forster's collection of short stories written
between 1902 and 1910.[52] In them the suburbs are everywhere, but
equally possibly nowhere, for the characters who find a momentary
escape. These fantastic tales, which play with the supernatural, the
mysterious and the anarchic, all revolve, in one way or another,
around middle-class products of suburban social conditioning being
confronted with cultural surprises in England or continental Europe.
The English travellers inevitably take their mental landscape with
them, but some of them are shaken into a moment of emotional
vagrancy by the 'view' they discover ahead of them. The English suburban body, relocated to Italy and Greece, is metamorphosed into
nature's constituent elements – water, trees, mountains – which are

then inscribed with mythic significance. Mr Lucas in 'The Road to Colonus', Eustace in 'The Story of a Panic' and Evelyn in 'The Other Kingdom' all break out of suburban stasis to experience uninhibited physicality. Forster uses a familiar device in these stories, one that he later abandoned: the perspective of a child. Eustace, the boy in 'The Celestial Omnibus', and the unformed, virginal Evelyn, are children with a clear eye, for whom 'home' remains possible because they have yet to be 'fully conditioned'. As the Faun says in 'The Curate's Friend', 'children listen until grown up'.[53] The adult men in these stories – the priest, the generals, academics, the 'measurers', the artists – may guess at what they have lost, but seem incapable of rediscovering it.

In these stories, Forster deploys a strategy of narrative delusion in which a critique of social behaviour fulfils readers' expectations while providing access to the non-rational. In his own words: 'I have been forced to use the unworthy medium of a narrative, and to delude you by declaring that this is a short story, suitable for reading on the train'.[54] He is right that the realistic narrative can be a sub-urban form ('Yes, oh yes, a novel tells a story'),[55] and the short story a suburban form particularly suited to commuters, but the suburbs of the early novels and stories are true borderlands between the geo-graphies of the Home Counties and of individual desire. Where the reader learns to take a different view of reality there are fissures that provide entrances to a different kind of experience. Whereas the suburban railway's function is to get a commuter from A to B, the alleyway in 'The Celestial Omnibus', the tree in 'The Road to Colonus', the bridge in 'The Other Kingdom' and the hedgerow in 'The Other Side of the Hedge' are all stargates out of the material suburb into sexual and ecstatic awareness.

In the three earliest novels Forster published – *Where Angels Fear to Tread* (1905), *The Longest Journey* (1907) and *A Room with a View* (1908) – the fantastic and ludic elements of the short stories, that explode the boundaries between suburban existence and individual imaginative and erotic revelation, are internalised as individual moments of insight in the face of the unfamiliar. The realistic inter-face of the narratives offers a social critique of materialism and con-ventionality set in a domestic framework where women emasculate men by establishing behavioural boundaries – although the polarities are never as simple as this would suggest. Windy Corner, in *A Room with a View*, is a case in point. It exemplifies the suburban home, but its name, as I have already noted, suggests instability. This ambiguity reveals itself in several forms, as the following extract demonstrates:

> Cecil's first movement was one of irritation. He couldn't bear the Honeychurch habit of sitting in the dark to save the furniture. Instinctively he gave the curtains a twitch, and sent them swinging down their poles. Light entered. There was revealed a terrace, such as is owned by many villas, with trees either side of it, and on it a little rustic seat, and two flower-beds. But it was transfigured by the view beyond, for Windy Corner was built on the range that overlooks the Sussex Weald. Lucy, who was in the little seat, seemed on the edge of a green magic carpet which hovered above the tremulous world.[56]

Here we have the familiar suburban image of a tidy house, economically run (saving the furniture) but comfortable, a tended garden in contemporary style ('such as is owned by many villas'), a 'little rustic seat' paying homage to suburban *rus in urbe* aspirations and, in the centre, a woman, fixed as if in a painting, presiding over the home. But the scene beyond reveals its borderland nature: the confined terrace and flower-beds of suburban artifice are juxtaposed with the openness of the Sussex Weald, the stasis of the rustic bench with the flight promised by 'the green magic carpet', and the heavy living-room furniture with the fluidity of emotional adventure ('tremulous world').

The two visions are inseparable – it is the suburb that has made possible the larger vision and home is necessary to the orientation of the view – but it is Lucy's quest to find out how they might be combined in one meaning, how she might transform herself from the work of art that Cecil perceives her to be into an inhabitant of the 'tremulous world'. Forster's emphasis on the 'view' in his novels is not on what you see but on how you see it: the world, and the suburbs, are chameleon and open to the shaping of those who live in them. So, after her visit to Italy, Lucy can think 'One could play a new game with the view, and try to find in its innumerable folds some town or village that would do for Florence. Ah, how beautiful the Weald looked!'[57] In contrast, Cecil, who opens the curtains but wishes only to see a sophisticated picture, deliberately avoids experiences which are 'absolutely out of our suburban focus'.[58] The pool in the pine woods where George, Freddy and Mr Beebe bathe has a similar dual identity and meets a similar fate. Retained as a token rural feature in a suburban development, it becomes the space beyond the suburbs where they enter into an eroticised seascape, while simultaneously recovering a kind of prelapsarian innocence, 'racing' and 'playing

Indians' in the Garden of Eden. Later the reader discovers that it has been drained to accommodate new building, cutting off an avenue to self-discovery.

The Longest Journey also opposes the world of the suburbs to the wildness of a classicised and eroticised landscape that offers a return, 'to the Greek ideal of beauty as a panacea for the ills of modern society', as one reviewer commented when it was published in America in 1922.[59] However, the element of play, which is such a distinctive feature of the short stories, is overshadowed in what is Forster's darkest novel. The suburbs in this novel imply a failure of choice: suburban life handicaps Rickie's development and spells the slow death of Agnes Pembroke. Rickie's father lived in a suburb 'not for any urgent reason', and he subjects his son to 'filmy heavens', and to taking 'his first walk on asphalt'.[60] The effect intensifies as the narrative moves to the Pembrokes' home in the suburb of Sawston, pretentious, self-regarding, and dubbed 'sububurb' by Forster.[61] The account of Rickie's marriage, his work as a school teacher and the daily life of the Sawston world makes a well-aimed attack on a cruel and narrow-minded society that deliberately blinds itself to suffering, greed and dishonesty.

So what perspective yields so savage a view? In The Longest Journey Cambridge is Rickie's true home, a place of physical and intellectual repose and of intimate male relationships uncluttered by the conventions of female society. In this novel, Cambridge University is the ultimate judge and jury on two alternative modes of social existence – in the suburbs of Sawston and in the fields of Wiltshire. Cambridge (Forster's own spiritual and intellectual home) and Oxford were themselves 'steadily becoming the academic suburbs of metropolis and Empire',[62] and they allowed Forster to view the world from what was arguably his own suburban idyll. Liberated by his secure location in the community of Cambridge University, he was able to avoid the disadvantages that he perceived in the actual suburbs (feminisation, domestication, commuting, monotony), and to achieve an intellectual, masculine, self-contained rus in urbe environment, such as Jefferies and Thomas could only dream about in the fragile havens of their imaginations. Intellectually, he was able to sustain overt social critiques of the suburbs because he was insulated by the narrowly defined and covert landscape of a homosocial/sexual community.[63] Both Rickie, who opts for marriage, and his friend Ansell, who fails his exams, are kicked out of the Garden of Eden that Cambridge represents. From then on, the only reality left is that innermost space described by Ansell, 'the one in the middle of everything, that there's never room enough to draw'.[64] In this novel, Forster seems to suggest that there is no single 'innermost space' large enough to encompass both the geographies of modern suburbia and Wiltshire's ancient landscapes.

A discussion of *Howards End* and *The Happy-Go-Lucky Morgans* acts as a coda to this chapter and to the first stage of my argument. Both novels move away from any form of utopian dream as a personal vision or a cultural intervention, exploring instead reconciliation and acceptance, compromise and pluralism as society's best hope for the future. They convey a full appreciation of cultural loss and, in particular, of the strain of sustaining ideals whose articulation has become marginal and/or irrelevant to cultural discourse. Their mood is predominantly reflective, even resigned. Though both novels pay homage (directly in the case of *The Happy-Go-Lucky Morgans*; indirectly in the case of *Howards End*), to childhood memories of beauty and to the integrity of individual dreams, these works assume a mature viewpoint that refuses any longer to privilege what have become mere avenues of avoidance as a deeper reality. Today the critical reputation of *Howards End* is assured, but *The Happy-Go-Lucky Morgans* has slipped from public view, out of print for most of the second half of the twentieth century. Perhaps this situation reflects a fair assessment of their respective achievements, or perhaps a television adaptation could change *The Happy-Go-Lucky Morgans'* publishing destiny and invite a reappraisal. In any case, both novels are equally important to my argument, because both put the suburbanisation of landscape and culture to the test and acknowledge that the suburbs are the social formation of the future.

There is a schematic deliberateness about the structure of *Howards End* which seems to mark a taking-in of breath as Forster prepares to engage with the modern on its own terms, and to work out, as David Medalie puts it, 'what can and cannot be salvaged from the interregnum that precedes what is deemed to be a terminal sociohistorical period'.[65] Although it is less overtly concerned with the suburbs as location than *Where Angels Fear to Tread*, *A Room with a View* or *The Longest Journey*, *Howards End* is, as Forster was later to claim, a novel about finding where to belong in a world of flux. Howards End itself, Honiton, and the London apartments where the

Schlegels and the Wilcoxes live, are all examples of the destabilisation of the idea of home, even while their material reality appears to substantiate it. Realism and the novel as social critique prevail, and only vestiges of the ludic landscape of the short stories remain; the folk story of the pigs' teeth in the wych elm is one such remnant. The encounter with the 'wild' is bathetically reduced to Leonard Bast's earnest desire to 'get back to the earth', aided by the books that he reads and an unsatisfactory walk through Wimbledon woods. Home is the true focus of *Howards End* – a sober holding space in which it is possible to accept social change without the sacrifice of human feelings and instincts. The text is further suburbanised by its abdication to the feminine. The liminal misogyny of, for instance, *The Longest Journey*, is replaced by a reconfigured feminine that has colonised the masculine realm, a feminine of whose reflective and affective integrity the characters of Mrs Wilcox and Margaret and Helen Schlegel are different versions.

The idea of the countryside, despite the importance that Forster claims for it, has little power in *Howards End*; the country landscape exists only in pockets to be viewed from a hill, managed in a country estate, or besieged by suburban developments as Howards End itself is. Forster famously declared that, 'those who care for the earth with sincerity may wait long ere the pendulum swings back to her again', but it is hard to resist the hint given by the archaic or poetic 'ere' that this time can never come again.[66] The last refuge of the countryside is in art, for, as Forster recognises, the earth had become an aesthetic construct during his own lifetime. Yet Forster challenges even this vestigial rural identity by deliberately allowing art to fail in the well-known opening to chapter 19. His description might initially remind the reader of John of Gaunt's panegyric to 'this precious stone set in the silver sea' in Shakespeare's *Richard II*, as he heaps up references to an archetypal English landscape which climax in a stirring rhetorical flourish on the totality of England. But this is all that the passage is – a mere series of flourishes, self-consciously emptied of meaning. At the heart of the passage, strategically placed at the halfway point, is the negative and bathetic half-sentence 'Nor is Suburbia absent'.[67] Between the folds of the hills, among the woods and the streams, invisible to the eye, lies the concrete manifestation of modern England. The transcendence of the final sentence is delusory. It is not Romantic sublimity but a transparent artifice which pretends ironically to restore the reader to an untouched island idyll.

Edward Thomas's only novel, *The Happy-Go-Lucky Morgans*, stands apart from the rest of his prose writing. It is the most satisfying example of the suburban mode I have encountered and its achievement adds a further dimension to the argument of this chapter.[68] Between the opening sentence, 'My story is of Balham', and the conclusion, in which the narrator returns many years later, the 'story' expands from a house and its place in the history of suburban change to take in the sum of British history, culture and landscape that is carried in the collective memory of Abercorran Street's motley community. Each chapter tells its own story, and as these different stories are shared in the sociable atmosphere that characterises the Morgans' household, they weave together 'an overlapping of imaginative worlds' bringing the past into the present of a London suburb.[69]

Memory is the single most influential factor in shaping the characters' perceptions of the present. Childhood memories are again seen to create a landscape in which everything afterwards is located and by which everything is measured. Cultural memories of any kind, whether they are legends, traditions, folklore or the more formal culture of books, heighten, interpret and give a language to present experiences. Life memories are the sum of individual identity – a mental record of how and why someone is where they are and who they are. Because of this, there is no separation between past and present, just a shifting of perspective. In Abercorran House, 'At one moment the past seemed everything, the present a dream; at another, the past seemed to have gone forever'.[70]

Abercorran House enters the narrator's consciousness through a chance encounter with Philip Morgan, who introduces him to his family and the friends who regularly drop in for a chat. Another chance event, when they lose their way together on a school cross-country run, leads to the discovery of 'Our Country', a den on the edge of the countryside where it merges into the edges of suburban development. In a long passage, Thomas traces the workings of the child's imagination and the way in which he internalises the external world as an enduring mental and emotional landscape.[71] It is surely the same process which invests with such power the children's stories of Kenneth Grahame, Beatrix Potter, Rudyard Kipling and Edith Nesbit, all of whom were Thomas's contemporaries.

In *The Happy-Go-Lucky Morgans*, the young boy's first response to his discovery is like that of Mary in Frances Hodgson Burnett's famous novel, *The Secret Garden* – that 'the place had been deserted, overlooked, forgotten, that it was known only to us'. Excited by the discovery, and with all his senses heightened, he knew that it was not like 'ordinary country. The sun was peculiarly bright. There was something unusual in the green of its grass.' Later, when as an adult he reads the *Odyssey*, he is reminded of his boyhood den, and the 'remote and holy isles' of Ulysses and Circe are visualised in his imagination as 'those little round islands of ash and hazel'.[72] As time passes, his vision of the den increases in imaginative intensity, 'extraordinary in its beauty', and gaining a mythical dimension as he realises that he 'did not fully believe that it existed'. The passage concludes both with a surrender to what has become an ineradicable mental image and with a rationalisation – a balance between the Romantic sensibility nurtured in childhood and the adult's maturer view:

> No wonder Our Country was supernaturally beautiful. It had London for a foil and background; what is more, on that first day it wore an uncommon eternal splendour, so that I cannot hope to meet again such heavenly gilded elms smouldering in warm, windless sunshine, nor such bright meadows as they stood in, nor such blue sky and such white billowy cloud as rose up behind the oaks on its horizon.[73]

If this portrayal sounds more like the Wordsworthian Lake District than Balham, it is worth noting Glen Cavaliero's comment (linking Edward Thomas with Edith Nesbit): 'how essentially understanding and tender toward youth both writers are'.[74] Thomas convincingly conveys children's double perspective, which can exchange reality and fantasy without noticing, and their intrinsic curiosity, which stores up the stories of their elders, the books that they read and the places where they live against the future that they will encounter.

The adults who tell their stories in *The Happy-Go-Lucky Morgans* are already storehouses of memory. Although they carry social labels (Aurelius is the 'Superfluous Man', Mr Stodham the 'Respectable Man', Mr Torrance the 'Cheerful Man'), Thomas sees the extraordinary in these ordinary people with a conviction of human value which is shared by a very different group of realist suburban writers, among them Arnold Bennett and G. K. Chesterton. Mr Stodham, for instance, is the very epitome of clerkdom, a topic I will return to in a later chapter. He is 'nearly a middle aged clerk, disappointed in a tranquil style' who prided himself on having talked in his youth 'of going to the colonies': the fact that he did not go does not alter 'a sort of shadowy grandeur' that he retains because he had even considered it.[75] The inner extraordinariness of Mr Stodham is defined, not by such obvious attributes, but by two significant life events. In the first, afraid that his house is in danger from fire Mr Stodham faces the ultimate existential dilemma: 'which book shall I save?' After long deliberation, he is incapable of choosing, and finally grabs a book at random. The joke is that the fire never reaches his house; the grandeur lies in the impossibility of his choice. Every book represents a portion of his history and of his psychological makeup, acting like a diary to remind him of past experiences. They are an externalisation of himself and cannot be isolated from each other. The second incident tells of his encounter with a dryad. In his attempts to rescue her from the stifling suburban bedroom where she is trapped, he nearly sets fire to himself. Again the story is absurd. Again it has grandeur, pointing to Mr Stodham's capacity for visions of beauty, for freedom and for selflessness.

Although Abercorran House might seem like a peg to hang a series of varied stories on, this is far from being the case. Abercorran House, which at the opening of the book already holds the histories of Wales and of the Morgans in its name, absorbs all the stories and, by the end of the novel, is the sum of what has been shared inside its walls. It is also part of Balham. Threaded throughout the fantastic and evocative stories is the insistent presence of a constantly changing suburban landscape which Thomas describes in meticulous detail. From the first, the reader knows that this is a story of change. From being a large house, on the corner of Wilderness Street (which ran out into countryside) and near a pond full of carp, Abercorran House ends up sandwiched between other houses, one of which 'probably has the honour and misfortune to stand in the pond's place'.[76] We have already encountered a similar shift from pond to building plot in Forster's A Room with a View and in Keble Howard's Smiths of Valley View, and it will occur again in H. G. Wells's The New Machiavelli: it was clearly perceived as a potent image of social change. Abbey Road, where Mr Torrance lives, is described with the detail of a set of directions. It maps out the whole history of urban development. It 'ran into pure London' at its north end, and into carved up and industrialised countryside at the other, with every turn of the road taken up with a different kind of development, of a different age or class status.

In his essays, Thomas writes about the masculine world of the rural ramble, but in The Happy Go-Lucky Morgans, he is able to break away from a narrowly masculinist perspective, as Forster does in *Howards End*. Ann, the housekeeper at Abercorran, who came from Wales with the Morgan family and stays in Balham when they leave, is the feminised heart of suburbia. She is also the spirit of history. She is not interested in particular dates and facts, but she is a conduit for stories and memories. She exemplifies the modern condition that must reconcile the dualism of suburban life. Ann, the reader is told, 'likes the new houses as well as the old elm trees, and the hundreds of men, women, and children as well as the jackdaws'.[77]

The opening sentence of *The Happy-Go-Lucky Morgans* locates the narrative in Balham; at its conclusion, Ann claims that Balham is the best place in the world. Between these two points we learn what such a claim means. All the people who fetch up in Abercorran House are migrants, but when they arrive they bring the landscapes, the traditions, the myths and the histories of their former lives with them. Stories from Wales, Essex, Wiltshire and Hampshire are woven together into the texture of London suburban life, for the suburbs are the sum of mobile peoples. But this Balham is also a literary suburb, since it is Thomas's dual vision of the limited material location and the immensity of its world that makes the fragments cohere. The novel straddles the rural and urban, it contains the oral and mythical. Each similar house in a similar street, the reader infers, contains vibrantly different individuals, whose characters are their stories and whose mental landscapes become suburban dreams.

The works of Richard Jefferies, Edward Thomas and E. M. Forster mark stages in a Romantic and masculinist cultural struggle. Many of these novels and essays turn their faces outwards from the suburbs to recover nature and, by implication, the wildness of masculinity in the displaced location of the imagination. In Jefferies' work, we see the remnants of a past age. His neo-Romantic writings struggle to understand and to articulate the collapsing boundaries between countryside and city, between real and imagined landscapes. The power and suggestiveness of Wordsworth's poetry, which holds 'what we see and half-create' in such a fine balance, is diffused in Jefferies' prose into a sentimental sensuality and into descriptions of feeling that struggle for effect. Outside both country and city by education and by inclination, he occupied a space in the new literary suburbs that was doomed to be temporary. Edward Thomas seems a world away from Jefferies, yet he too, in his early writing, used the Romantic tradition as a way of interpreting the clash of city with country. Later, in *The Happy-Go-Lucky Morgans*, as his own voice grew more assured, the Romantic tradition became no more than a step on the way to understanding the extraordinariness of the human personality within the ordinariness of the human environment, a humanist perspective which was already emerging as a defining characteristic of many contemporary realist novels.

Forster also abandoned the diluted Romanticism and paganism of his early works. Suspicious of feelings which had been diverted from their emotional sources into fashion and self-obsession, he initially depicted the conventional repressive suburb as a negative image that concealed a world of passion, freedom and self-expression. In *Howards End*, he tried to bring country and city and passion and progress together. In the late 1880s, William Morris and Jerome K. Jerome had envisioned their dream of a happy, egalitarian society in suburban terms. In 1910, Forster could only appeal to a cultured few through the overarching and talismanic phrase, 'only connect', with which he attempted to reconcile those antagonisms of class, education and history that seemed irreconcilable in life. Thirty years and a collective failure of confidence separated them.

Notes

1   The link between childhood, the countryside and home is pervasive in fiction for children during this period: see Kenneth Grahame, [1908] *The Wind in the Willows*, Rudyard Kipling, [1906] *Puck of Pook's Hill*, E. Nesbit, [1899] *The Story of the Treasure Seekers*, and Frances Hodgson Burnett, [1911] *The Secret Garden*. As recently as 2000, the conservative philosopher Roger Scruton lamented the death of the extraodinarily tenacious cultural myth which conflates England, the countryside and childhood, claiming that a child's England is an 'Arcadian countryside' and an 'enchanted realm' (Roger Scruton, *England: An elegy* (London: Chatto and Windus, 2000), 12, 60).
2   Cavaliero, *The Rural Tradition*, 15.
3   Letter from Mrs Beresford to Richard Jefferies, cited in Samuel J. Looker and Crichton Porteous, *Richard Jefferies: Man of the fields: A biography and letters* (London: John Baker: 1964), 116.
4   Patricia Merivale, *Pan, the Goat God: His myth in modern times* (Cambridge, MA: Harvard University Press, 1969), 140.
5   Ronald Pearsall, *Edwardian Life and Leisure* (Newton Abbot: David and Charles, 1973), 119.
6   Henry Rider Haggard, [1902] *Rural England*, cited in Pearsall, *Edwardian Life*, 11.

7   Oscar Wilde, [1891] 'The Decay of Lying' in *The Works of Oscar Wilde*, edited by G. F. Maine (London and Glasgow: Collins, 1948), 909–931 (909).

8   The domestication of the sublime needs to be seen in the context of the increase in travel which was aided by the expansion of the British Empire, and of the role of explorers, adventurers and scientists in bringing the exotic into the domestic arena.

9   Edward Thomas, *Richard Jefferies: His life and work* (London: Hutchinson, 1909), 323.

10 London as the abyss became an obsessional trope that continued well into the 1890s. See Andrew Mearns, [1883] *The Bitter Cry of Outcast London*; George Sims, [1889] *How the Poor Live and Horrible London*; and novels such as George Gissing, [1889] *The Nether World* and Margaret Harkness, [1889] *In Darkest London*. These were counterpointed by slum romances such as Walter Besant, [1882] *All Sorts and Conditions of Men*, but dystopic fantasies of the future grew in popularity during the 1890s.

11 Richard Jefferies, 'Author's Preface' in *Wild Life in a Southern County* (London: John Murray, 1879), vii.

12 From Jefferies' notebooks for 1881–83, cited in Looker and Porteous, *Richard Jefferies*, 134.

13 Looker and Porteous, *Richard Jefferies*. In fact, no one could have been less of a man of the fields than Jefferies. He had no desire to be of the earth, to work and co-operate with nature as an agricultural labourer or as a farmer in his own right, and he never returned to the Wiltshire countryside once he had moved as an adult to live in the London suburb of Surbiton.

14 Walter Besant, *South London* (London: Chatto and Windus, 1899), 316.

15 These articles were collected in Richard Jefferies, *Nature Near London* (London: Chatto and Windus, 1889).

16 Jefferies, *Nature Near London*, 199, 197.

17 Jefferies, *Nature Near London*, 50.

18 Jefferies, *Nature Near London*, v.

19 Jefferies, *Nature Near London*, 102.

20 Richard Jefferies, 'Outside London' in *The Open Air* (London: Chatto and Windus, 1905), 231–251 (250).

21 Thomas, *Richard Jefferies*, 327.

22 Richard Jefferies, letter to C. J. Longman, cited in C. Henry Warren, 'Introduction' in Richard Jefferies, *The Story of My Heart* (London: Eyre and Spottiswoode, 1949), xv.

23 Looker and Porteous, *Richard Jefferies*, 26–27.

24 Jefferies, *The Story of My Heart*, 157.

25 Looker and Porteous, *Richard Jefferies*, record the low level of sales when it first appeared (153). C. Henry Warren notes different critical opinions in his introduction to the 1949 edition and, in particular, D. H. Lawrence's, George Saintsbury's and W. H. Hudson's objections to it (xii).

26 See e.g. 25, 31, 56. Contrast 'Lines composed a few miles above Tintern Abbey' (1798), from which the phrase 'living soul' is quoted, where Wordsworth's experience is communicated by a directness of expression that conveys a dynamic interaction between himself and nature ('I hear',

'I see', 'I behold', 'I stand'), in contrast to Jefferies more passive receptiveness.

27 Jefferies, 'The Modern Thames' in *The Open Air*, 112–138 (137).

28 Jefferies, *The Story of My Heart*, 143.

29 Helen Thomas, [1926] *As It Was and World Without End* (London: Faber and Faber, 1972), 20.

30 Jefferies, *The Story of My Heart*, 116.

31 See chapter 1, note 22.

32 Looker and Porteous, *Richard Jefferies*, 211.

33 Looker and Porteous, *Richard Jefferies*, 159–160.

34 Thomas, *As It Was*. Helen Thomas comments on the importance of Richard Jefferies' work for the young Edward Thomas's imaginative development and, in particular, on the impact of Jefferies' essay 'On Beauty' on the emotional context of the beginning of their sexual relationship (33).

35 Edward Thomas's poetry lies beyond the scope of this discussion because it was not published until after the First World War.

36 Thomas, *As It Was*, 13.

37 William Cooke, *Edward Thomas: A critical biography, 1878–1917* (London: Faber and Faber, 1970), 18.

38 [1907] *The Pocket Book of Poems and Songs for the Open Air*, compiled by Edward Thomas (London: Jonathan Cape, 1928). The quotation is taken from The Travellers' Library Series' heading.

39 Edward Thomas, [1911] *Light and Twilight* (Holt: Laurel Books, 2000), 14.

40 Thomas, *Light and Twilight*, 34.

41 Thomas, *The Heart of England*, 3.

42 Masterman, *The Condition of England*, 65.

43 According to W. H. Hudson, Thomas was a mystic but 'was shy of exhibiting it, and either disguised it or attributed it to someone he meets and converses with in his rambles' (W. H. Hudson, 'Introduction' in Edward Thomas, *Cloud Castle and Other Papers* [London: Duckworth and Co., 1922]).

44 Thomas, *The Heart of England*, 5.

45 See 'Arcadian Recourse' in Paul Fussell, *The Great War and Modern Memory* (Oxford: Oxford University Press, 1977), 231–269.

46 Stan Smith, *Edward Thomas* (London: Faber and Faber, 1986), 13.

47 Andrew Radford makes a similar point about the symbolic function of the countryside in 'The Gentleman's Estate in Ford's *Parade's End*', *Essays in Criticism*, 70: 4 (October 2002), 314–332. He argues that after the First World War, images of the rural, however nostalgic and conservative they can appear today, still offered the only available culturally collective resistance to the devastation of the natural world on the western front.

48 Looking back from 1931, W. B. Yeats summed up the prevalent feeling that civilisation was founded on a stability and continuity embodied in the integration of house and home ('A spot whereon the founders lived and died Seemed once more dear than life'), and that it was betrayed by social mobility ('We shift about – all that great glory spent Like some poor Arab tribesman and his tent') in W. B. Yeats, 'Coole Park and Ballylee, 1931' in *Collected Poems* (London: Macmillan, 1967), 276.

49 Thomas Hardy, [1883] 'The Dorsetshire Labourer' in H. Orel (ed.),
    Thomas Hardy: Personal writings (Basingstoke: Macmillan, 1967), 180 ff.
50 Robert K. Martin and George Piggott (eds), *Queer Forster* (Chicago and
    London: Chicago University Press, 1997), 18.
51 See D. H. Lawrence, letter to Bertrand Russell, 12 February 1915 in
    Henry T. Moore (ed.), *The Collected Letters of D. H. Lawrence*, vol 1.
    (London, Melbourne, and Toronto: Heinemann, 1962), 316–318 for
    Lawrence's account of Forster's three-day visit when they seemed to be
    constantly on the verge of quarrelling.
52 E. M. Forster, *Collected Short Stories* (Harmondsworth: Penguin, 1954).
53 Forster, *Collected Short Stories*, 90.
54 Forster, *Collected Short Stories*, 94.
55 E. M. Forster, [1927] *Aspects of the Novel* (Harmondsworth: Penguin), 5.
56 E. M. Forster, [1908] *A Room with a View* (Harmondsworth: Penguin,
    2000), 105.
57 *A Room with a View*, 175.
58 *A Room with a View*, 197.
59 Unsigned notice in *Boston Evening Transcript* (19 April 1922), cited in
    Philip Gardner, *E. M. Forster: The critical heritage* (London: Routledge
    and Kegan Paul, 1973), 98.
60 E. M. Forster, [1907] *The Longest Journey* (London: Edward Arnold,
    1964), 29.
61 *The Longest Journey*, 41.
62 Harris, *Private Lives*, 21.
63 See Lois Cucullu, 'Shepherds in the Parlor: Forster's apostles, pagans,
    and native sons', *Novel: A forum on fiction*, 32: 1 (Fall 1998), 19–47, for a
    discussion of the hellenisation of the English countryside with particular
    reference to *The Longest Journey*.
64 Forster, *The Longest Journey*, 24.
65 David Medalie, *E. M. Forster's Modernism* (Basingstoke: Palgrave, 2002),
    3.
66 E. M. Forster, [1910] *Howards End* (Harmondsworth: Penguin, 1989),
    116.
67 *Howards End*, 170.
68 Edward Thomas, [1913] *The Happy-Go-Lucky Morgans*, with an
    introduction by Glen Cavaliero (Suffolk: Boydell Press, 1983).
69 Cavaliero, 'Introduction' in *The Happy-Go-Lucky Morgans*, vii.
70 *The Happy-Go-Lucky Morgans*, 25.
71 *The Happy-Go-Lucky Morgans*, 35–38.
72 *The Happy-Go-Lucky Morgans*, 37.
73 *The Happy-Go-Lucky Morgans*, 38.
74 Cavaliero, *The Rural Tradition*, ix.
75 *The Happy-Go-Lucky Morgans*, 90.
76 *The Happy-Go-Lucky Morgans*, 2.
77 *The Happy-Go-Lucky Morgans*, 3.

Part II

✳

SUBURBAN DREAMS

4

✳

THE SUBURBAN GARDEN

Elizabeth von Arnim and the garden romances

T HE small garden, which 'attained the zenith of its popularity' during the 1890s and the Edwardian years in the suburbs, generated a new genre – the garden romance – which,
in turn, fuelled the growing passion both for gardens and writing about
gardens.[1] Writing about domestic gardens created a new aesthetic
drawn from perceptions of nature, which, while it acknowledged the
attractions of Romanticism, flourished in less exalted female literary
and domestic spaces. Barbara T. Gates compares such writers favour-
ably with male nature-writers such as Richard Jefferies, whom she
sees as nostalgic for a vanished literary and rural past, unlike women
who were more 'involved in the business of describing, discussing,
and theorizing beauty per se'.[2] In reinterpreting nature and the rural
world, she rightly concludes that 'nineteenth-century men told one
story, nineteenth-century women another'.[3] The garden stories told
by Elizabeth von Arnim, Barbara Campbell, Kathleen L. Murray and
others are the subject of this chapter.

   The long-neglected garden which the orphan Mary discovers in
Frances Hodgson Burnett's famous story for children, *The Secret
Garden* (1911), is one of the few familiar surviving indicators of this
fictional moment. Burnett's description of Mary's experience resonates with meanings which had long been important to England's
psychic landscape, but which assumed specific forms at the turn of
the twentieth century. Mary's garden is at once domestic and wild,
real and magical. It is spatially fluid: contained within its walls but
limitless in its suggestiveness. Mary controls it – it is hers to enter as

she wishes – but the garden contains her and shapes her identity. Fresh from England's foreign colony of India, she is herself colonised by the English countryside, which gives her the psychic space for self-invention and liberation. In particular, she learns about the power of nature to grow and regenerate, and her own power to nurture, heal, and, by implication, to love: in Barbara T. Gates's words, 'Her female agency allows for the appropriate taming of the wildness that the garden has become.'[4] Mary's garden is, in fact, a walled garden within a large country estate in Yorkshire. On the surface this is a long way from the suburban gardens of late nineteenth-century and early twentieth-century London, but the motifs with which Hodgson Burnett constructed her garden were already familiar to suburban designers and suburbanites.

In the garden romances, the process of colonisation is similarly twofold. While gardens hold the power to influence and shape the identity of the women who care for them, women occupy their gardens in an act of imaginative colonisation (as Burnett emphasises, Mary 'was standing *inside* the secret garden'), making them vantage points for surveying their own lives, cultures and locations.[5] Often, as they followed in their husbands' or families' footsteps, they reclaimed the England that they had left behind by creating gardens around the world, asserting their desire for continuity and their right to a personal history. This gendering of gardens as a female sphere of activity and psychological landscape may seem reactionary: it is certainly rooted in cultural and personal tradition. Childhood memories, reminiscent of the rural visions of Richard Jefferies, Edward Thomas and E. M. Forster, also characterise the garden romances. It is not surprising, as Jacqueline Rose argues, that ideas of childhood are closely associated with the discourse of colonialism, which 'identified the new world with the infantile state of man' and then furnished it from cultural memory.[6] The literature of the past informs the pleasure that women gain from their gardens, and sustains an image of an idealised rural England – an England of delicate flowers, gentle fragrances and abundant growth.

Despite their strong links with the past, these romances are stories of female empowerment and progress. Horticultural books are shelved alongside Shakespeare, Whitman and Keats; the freedom of the garden allows intimations of the primitive and the erotic to mingle with daily activity, and the garden territory symbolises a woman's right to her individual identity. Formally, the garden romances constitute a rebellion against the literary tradition that their writers had enjoyed, and by which they had been shaped, but which had made little room for their perspective. Variously composed as diaries, journals, letters and personal reflections, and often structured around the months of the year or the seasons, these romances constitute a distinctively female literary form. Nothing points so clearly to the changing relationship between the old high culture of educated men and the popular writings of early twentieth-century women garden writers than these writers' acknowledgment of the masculinised past alongside their pleasure in their newly defined feminised present.

The garden romance emerged in response to a particular cultural moment. The ambiguity conveyed by the phrase *rus in urbe* was to spin a web of complexity and significance around the suburban garden. The garden paid homage to nature, healing the sense of rupture between human beings and their environment, and ameliorating the loss of self-determination created by an urban environment. The smallest suburban garden could make a powerful connection with the past, as its owner filled its space with roses, lilies and other perennials, adding cabbages and potatoes if there was room for a vegetable garden, as well as garden furniture that reflected 'the homely beauty of the cottager's ideal'.[7] Even 'a tiny strip . . . situated amid smoke and dirt', as a contemporary garden writer encouragingly commented, 'invariably looked bright and pretty, reminding one somehow . . . of the days of long ago'.[8] A garden could simultaneously be entirely up to date, full of exotic imports and displaying elaborate bedding schemes. It could always be an arena for dreams of the future, a safe and private place in which to daydream, if only of simple plans for the following year. Lawns, flowers and shrubs, whether in gracious middle-class retreats or in handkerchief-sized rectangles at the fronts of terraced working-class houses, became the hieroglyphics of a horticultural text, giving a formalised statement of individual social identity and a way into the vast hinterland of individual desire.

The social significance of gardens was partly influenced by aristocratic ideals. In a succession of building developments from the mid-nineteenth century, wealthy businessmen's houses, often built on carved-up country estates, translated the style of the landed gentry into the more pragmatic mode so disliked by Richard Jefferies.[9] The garden idea filtered down through the diminishing plots of the middle class and of aspirants to the middle class, to the tiniest of terraces. The smaller the garden, the more the aristocratic notion seems to have been complicated by the equally potent ideal of the rural cottage garden. Where there was no garden at all, there were window boxes.[10] Quoting from interviews conducted during the 1890s, Charles Booth records the desire people had to recover the countryside in a suburban equivalent – the garden. 'Houses with good gardens at the back' were what the suburb-dwellers told him that they wanted, but these were 'seldom empty and hard to get', while 'houses with porches creeper-covered' were 'eagerly tenanted'.[11] For a time during the early 1890s, *Punch* regularly ridiculed those upwardly mobile suburbanites whose gardens showed any sign of social aspiration, whether this took the form of pretentious names like 'Fontainebleau' (which 'deserves its name from two remarkably fine plane-trees at one end of the lawn'), or neat rows of mustard and cress mimicking the kitchen gardens of the landed gentry.[12] This strain of satire has continued unabated for over a hundred years. Commentators today who mock the 'unfashionable' flowers which 'suburbanites in their hundreds [are] carrying away' also fail to grasp the difference between the social and the personal meanings which gardens uniquely express.[13]

Not all observers have been so unperceptive. Viscountess Wolseley, one of the earliest women garden writers, recognised the distinctiveness of the small suburban garden, in a striking image which suggests that its meaning could only be revealed to outsiders in a rare moment of insight transcending time and space:

> In these days of motors, when we are quickly whirled through the approaches to London and other towns, we do not see as much of suburban gardens as when the train slowly slackens speed upon a high railway-embankment and we look down from it upon rows of small houses. The buildings may be all alike, but how varied in taste, order, and arrangement is each plot of ground.[14]

This variety, energetically encouraged by the forces of consumerism through the gardening advice which was freely dispensed in women's magazines, gardening magazines and a wide range of 'How To' books, was a form of self-expression. 'Be original', exhorted Violet Biddle, in terms that would not be out of place today. 'Each garden, however small, should possess an *individuality* of its own – some feature that stamps it as out of the common run.'[15] Women frequently expressed guilt over the extravagance into which their gardens drew them but planning, poring over seed catalogues, ordering, receiving, planting, watching and anticipating results were crucial aspects of gardening which pleasurably mingled the practical with the imaginative.

Viscountess Wolseley and Violet Biddle were only two of a number of women gardeners and garden writers who began to establish the garden as a peculiarly domestic and female space. Wolseley also saw the potential of gardening as a means of female employment, and set up a gardening school in 1910 to encourage middle-class women to take up country pursuits as an alternative to employment in the city. Deborah Kellaway notes the connection between the writing of women garden writers and 'the story of her own garden', as well as 'an underlying happiness' which is the the keynote of their writing and an opportunity for suburban fulfilment.[16] The predominantly domestic role that still defined women during this period appears to have been transformed by the discoveries of active gardening and of garden writing, through which they contributed significantly to what Gates calls 'the intellectual construction of nature'.[17]

The joy and delight conveyed in garden writing, which are more akin to the spirit of William Morris than to the social scepticism of *Punch*, are one of its most important aspects. For women, a garden provided the space to create beauty out of nature and, in so doing, to experience happiness – not necessarily in evasion of social realities, but certainly in counterpoint to them. Of course, many women garden writers, such as Vita Sackville-West, Gertrude Jekyll and Kathleen L. Murray, were prosperous and privileged, but their focus on the individual garden as an act of creation offered a practical and feasible resolution to the *rus in urbe* conflict and a new humanised connection with nature. Paradoxically perhaps, the dreams that their work fostered contributed to the democratic spirit of the suburbs. Intensive land redistribution (albeit haphazard and often exploitative) in the steadily expanding suburbs made the garden dream possible for an increasing number of people, turning the countryside and country estates into 'a multitude of houses' and 'a set of discrete assertions'.[18] Mass home-ownership, or tenancy of suburban units, was a reaction to the inhuman scale both of the cities and of the aristocratic estates. By implication, it was also an imaginative shift from the heroic to the ordinary. 'Mass' and 'ordinary' are culturally treacherous words which are often used to imply mediocrity, but in suburban territory they invest power and value in the individual.

Suburban gardens became the topography of the future and changed the physical landscape forever; but they also made a considerable contribution to the rewriting of the pastoral and Romantic traditions, of which their very existence was a redefinition.[19] The semantics of both *rus* and *urbe*, which were themselves highly aestheticised concepts, merged to create a hybrid which was embodied in the idea of the suburban garden. This new garden-meaning successfully leeched out the morality of the Garden of Eden. Although images of Eden abound – there are examples in the suburban idyll fiction of Conan Doyle and Keble Howard, and they occur frequently in garden writing – the meaning of Eden is secularised and generalised, and it becomes a code word for ineffable beauty, spiritual uplift and individual worthiness. Likewise, the classical metamorphic world, whose sexual anarchy Forster struggled ineffectually to bring to the countryside of Wiltshire, is dissolved into logical botanical taxonomies and its sexuality is civilised into a paradigm of heterosexual love characterised by natural feeling and socialised in marriage.

Other Romantic concepts of grandeur were also rewritten. As Andrew Griffin argues, in relation to John Stuart Mill's *Autobiography* (1873), 'the self will be, when it is "most itself", not freely wandering but enclosed, shielded, withheld; not supported and nourished by the "God of Heaven" but self-cultivated, carefully tended, watered, and weeded'.[20] Griffin exposes here the inadequacy of Wordsworth's version of the Romantic sensibility which, in the face of a scientific rationalism that had ruptured the vitality of the relationship between the natural world and the imagination, was transformed from a wilderness into an 'interior garden'. Michael Waters writes: 'The prominence of gardens in Victorian literature has much to do with the declining imaginative and inspirational potency of wilder, natural landscapes, and with the rejection or modification of the aesthetic interests responsible for their earlier exaltation.'[21] There is no doubt that, in a remarkable cultural reconfiguration, the imaginative territory marked out by the proliferating private gardens of the suburbs marked the displacement of Romanticism and Victorian neo-Romanticism in the English literary and cultural imagination.

The increase in the number of popular gardening magazines is further testimony to the domestication and, therefore, personalisation of nature. Garden centres were a feature of suburban life from the mid-nineteenth century, and plants from the furthest parts of the globe continued to be brought home and cultivated for domestic gardens in ever greater numbers.[22] The joint bequest of Wordsworth

and Darwin to the suburban gardener was, on the one hand, an emotionally convenient set of 'symbolic representations and sacramental
meanings', and, on the other, a growing fascination with all branches
of horticulture.[23] Cultivating a garden offered women not only scope
for an imaginative life, but also an opportunity to enjoy the pleasures
of science, and (a particularly important element in women's gardening pleasures), physical activity.

Although the garden romance rapidly became exclusively identified
with women writers, I want to begin with Alfred Austin, whose *The
Garden that I Love* (1894) translated the garden tradition of Victorian
poetry into novel form and set up a template for the garden writing
which became something of a vogue from 1898 to 1914.[24] Austin's
chief distinction was as a prolific but bad poet and as a worse Poet
Laureate (he was appointed in 1896). His main excursions into prose,
other than his autobiography, were two garden novels which are
chiefly interesting for the way they bring together the dominant
motifs of late nineteenth-century aestheticised gardens.

The style and form of *The Garden That I Love* are consciously
demasculinised. The first person narrator lives with his sister, whose
interests he always puts first and to whom he defers as a superior
version of himself. When she marries, he acknowledges that she, as
a woman, has the right to remain, for the house is a woman's place
where 'Grandmothers, great-mothers, great-great-grandmothers . . .
had sat in the ingle-nooks', while he prepares to move on.[25] The book
is addressed through an epistolary introduction to 'Madeleine and
Dorothy', and the narrative is structured in a loosely meandering way
through journal entries from autumn to autumn of a twelve-month
period. In addition, rather like an Elizabethan commonplace book,
the text is a potpourri of conversations, reminiscences, poems, and,
of course, horticultural information about planning, planting and
seasonal developments. Austin's adoption of these intimate and
feminised forms locates the garden as a woman's world even though
he, the narrator, is the one who does the physical work.

The garden is a synthesis of nature, of his identity and of the
human community. The book's illustrations evoke the English rustic
dream of picket gate, rambling climbers over the front door and a
profusion of shrubs and flowers. In a reference to the contemporary
'cottage v. palace' debate, the narrator later tells his friend Lamia
that, given the choice, he would probably choose a cottage even over

Chatsworth.[26] Nature, in a backward look to Wordsworth and the
Victorian moral imagination, has an implicit moral force in that it
'admonishes one to be continuously patient, to trust, to hope, to have
implicit faith in the capacity of time to work wonders . . . and, after
repeated failure cheerfully to try again'.[27]

But there is also considerable human agency at work, since the
building of a garden is analogous to 'a sort of unwritten, but withal
manifest, autobiography'.[28] The beauty of the narrator's garden
ultimately makes possible the happy endings to two love stories –
his own with the talented, clever Lamia, and that between his sister
and their friend, the Poet. The garden, in its role as the external and
natural space around the domesticated home, brings passion and
marriage together. Love is the force that domesticates nature, and
the love that grows through nature has the power to transcend the
material world. Through love, gardens are classless spaces, for while
actual gardens may be as different as the worker's garden described
in the opening pages and the narrator's own, the emotions that they
inspire and embody create a common human bond: 'I could live in
it', the worker declares passionately of his fifteen-foot square plot,
which is 'noticeably neat and lovingly ordered'.[29] Austin's vision
is a deeply traditional one, a kind of *Sesame and Lilies* brought up
to date for contemporary tastes. Yet the form that he uses, and his
literary, horticultural and personal depiction of an individualised
garden, acknowledge a feminine realm and anticipate a new popular
genre.

It was Elizabeth von Arnim's account of her first garden that, according to Rachel Anderson, 'sparked a trend'.[30] *Elizabeth and Her
German Garden* was instantly popular, being reprinted eleven times in
the year after publication, going into twenty-one editions by 1899
and triggering a number of similar works.[31] The book was published
under the pseudonym 'Elizabeth', speculation as to the identity of
the author was rife, and Alfred Austin was suggested by some as a
possible candidate.[32] However, although the form and theme appear
similar, von Arnim's text is fundamentally different from Austin's. An
Australian who grew up in England, she married the Count von
Arnim when she was twenty-four, and lived in Switzerland where,
within three years, she had had three children. In 1895 she persuaded
her husband to move to live in his run-down estate in Prussia, and
there she discovered her garden, with all the instant recognition that

Mary had as she pushed through the door under the ivy into the secret garden for the first time. This real-life event, the discovery of a forgotten and neglected garden, coincided with what Jane Brown calls 'one of the most powerful ideas in cultural history', that is, 'the secret garden, a hidden place of enchantment and peace, where all our ills can be cured', and it guaranteed the novel's success.[33]

One of the main motifs of *Elizabeth and Her German Garden* is the rediscovery of childhood and the significance that this has for an adult in regenerating the life of the emotions and the imagination:

> until, at last, . . . wandering out afterwards into the bare and desolate garden, I don't know what smell of wet earth or rotting leaves brought back my childhood with a rush and all the happy days I had spent in a garden. Shall I ever forget that day? It was the beginning of my real life, my coming of age as it were, and entering my kingdom.[34]

In part, the garden romances grew out of the need to retain the child in the adult and to legitimate the rediscovery of physical abandon, gaiety and carefreeness for women in particular. Elizabeth includes her babies (she always calls them 'babies' although they are also nick-named April, May and June after their birth months) in her garden and shares their responses: 'We made cowslip balls sitting on the grass', she tells us. She daydreams with them about building 'a little cottage' with 'daisies up to the door' and 'close to the stream so we might wash our plates among the flags'.[35] On other occasions, when she is depressed or overwhelmed by playing hostess to her husband's guests, she runs like a guilty child to the garden 'for refuge and shelter'.[36] It is her 'Eden without Jehovah'.[37]

The association of gardens and childhood memories emerges strongly in a number of women's memoirs. In Alice Morse Earle's *Old Time Gardens* (1901), the idea of a garden seems to have become part of a cultural collective unconscious: 'Somewhere, in my childhood, I saw this beautiful garden . . . and when I was grown I asked where it was, describing it in every detail, and the only answer was that it was a dream, I had never seen or played in such a garden'.[38]

Barbara Campbell muses on the fate of the city child, who is deprived of that experience of mystery, beauty and adventure which encourages impressionable children to follow the path: 'that reaches under the trees and through the long meadow-grass where the red-gold lily bells tinkle, up the brook to the great flat mossy rock, beneath which is the door to fairyland'.[39] Gertrude Jekyll, who was to

become such a significant influence on garden design, never forgot
that children and gardens belonged together, and she mourned her
own strict upbringing which robbed her of such freedom. In her book,
Children and Gardens (1908), a kind of instruction book to help
children learn to garden, the garden is a place of liberation and fun,
a parallel world where children can dig, climb, make dens, cook on
open fires and invite grown-ups to join them if they happen to feel
like it. The delightful illustrations such as 'A grown up wheelbarrow
is a good place to sit in', 'In the sand pit', and the picture of a garden
bench with shoes and stockings strewn haphazardly over it, seem to
have been created out of the same psychology that inspired Kenneth
Grahame's *The Golden Age* and *Dream Days*, and Edith Nesbit's
Bastable stories. It is not surprising to discover that Gertude Jekyll
included a picture of von Arnim with her children outside their
garden house in *Children and Gardens*.

For Elizabeth, reaching back into childhood was also part of
reinventing her adulthood. When she first found her garden, she
was alone for six weeks, ostensibly supervising the redecoration of the
house but actually living almost wild in the neglected, overgrown and
unknown garden. There she was 'most herself', reading, gardening,
dreaming of the garden's future or simply forgetting 'the existence
of everything but the green pastures and still waters and the glad
blowing of the winds across the joyous fields'.[40] She broke down the
boundary between house and garden, filling the house with lilacs,
flinging the windows open and positioning her dressing table so that
she could see aspects of the garden at all times.

Her book is characterised by suburban informality and access-
ibility. It is written as a journal of the seasons but it digresses, as
any diary does, into other subjects – family anecdotes, accounts of
visits and of a family Christmas. Although published as a novel, it is
actually a medley of forms: romance fiction, fictionalised autobiography and memoir. Terence de Vere White's description of the book
as 'an imaginative biography' is probably the best assessment, although
I would prefer to call it 'a biography of an imagination'.[41] Von Arnim's
style is fluent, never giving the reader time to stop and ask, 'Is this
true?', and never needing to, since the garden is truly the landscape
of Elizabeth's emotional life. H. G. Wells, whose good opinion of the
book may well have been influenced by the fact that he had had an
affair with its author, took the opportunity to justify his own literary
methods in celebrating hers: 'in some cases the whole art and delight

of a novel may lie in the author's personal interventions; let such novels as *Elizabeth and Her German Garden* . . . bear witness'.[42]

Von Arnim's garden is as much a literary garden as a realistic one. She enjoys sharing with her readers, not so much the garden itself as what the garden means to her. In her turn, she interprets her experiences of the garden through the words of others, just as suburban men walking in the South Downs clutch their pocket books of poems. In the chapter 'May' of *The Solitary Summer* (1899), for instance, she explains her intellectual growth through the works of Goethe, Thoreau, Keats, Johnson, Boswell and Spenser, and amuses herself, and us, by testing each of them out against her own garden experience. Thoreau, with his commitment to Walden, nearly out-does her own sense of devotion to her garden, until she forcibly reminds herself that Thoreau also had an ordinary domestic life out-side Walden. During the winter she plunges into gardening books, improving her own garden in her imagination and entering the gardens of others, until writing about 'roses and all the other summer glories' cheers her up.[43]

The Solitary Summer is not, I think, as successful as *Elizabeth and Her German Garden*, but it contains one long sequence which brilliantly evokes what is perhaps the most important aspect of von Arnim's writing – a woman's sensuous pleasure in freedom from social constraints and the potential that this gives for freedom of thought and action. She gives an account of creeping out of the house in June, just before dawn, and wandering around the garden which is both real and surreal. She witnesses the garden at work, growing and flowering, with the birds singing and fragrances being released as she moves among the plants, the grass soaked with dew. Under the moonlight, she feels that she has been given a vision of the world. Unlike Edward Thomas and Richard Jefferies, who feel that nature fails them in their search for transcendence, in a sudden fullness of understanding she allows herself to acknowledge thoughts of suffering, of death, of futility that she would normally push away. Her account of this moment acknowledges its importance, but, characteristically, she personalises rather than universalises her experience: 'I shall not soon forget . . . a feeling as though I has taken the world by surprise, and seen it as it really is when off its guard – as though I had been quite near the very core of things'.[44]

Of von Arnim's work, *Elizabeth and Her German Garden*, in particular, is still an exhilarating experience to read today – a celebration of a private world of spiritual and mental restoration that sustains her individuality and invigorates her energies. Even though Elizabeth wrote about a neglected aristocratic garden in northern Prussia, her account spoke to the needs of the time, to grasp the vanishing remnants of a lost golden age and integrate them into the new social formations, and to legitimise women's need for an identity beyond that of wife and mother. It is interesting to speculate whether E. M. Forster, who, in one of those bizarre interconnections that occur so frequently in the early twentieth-century literary scene, tutored von Arnim's children during 1905, would have identified with the erotic elements of von Arnim's romance or would have resisted the implications of her feminised world and, indeed, whether he was allowed to enter the garden that she wrote about. Another oddly appropriate footnote to her story is that the von Arnim estate was sold off because of debt in 1908; her husband died in London in 1913. Within a few years, as the First World War swept across Europe, Prussia no longer existed and the already weakening aristocratic families of Europe were finally marginalised. But by then Elizabeth's dream had been translated into thousands of suburban gardens. It was not surprising that demobbed soldiers, returning to England and promised 'homes fit for heroes', felt that '"a garden" summed up the space, air and privacy for living they felt they had earned'.[45]

Barbara, or Barbara Campbell (whose real name was Mabel Osgood Wright), acknowledges her debt to Elizabeth von Arnim in her own account of cultivating a garden, The Garden of a Commuter's Wife (1901), but her story is of continuity rather than discovery.[46] Her garden is also overseas, in the United States, and it is the garden of the house where she grew up. After her marriage to an Englishman, whose own childhood home had a garden that he remembers with affection, they have to decide where to live. He leaves the decision to his wife since, he says, the choice of home is a woman's prerogative; but when she chooses America she brings ideas and plants from his old garden to make an English garden overseas. Like Elizabeth and Her German Garden, Barbara's novel is organised as a diary, full of small daily events, hopes and pleasures in a way which is also reminiscent of the mood of Doyle's and Howard's suburban novels. The relationship between her father, her new husband and herself is framed by the memory of her dead mother, and is charted in the growth of the garden as she reshapes it according to her dreams.

Barbara's garden is conveyed in strongly feminised terms. The original layout had been designed by her mother, and this fact provides her with a sense of mission and continuity. An old apple tree, nicknamed 'The Mother Tree', is the central point of the garden where she rests, reads or daydreams. Her husband (a thoroughly new man who takes time off work to help shift rockery stones or receive a delivery of manure) and her father are welcome in the garden, but they can only be appreciative observers and instruments in helping her to execute her plans. The garden which was the playground of her childhood becomes the fulfilment of the mature woman, since gardening allows her self-discovery and a creative outlet for her energies. Inhabiting a garden gives rein to a delicious sensuousness as her husband Evan put roses in her hair, and she plays with ideas of a primitive or a Bohemian existence in the open air.

A large part of the garden's female identity comes from its power to sustain love. As Barbara weaves her husband's English garden into her American one, she weaves their marriage together. The sundial that they transport from Evan's garden to America continues to tell English time, reminding them of their joint inheritance, and one of her first plantings is of the primrose and cowslip roots that successfully survived the journey. While the outline of the garden is drawn on American soil, the colours that fill it come from an English cottage tradition:

> There was a broad band of hollyhocks, too well placed against the honeysuckle bank to be disturbed, straggling helter-skelter were foxgloves, Canterbury bells, larkspurs, phloxes, sweet William, columbines, white anemone, japonica still in bloom, in company with monkshood, hardy coreopsis, evening primroses, honesty, and sunflowers.[47]

Later in the novel, Barbara's husband gives her a case made from the wood of the Mother Tree, in which he has put a copy of the book that had first brought them together inscribed 'Blessed is she to whom it is given to link the new love with the old'.[48] In a later novel, *The Open Window*, nature and love, bounded by the garden, are brought together in a pre-lapsarian vision of herself and her husband as 'a couple of carefree children playing at going on a journey to seek the Tree of Life'. This game is based on her reading of Edmund Spenser and John Bunyan, and she had played it as a child during 'days spent alone in the garden'.[49] In this literary and Edenic setting innocent love thrives. Even Martha Corkle, Evan's old nurse from *The Garden of a Commuter's Wife*, who is (reluctantly) transplanted to American soil, finds love with the local handyman, Tim Saunders. The concluding sentence of the book tells of their sealing their commitment to one another with a kiss.

The full meaning of Barbara's garden is revealed in an evocative illustration of a woman seated casually in a window, staring dreamily out at the garden which is the source of her imaginative life, her language and her way of understanding herself and her world. Her book shelf is described in horticultural terms, laden with gardening books which she has 'planted' in carefully chosen sequence and which will be her 'garden of remembrance' until spring comes; the books will provide 'main roads, bypaths, and endless vistas' to her garden of the imagination.[50] A similar passage in a later novel, *The Garden, You, and I* (1906), in which Barbara looks out at her garden from her bed, underlines how the garden breaks through the barriers between indoors and outdoors, and nurtures the health of the imagination with its physical presence:

> To keep in touch with earth and sky, I raise myself comfortably, elbow on pillow, and through the window scan the garden, wild walk, and the old orchard at leisure, and then let my arm slip and the impression deepen through the magic of one more chance for dreams.[51]

The interweaving of an English, a foreign and a personal garden is further complicated in Kathleen L. Murray's accounts of her garden in India, *Letters from the Wilderness* (a collection of articles first published in the *The Statesman*), and *My Garden in the Wilderness*, published in 1913 and 1915 respectively.[52] Von Arnim's garden is never significant specifically because it is German and there is no deliberate attempt to anglicise it; perhaps its northern European location is in harmony (ironically given the events of the following years) rather than in conflict with British gardenscapes. In any case, Elizabeth's experience of it is primarily one of personal liberation. By contrast, Barbara's garden is a deliberate horticultural reflection on a transatlantic marriage; and the ability of nature to accommodate plants from different bio-contexts in a single whole is a metaphor for cultural assimilation and sexual happiness. But Murray's garden occupies more problematic colonial territory, although she remains at one remove from the military and governmental structures of the Raj, as well as from the upheavals of western Europe at the time of the First World War. She lived in the family house with her brother, who worked in indigo production in the small, remote town of Behar in the years preceding and during the war. There are no hints in the text of any power struggles, so it is difficult to assess how far the garden images were offered as imaginative escapes (for the author and/or the reader), and whether Murray's socially privileged status, coupled with her distance from the centres of power, enabled her to put a bracket around international events. There is, of course, another explanation of her seeming detachment. For all her affluence and privilege, Murray was socially isolated and effectively redundant, in a social context where her every need was provided for and her sole function was to occupy her time. She is sensitive to the implied pity expressed by people 'who openly wonder "what can you find to do with yourself all day"', but she also acknowledges that such freedom is defining, making unique demands on a woman's inner resources if she is to live a satisfying and creative life.[53] The garden that she created in what she terms the 'wilderness', and the writing that it inspired, began to resolve for her these problematics of culture and gender.

At first, India is represented as the 'land of regret', the 'wilderness', a home that sometimes seems a place of exile from Scotland and London despite the length of time that her family has lived there. The garden, however, rejects such historically and geographically specific divisions. Refusing to be constrained by notions of nationality or global space, Murray's garden flamboyantly demonstrates its international status, allowing the changing seasonal conditions and its own different aspects to display both the massiveness and brilliance of Indian trees and flowers and the delicacy and variety of English species to their best effect. The mingling of the plant names – the Indian peepul, sissoo and teak trees, the mustard, poppy and chilli flowers, and the English cosmos, candytuft, sweet peas, hollyhocks and roses – creates an almost surreal environment, a kind of surprising familiarity or exotic homeliness in which Scotland, England and India are all elements of one mental and emotional landscape.

Murray's Indian garden gradually colonises her British-educated imagination, integrating the past impressions and history of the colonising writer into its present significance for her: like von Arnim and Campbell, she finds that the spirit of the garden is the sum of her experiences and liberates her to be fully herself. In *Letters from the Wilderness*, her growing involvement with the garden parallels a vestigial narrative of missed opportunity and lost love which allows her to discover another independent, mature (what she calls 'worldly')

4

'through the window I scan garden, wild walk, and the old orchard at leisure'
Illustration from Barbara Campbell, *The Garden of a Commuter's Wife*

version of herself. Although when she begins gardening she does not fully realise the gendered implications of her engagement, with hindsight she claims, in an echo of Mrs Wilcox in *Howards End*, that 'there is a heart in this garden, the heart of the woman who lived here before we did, and who planned it all'.[54] And only later does she recognise fully the profound alliance between gardens, women's emotional and psychological needs and their specific situation in history. 'I did not know I was obeying a primitive instinct in making myself a garden in the wilderness', she wrote in her introduction. She continues:

> But now the thought comes that the instinct goes deeper, and that we are all mentally creating for ourselves some little, lovely garden in our especial wilderness – a garden of dreams, of hopes, of ambitions, of love – and that without these gardens in the wilderness life would be scarcely tolerable, and exile be bitter indeed.[55]

Like von Arnim and Campbell, she creates a vantage point, placing a seat so that it is 'shaded by the teak trees and closed in by a shrubbery', where she can occupy the same threshold between domestic and wild that Lucy Honeychurch glimpses in her view through the window in *A Room with a View*. Murray's new experiences inspire memories of childhood and thoughts of favourite poets and novelists; she studies horticultural catalogues and imports European plants. The outdoor garden of her physically active life and the interior garden of her imagination become interchangeable, even indistinguishable. A description which echoes Campbell's in the way it legitimises idleness, or 'woolgathering' as Edward Thomas calls it in *The Happy-Go-Lucky Morgans*, makes clear that the reality of the garden is as readily apprehended by the inner as by the outer eye: 'But I like best to lie late in bed, with the scent of belated wallflowers and a babel of bird cries coming in at the open window, and to watch the broad plantain leaves swaying across the square of turquoise sky that bounds my early morning vision.'[56]

The garden romance was not exclusively the domain of affluent upper-middle-class writers. The model of gardening that these books described was also a powerful image of modern womanhood – an apparently irresistible combination of practicality and poetry, of physicality and idleness, of science and imagination, of assertiveness and nurturing, of continuity and regeneration, of security and beauty. It was an ideal enthusiastically rehearsed in the growing body of garden writing, whatever the size of the garden concerned. Mrs Leslie Williams's *A Garden in the Suburbs* (1901) is an early example of the garden romance adapted for the small suburban gardener. The hard cover of the first edition shows the panoramic view out of a window over an elegant balustrade, across a sloping lawn, to a 'borrowed' vista of gently sloping fields patterned with hedges.[57] The frontispiece inside is a diagram of 'The real garden'. With its gravelled area, rockery, tiny greenhouse, wire rose arch and laburnum tree, a lawn sandwiched between two flowerbeds and bounded on either side by neighbours' gardens, the ground plan is recognisable today as that of the archetypal suburban garden. There is, of course, a gentle joke in the juxtaposition of the two gardens, just as there is in Williams's nickname for her own garden, 'The Oblong'. But the illustrations are also an acknowledgement of the existence of two gardens – one that the reader is invited to plant, nurture and live in, and another that she is encouraged to cultivate in her imagination.

The acknowledgment of this dichotomy is not the only way in which Williams's idea of the garden differs from von Arnim's and Campbell's. It is considerably harder work, with no space for vigorous growth or rambling plants; and, with a family of husband, children and a dog to accommodate, there is a daily struggle to produce the illusion of fecundity and the actuality of control. Cats have to be kept out, the dog kept in and her husband encouraged to do something other than sit in the deckchair under the apple tree. Williams does most of the garden labour herself, going round 'every day with my poor humble margarine bucket full of best potting soil, my trowel, grubbing mat to kneel on and sundry boxes of seedlings', and calling into question the sincerity of Elizabeth's cry in *The Solitary Summer* that she 'aches with envy' when she watches the gardeners 'turning up the luscious damp earth'.[58] Williams does, however, have to rely on outside help to get building rubble moved when it is discovered under the poorly performing lawn. Perhaps the greatest difference is that she must take into consideration the buildings which surround her so that she can combat what Walter Creese calls 'a mass deprivation of sight' with the colour and design of her planting.[59]

Nevertheless, it is clear that Williams's book pays tribute to von Arnim. She has her 'own little private dream of a heavenly mansion' that she strives to replicate in 'The Oblong Eden'.[60] Her husband is tolerated and sometimes compelled to contribute, but The Oblong is a feminised space where both her traditional nurturing role and her modern independence can be satisfied: its 'walls enclose a little area where female suffrage reigns, and deserves to do so, for its pains', but it is also 'like a child – it must be fed'.[61] Within the confines of her garden, she paints a picture of colours and shapes throughout the seasons, reading books, searching catalogues and passing the winter reading about gardens and gardening. Although the small garden limits the numbers of flowers and the size of the trees, it does not limit imaginative possibilities: 'the difficulties . . . are a spur to the hope that on that blissful "someday", which for most of us holds so much more than is possible in the present, garden boundaries may widen and garden opportunities increase'.[62]

It is not surprising that Leslie Williams's book is more of a gardening book than von Arnim's and Campbell's. The privilege of allowing dreams and realities to be inextricable belongs to the rich and secure. A suburban gardener needs advice and practical hints to start her off as well as dreams to sustain her efforts. But A *Garden in the Suburbs* is primarily a garden romance. Williams adopts the journal mode, making monthly records of her garden tasks and achievements in the first person; and the chapters (though some more than others) read like a sequence of letters. The reader is addressed in a conversational tone as a friend, as if she shares knowledge of the garden and common assumptions about gardening. The text is scattered with personal anecdotes and thoughts triggered by gardening, while her imaginary garden is always as real as 'The Real Garden'.

The garden romance was a genre as short-lived as its masculine equivalent, the rural ramble. It was a response to a deep need to avoid a social rupture between past and present, perceived in terms of country and city, and to find a dynamic connection between 'woman' and 'wife', in a domestic situation which promised women better material conditions but made for a potentially stultifying existence. Men are always outsiders in the Edwardian woman's garden. For Elizabeth, her garden represents an escape from being a wife, and von Arnim's most powerful writing is found in those passages in which she is alone and sure that she cannot be touched by wifely duties. Even so, she dedicates *The Solitary Summer* to her husband, and the closing passage describes their affectionate embrace. Barbara's garden is more self-consciously a feminine arena, but part of its pleasure for her is the admiration and support of her father and her new husband for her activities. Leslie Williams, too, dedicates her book to her husband. The statements of independence that these writers' gardens represent as actual and private spaces, and as literary achievements, are mitigated in wifely fashion. However, the style of the garden romances entirely escapes the imprint of a masculine literary tradition. Their literary mode suggests models of communication between women to which men are irrelevant. The language is informal, personal and immediate. Digressions, anecdotes, reminiscences and personal reflections mingle with horticultural notes, garden descriptions, reading records and accounts of visits, journeys and family histories. These texts transgressed the privacy of the gardens that they described to make a dream of women's empowerment shareable with suburban women readers.

In *The Waste Land* (1922) T. S. Eliot depicted a culture which had lost its way, a world whose symbols had lost their spiritual and cultural history and had surrendered to an endemic and enveloping ugliness: in this poem, April is (famously) 'the cruellest month'. However, to most suburbanites of both sexes and all classes who had escaped from the city, qualified by improved education and wages to begin to make their own dreams, such doomful prophesying would have made no sense. Gardens, which were often mere squares of uncultivated earth on new estates, may well have been a jerry-builder's confidence trick to appeal to class aspiration and snobbery, and their designs were often thoroughly vilified. But the democratic undertow of the early twentieth century, when individuals staked their claim to the land, was to prove more enduring than such passing criticisms. The tree on the avenue and the gardens that bordered it were not simply decorative devices to those who bought or rented the new properties. They became symbols that harnessed and democratised pastoral, picturesque, sublime and Romantic views of nature. For suburbanites they acted simultaneously as a connection to the myths of the Golden Age and a reassurance that the lost domain had been restored, as reminders of childhood memories and promises of a new future. In both their actual and symbolic existence, gardens embodied (en-natured) and feminised the suburban new.

Notes

1 Brown, *The Pursuit of Paradise*, 157. Brown calls Letchworth Garden City, designed by Raymond Unwin in the spirit of Ebenezer Howard and built in 1903, as the 'apotheosis' of the small garden, 'designed for thirty thousand small gardeners at about five houses and twenty-four people to the acre' (154).

2 Gates, *Kindred Nature*, 197. Gates also includes women's travel writing in a fascinating essay on the female sublime.

3 Gates, *Kindred Nature*, 8.

4 Gates, *Kindred Nature*, 241.

5 Frances Hodgson Burnett, [1911] *The Secret Garden* (London: Penguin, 1995), 74.

6 Jacqueline Rose, *The Case of Peter Pan, or, The impossibility of children's fiction* (Basingstoke: Macmillan, 1984), 50.

7 M. H. Baillie Scott [1906], *Houses and Gardens: Arts and crafts interiors* in Brown, *The Pursuit of Paradise*, 156.

8 Violet Purton Biddle, *Small Gardens and How to Make the Most of Them* (London: C. Arthur Pearson Ltd, 1901), 17.

9 See Joan Morgan and Alison Richards, *A Paradise out of a Common Field: The pleasures and plenty of the Victorian garden* (London and Sydney: Century, 1990) for a discussion of the relationship between garden design and garden products, and country house status in the mid-Victorian period.

10 See Sue Bennett, *Five Centuries of Women and Gardens* (London: National Portrait Gallery Publications, 2000), 82.

11 Booth, *Final Volume*, 178.

12 F. Anstey, *Voces Populi* (reprinted from *Punch*) (London: Longman, Green and Co., 1890), 1.

13 Michael Leapman, 'Snobbery Blossoms in Borders and the Shrubbery', *Independent on Sunday* (17 April 1994), 7.

14 Viscountess Wolseley, *Gardens, Their Form and Design* (1919), cited in Deborah Kellaway (ed.), *The Virago Book of Women Gardeners* (London: Virago, 1997), 141.

15 Biddle, *Small Gardens*, 17. Emphasis in original.

16 Kellaway (ed.), *Women Gardeners*, xvi, xvii.

17 Gates, *Kindred Nature*, 8.

18 Walter L. Creese, 'Imagination in the Suburb' in Knoepflmacher and Tennyson, *Nature and the Victorian Imagination*, 44–67 (50).

19 See the introduction to Knoepflmacher and Tennyson for an analysis of neo-Romanticism in the mid-Victorian period.

20 Andrew Griffin, 'The Interior Garden and John Stuart Mill' in Knoepflmacher and Tennyson, *Nature and the Victorian Imagination*, 171–186 (173).

21 Waters, *The Garden in Victorian Literature*, 183.

22 Two examples are Robert Fortune (1812–80) who introduced (among other plants) honeysuckle, weigala, forsythia and winter-flowering jasmine, and Ernest Henry Wilson (1876–1930) who introduced dogwood, clematis Montana, buddleia and azaleas.

23 Knoepflmacher and Tennyson, *Nature and the Victorian Imagination*, xxi.

24 Alfred Austin, *The Garden that I Love* (London: Macmillan, 1894).

25 *The Garden that I Love*, 35.

26 See George F. Ford, '"Felicitous Space": The cottage controversy' in Knoepflmacher and Tennyson, *Nature and the Victorian Imagination*, 29–48.

27 *The Garden that I Love*, 132–133.

28 *The Garden that I Love*, 112.

29 *The Garden that I Love*, 3, 1.
30 Rachel Anderson, *The Purple Heart Throbs: The sub-literature of love* (London: Hodder and Stoughton, 1974), 117. According to Elizabeth's entry in Kemp et al., *Edwardian Fiction* (114), Austin gave her a copy of his book when he heard about her enthusiasm for gardening, so he should perhaps get greater credit for being the originator of this genre.
31 Elizabeth von Arnim, [1898] *Elizabeth and Her German Garden*, with an introduction by Jane Howard (London: Virago, 1985).
32 Deborah Kellaway, 'Introduction' in Elizabeth von Arnim, [1899] *The Solitary Summer* (London: Virago, 1993), ii.
33 Brown, *The Pursuit of Paradise*, 50.
34 *Elizabeth*, 7.
35 *Elizabeth*, 35.
36 *Elizabeth*, 23.
37 Cavaliero, *The Rural Tradition*, 32.
38 Alice Morse Earle, [1901] *Old Time Gardens* in Kellaway, *Women Gardeners*, 231.
39 Barbara Campbell, *The Garden, You, and I* (New York and London: Macmillan, 1906), 204.
40 *Elizabeth*, 47.
41 Terence de Vere White, 'Introduction' in Elizabeth von Arnim, [1922] *The Enchanted April* (London: Virago, 1986), viii.
42 Wells, 'The Contemporary Novel', 198.
43 Elizabeth von Arnim, [1899] *The Solitary Summer* (London: Virago, 1993), 35.
44 *The Solitary Summer*, 62.
45 Brown, *The Pursuit of Paradise*, 159.
46 Barbara Campbell, *The Garden of a Commuter's Wife* (New York and London: Macmillan, 1901), 8.
47 *The Garden of a Commuter's Wife*, 131.
48 *The Garden of a Commuter's Wife*, 353.
49 Barbara Campbell, *The Open Window: Tales of the months* (London and New York: Macmillan, 1908), 120.
50 *The Garden of a Commuter's Wife*, 137, 183, 191.
51 Campbell, *The Garden, You, and I*, 7.
52 Kathleen L. Murray, *Letters from the Wilderness* (London and Calcutta: W. Thacker and Co., 1913) and *My Garden in the Wilderness* (London, Calcutta and Sima: W. Thacker and Co., 1915).
53 *My Garden in the Wilderness*, 143.
54 *Letters from the Wilderness*, 45–46.
55 Introduction to *Letters from the Wilderness*.
56 *My Garden in the Wilderness*, 171.
57 Mrs Leslie Williams, *A Garden in the Suburbs* (London and New York: John Lane and Bodley Head, 1901).
58 *A Garden in the Suburbs*, 54–55; *The Solitary Summer*, 14.
59 'Imagination in the Suburb', 49.
60 *A Garden in the Suburbs*, 1, 65.
61 *A Garden in the Suburbs*, 56, 142.
62 *A Garden in the Suburbs*, 195.

5

*

THE FEMININE SUBURB/1

Women readers and romance fiction

WOMEN's garden romances were part of a much larger story told by women. While male visionaries, escapists and idealists were free to travel where they pleased and to roam the universe of their imaginations, the majority of women suburbanites seemed doomed to live within rather more constrained boundaries. The smallness of suburban life – small houses, small minds and small concerns – was a popular joke at their expense. Men were sometimes the butt of the joke, but that was because they had been emasculated by the female world of the suburbs. The responsibility for suburban smallness was undoubtedly laid at women's door. Yet it appears that women transcended the constraints of small suburban houses and often undeveloped suburban communities to roam in their imaginations, in much the same way that better educated and more affluent men and women transcended their grander sense of cultural poverty. However, there was a fundamental difference. Whereas the writers whom I discussed in the first part of this book wrote about or created their own versions of the suburbs, the readers who lived in the suburbs devoured fiction that predominantly ignored the suburbs' existence. The fiction *in* the suburbs created a quite different imaginative landscape from the fiction *of* the suburbs. It is to this fiction, which was aimed at women at home although it was not read only by women at home or, indeed, only by women, that I want to devote the next two chapters.

In contemporary public opinion, the identification between women and the suburbs was initially forged, as we have seen, by the suburbs' essentially domestic function and by the endorsement of women's role as homemakers. This notion of the feminisation of the suburbs merged with contemporary fears about the feminisation of culture to identify particular kinds of reading and readers as 'suburban'. Popular fiction and in particular romance, were seen as the locus of suburban culture and as indicative of a range of social ills. As with so many controversial topics at the turn of the twentieth century, social anxieties about popular fiction can be traced to questions of scale and of gender. Popular fiction in magazines and books seemed to indicate the failure of universal education to deliver discrimination as well as skills. It signalled the commodification of culture, and was proof of women's intellectual weakness.

The dramatically increased scale of magazine and book production, and women's increased role as consumers from the 1880s, are not in dispute. It is generally agreed that, by the end of the nineteenth century 'women were consumers of magazines on a scale unimaginable a century earlier'.[1] Novels were equally popular. By 1923, two hundred novel titles were being published every week, and the advertisements that were common in the backs of these early popular editions testify that the majority of them were written by women for women.[2] Individual authors began to sell in numbers that we may still find staggering today. According to Annette Federico, Marie Corelli routinely sold 600,000 books a year after her fame was assured by *The Romance of Two Worlds*, which was published in 1886.[3] Some successful books were surprisingly enduring. Elinor Glyn had sold five million copies of *Three Weeks* (1907) by the early 1930s. Florence Barclay's *The Rosary*, published in 1909, was still selling well in 1928; while Ruby M. Ayres, who began publishing in 1912, is still reprinted today with only minor adjustments to modern taste.

Improvements in distribution were a crucial factor in expanding markets. The growth of libraries, which provided publishers with a regular and reliable market, was another. Richard Altick records that by 1900 the annual circulation of subscription libraries was thirty to forty million volumes, a figure that was considerably boosted by the widespread opening of public lending libraries early in the twentieth century.[4] Although not all the novels stocked by libraries were romances written by women and borrowed by women, they were certainly the largest single category. Nicola Beauman records that by 1923 the cheaper 2d libraries, which catered for working-class readers, had a clientele consisting equally of men and women, and that romances formed 30 per cent of their stock; in the more expensive libraries run by Boots and W. H. Smith, romance constituted 50 per cent of the stock and the clientele was 75 per cent female.[5] Other social factors probably played a part. The 1911 census showed that there were nearly one and a half million more women than men at a time when the average per capita income was steadily rising.[6] Charles Boon, who set up his own publishing company with Gerald Mills in 1910, gradually realised that women read the bulk of the books that his company published and were the chief library borrowers. Even before the First World War, he began to base his marketing strategy on that assumption.[7] Popular culture had been 'defined as feminine' as early as the mid-nineteenth century – in part to ring-fence and denigrate it.[8] By the late nineteenth century, the suburbs had become part of the equation. Suburbia and mass commodity fiction were similarly linked by association and by the contempt of the cultural elite. In a discussion of the reading public in the 1930s, Q. D. Leavis makes a jibe at the suburbs' expense, comparing the 'fantasy-spinning' of popular fiction to 'the romantic names on suburban gateposts'.[9]

Women clearly, if indirectly, exerted considerable power over the production and distribution of reading matter, but the notion of the feminisation of culture also suggests that they had power over what men read. The new phenomenon of the 'best-seller list', for instance, was dominated by male writers from 1903 to 1925, but by the 1920s it was perceived as 'a feminine artefact, produced by women for women'.[10] Men were not averse to enjoying fiction written by women, and they could even respond to it in a way usually labelled as feminine. A columnist for *Hearth and Home* recalled visiting a male member of her Literary Society, who had expressed dissatisfaction about the material selected for discussion, only to find him 'innocently engrossed in and enjoying a historical romance by an esteemed lady writer . . . whom we remember bedewing with appreciative tears in our tender adolescence'.[11] An amusing episode in Denis Mackail's *Greenery Street*, an affectionate satire on the common events of newly-married life published in 1925, describes a young wife's attempts to find just the right novels for her husband on her almost daily visits to the public library, and his pleasure in reading them despite stoutly maintaining that they were not his kind of novel.

From the advent of Marie Corelli to the present day, romance fiction for women has stirred up almost universal condemnation, and most that was written between 1880 and 1920, particularly in magazines, has been forgotten or ignored. The few dissenting voices at the time were often writers of popular fiction themselves, and they offer a valuable insider perspective. John St John Adcock, for instance, evocatively suggested the elusive meaning of the suburbs and its protean spatiality in his evaluation of Marie Corelli's work in 1909. Referring to the tag, 'idol of the suburbs', which had become attached to her, Adcock formulated a pertinent question – one that is still waiting for an answer: '[W]hen you find . . . that everything she has written has been translated many times into so many varied languages and dialects . . . you can only ask yourself, if this is suburban, which one of our novelists may be regarded as approximately cosmopolitan?'[12] However, the consensus among the literary classes was that romance fiction was the 'froth of the moment',[13] 'daydreaming fiction',[14] a morbid 'feeding of the imagination' liable to take workers from their duties and turn women into 'fiction-vampires'.[15]

The fundamental project of the romance was given a new impetus by a reaction against the moral seriousness of mid-Victorian writing and the dominance of the social problem novel later in the century. Interestingly, its revival in the 1880s was commonly associated with adventure, Empire and the reaffirmation of masculinity. R. L. Stevenson, a brilliant exponent of the romance genre, claimed that 'reading should offer a thoroughgoing holiday from our own intellectual nature, from the very limits indeed of our own subjectivity', that we should be 'rapt clean out of ourselves' and that we should leave the book 'incapable of sleep or of continuous thought'.[16] His success in achieving these ends in his famous South Sea adventure tales brought about what Nicholas Daly calls 'a tidal wave of romanticism'.[17] Although the critical reception of their romances was usually less positive, women writers had already entered the fray. When Marie Corelli published her first novel, in 1886, she wrote to her publisher in similar, if calmer, terms to Stevenson's: 'I want to make it [the public] also feel rested, invigorated, and rendered for a time oblivious of its troubles in the perusal of my pages'.[18]

Romance fiction for women provided a counterpoint to the testosterone-charged imperialist adventure, but they shared an oppositional position in the history of the novel. Romance reworked the collective emotion which had been played on by social problem novels as subjective feeling, making emotion so much the impulse of fiction that, for modernist writers, it became the defining difference between high and low culture, a mirror image of what Suzanne Clark calls a 'literary/non-literary dualism' and Q. D. Leavis called the 'antithesis between the novel of the heart and the novel of the brain'.[19] Romance became a critique of the kind of literary production that claimed aesthetic and intellectual superiority but seemed to fail to provide a satisfying imaginative experience for the vast majority of the new readership.

For this reason, romance also appears to have been an egalitarian project. Few women romance writers bothered about the world of the literary review as Marie Corelli did. Although some writers and books, such as Ethel M. Dell and her first bestseller, *The Way of an Eagle* (1912), would be drawn into the public glare because of their spectacular success, the vast majority relied on publishers' efficient distribution and publicity systems, on word-of-mouth recommendation and on a prolific output to keep their work known and read. New writers had to rely on submissions direct to magazine editors and publishers rather than networking London's literary coteries. In fact, many, if not most, of the women romance novelists began with magazine fiction and often continued to combine both kinds of writing throughout their careers. In addition, they seem to have had a strong sense of responsibility to their readership, a feeling suggested by Marie Corelli in the statement quoted earlier, and summed up by Bertha Ruck, whose first novels appeared during the First World War:

> I belong to the School of Thought (the Non-Thinking School, if you like) that considers 'compensating dream fiction', not as opiate, but as tonic ... People condemn the story-teller's cheerfully tied-up last chapter as a flight from reality. Personally, I regard it as the entrance into the original real world.[20]

This statement, like so much about romance fiction, inverts the common wisdom. The right to dream, which draws a line between the material reality and imagination with its narrative completeness, is part of the equipment required for dealing with the 'real world', and recognising this becomes a crucial part of the contract between reader and writer.

Romance, however, was not a monolithic genre, although it is often convenient to see it as such against the wider background of generic proliferation at the turn of the twentieth century. The period between 1880 and 1914 was one of innovation and development in literary genres – in science fiction, detective fiction, New Woman novels, colonial adventure and travel writings, to name only a few.

Many writers moved away from narrative realism and in so doing were part of a general search for innovation, for new ways to intervene in and interact with readers' hopes and fears. Within the specific genre of romantic fiction for women there was great diversity: mini-genres abounded, such as career, historical and desert romances; feminine versions of colonial and imperial adventures; the suburban idylls and garden romances which I discussed earlier; as well as the sexsation and exotic novels, such as Elinor Glyn's *Three Weeks* (1907) and E. M. Hull's *The Sheik* (1919), with which romance in this period is generally associated.[21]

If there was little formal innovation of the kind associated with modernism, there was radical change in the traditional use of plot. As David Trotter neatly puts it, 'The objective of Edwardian romance of womanhood was to *uncouple* event and meaning, temporarily'.[22] Writing about the romances published by Mills & Boon Jay Dixon makes the related point that the writers were not concerned 'with a precise vocabulary'; language, plot and location served to evoke, to suggest, and to arouse the reader, in an attempt at expressing the pre-eminence of inner feelings rather than constructing sequences of events.[23] While the modernists showed their modernity by subordinating plot to the exploration of consciousness, the romance writers showed their timelessness by subordinating plot to the exploration of emotion. Both groups of writers were attempting to articulate, from very different perspectives, the hinterland of daily life.

There are real problems in trying to understand the importance of women's romance fiction by applying current literary tools of analysis to the texts of individual novels. If romance novels are subjected to close reading practices, or to later Marxist, postcolonial or postmodern methods, many of them become unreadable, ridiculous, boring, and, on occasion, sexually or politically offensive. It seems surprising to me that feminist scholarship has not made greater efforts to subvert literary-critical orthodoxy and to recover this literature. 'There are limits to cultural empathy', the unarticulated and largely unacknowledged argument seems to run, 'and these are certainly exceeded by the implausible, over-emotional representation of women enslaved by love'. No formal textual approach that critics adopt will help them to understand the imaginative territory being constructed within this 'suburban' literature. As Jonathan Rose rightly warns, in his study of nineteenth-century working-class readers, it is a profound mistake for critics to 'try to discern the messages a text transmits to an audience by examining the text rather than the audience'.[24]

There are similar problems in identifying the readership of love-romance in terms of class and education, despite the consistent association of novels with middle-class readers, leisured women and domestic gentility, and of magazine fiction with the working- and lower-middle classes. This is partly because class terminology was being refined as the fiction was being published, with increasing precision but with less common acceptance.[25] In the early 1880s, the naming of classes was reasonably clear. Yet, by the end of the decade, a shift in terminology had begun to reflect changing social realities. The dividing line between the working classes and the middle classes was increasingly obscured, while a growing population of clerks seemed to constitute a new class in its own right. The idea of what constituted an educated person came under similar stress. The 'half-educated', and even the 'quarter-educated', were differentiated from the 'highly-educated' by those intent on keeping egalitarianism at bay.[26]

These increasingly complicated social variables make it difficult to pin down with any precision the class identity of the majority of women who bought, borrowed or lent these books and magazines. The numerous romances sold at W. H. Smith's railway stalls were bought by commuters to while away their daily journeys. Florence Barclay's *The Rosary* 'was said to have been read and wept over by every housemaid'.[27] In his survey of bestsellers between 1900 and 1939, which includes some of the most contentious romance fiction, Claud Cockburn assumes their readership to be the upper-middle or professional classes.[28] Q. D. Leavis, on the other hand, designates readers of bestsellers and romance fiction as 'the lowbrow public', although this group, as she goes on to argue, was beginning to include members of the middle classes as part of the 'levelling down' process she notes in chapter 4 'The Disintegration of the Reading Public'. Nicola Beauman's discussion of romantic fiction is based on a broad middle-class readership.[29] Kate Jackson argues that many of the new readers 'were members of the expanding lower middle class: a commuting, educated, urban, increasingly enfranchised and consumerist public, with access to leisure time'.[30]

These conclusions are based on economic factors, including the cost of books and of subscriptions to libraries. The proliferation of cheap editions by the end of the 1890s and the popularity of the 2d libraries indicates that access to books was extending down the social scale. Moreover it would be mistaken to assume that 'middle-class' was synonymous with 'leisured', that middle-class female readers were necessarily married, or that 'working women' were necessarily 'working-class'. The surest route to understanding this fiction is through readers' personal experience of, and pleasure in, the novels and stories in question. The most authentic analyses of romance fiction come from Jay Dixon and Nicola Beauman, both of whom write about this genre because they love reading it. Beauman's discussion is particularly enlightening in its emphasis on continuity between women and between generations. 'I love to imagine my mother and grandmother sobbing over books like this', she comments on Ethel M. Dell's *The Way of an Eagle* (1912).[31]

The most intractable question that we need to ask is how women understood these books. It is in this terrain of popular fiction that critics often fall foul of what Jonathan Rose calls the 'receptive fallacy' that is, the tendency to judge reader response through textual analysis.[32] In the face of almost complete lack of evidence from women readers themselves about their own responses, this sets us an impossible task. It is, however, worthwhile attempting to find some answers though any conclusions may turn out to be speculative. In 1888, for instance, T. H. Green suggested that the attractiveness of imaginative flights increased in direct relation to the security and predictability of social expectations, particularly in the suburbs where the worst of the urban conditions had been left behind.[33] Anthony Hope, the author of the bestseller *The Prisoner of Zenda* (1894), felt that fiction was aspirational and self-revealing in showing readers 'what they would be if they could, if time and fate and circumstance did not forbid, what in a sense they all are, and what they actions would show them to be if an opportunity offered'.[34] According to Annette Federico, Corelli's first book 'called out a widespread longing for moral certainty and spiritual assurance that had been left unfulfilled by the morbid frankness of the new fiction and New Woman novelists'.[35] None of these comments has the authority of knowing how contemporary readers responded, but what they all have in common is a recognition of the triangular relationship between women, their social context and their individual desires. At any point of personal need, hope or fear, women could try out possible alternative reactions through the medium of romantic fiction, in which they knew that their concerns would always be firmly located at the centre of the stage.

No doubt there are other models for reading practice, but in any case, none can be regarded as true of all women at all times. A woman sitting down at home to read a novel, a working woman reading the next episode of a magazine serial or a further chapter of her latest cheap edition, or a scullery maid rapidly reading a short story during a lull in her work might be seeking any one of a range of pleasures, or a combination of pleasures, or different pleasures at different times. More than that, any of their responses might also be mediated by their daily experiences, so that the entertaining, escapist or imaginative aspects of their reading would always interact with their reality. As Bertha Ruck suggested, reading is a way out of daily reality, but also a way of re-engaging with it differently. In discussing the whys and wherefores of popular fiction, the critic must be careful to acknowledge the power that readers have already taken as they pick up their book or magazine. I have no easy answers. I have no cache of diaries, memoirs or letters which could illuminate women's reading such as Rose was able (after much diligent research) to draw on in the case of self-educated working men. In fact, it is very possible that this silence is a factor in itself. Women's reading may well have gone largely unrecorded because its pleasure was deliberately sited 'outside' daily life, rather than acting as an element within it, as was the case for men seeking self-improvement. Arguably, women's own potential for interrogative thought, for formulating notions of value and for punctuating the familiar routines of daily life with imaginative experiences, was developed through the act of reading itself, both as an individual activity and as one shared with other women, rather than through describing it in letters or diaries.

Whatever the reason, what I am looking for – evidence of how suburban life was transformed through fiction into an imaginative territory – seems almost impossible to find directly from the readers themselves. However, we can learn from Rose's study not to commit the sin of allowing unsubstantial assumption or subjective judgement to masquerade as critical objectivity. We can also learn from Jay Dixon and Nicola Beauman, who make strong cases for untheorised personal experience as the only valid way to approach this fiction.[36] I want to build on both of these ideas and argue for a new theory that sidesteps current literary practice in order to offer a way of understanding the nature of the engagement between women readers and romance fiction. This theory valorises the contractual nature of women's reading, whereby the reader becomes an affective participant in an open-ended fictional discourse within which writer and reader seek a point of exchange where meanings can be negotiated. In this model the writer abjures the self-affirmation of artistic and aesthetic detachment to explore, create and mediate imaginative proving-grounds for their readers' experience.

The woman's world of the suburbs and what Margaret Beetham calls the 'feminised space' of the magazine are inextricable from one another. Although the suburbs were not the sole target of these publications, in her comprehensive analysis of the role of women's magazines in shaping feminine identity in the period under discussion, Beetham specifically links them with a suburban readership, partly because of the growth of the suburban population and partly because the greater spending power of suburb-dwellers made them an obvious market.[37] We can easily recognise the suburban idyll novels discussed earlier in Beetham's analysis of My Weekly, in which the construction of the domestic was 'not as the site of woman's work and the product of her skills, but as the theatre of human nature defined in terms of feelings – or the heart'.[38] Acting somewhat after the fashion of the mid-century evangelicals, the magazines set about constructing a secular model of domestic womanhood for the new century; they provided light-hearted entertainment but also recognised the diversity and complexity of individual situations and their focus was always on the world of emotions and relationships. While all the magazines, in their different styles, advised women how best to manage servants, to produce varied meals, to dress elegantly and appropriately, to deal with relationships and to clothe and look after children, setting a model of competence and beauty for all women to aspire to, they also all included fiction to a greater or lesser extent specifically aimed at women. This fiction empowered women to be heroines in their own scripts and to test the boundaries of their known world.

Magazine editors had carefully to walk a line between including the fiction that they knew would attract women purchasers and producing material that would acceptable in every home. Richard Altick records the century-long struggle to circumscribe young women's opportunities to read fiction, and to encourage them to resist its temptations, which might inflame their imaginations and undermine their sense of the real world and their role in it.[39] Comments on women as readers in the 1890s still reflected the anxiety of that struggle, as well as a literary snobbishness and a fear that the increasing literacy of both genders of the lower classes would taint established cultural criteria and lessen their validity. A not untypical editorial in *Hearth and Home* reminded its readers of the 'pernicious' effect of 'these hysterical stories . . . upon the minds of young girls, and even older women'.[40] Whereas fear of fiction in the early part of the nineteenth century was generally motivated by religious considerations, later in the century it was concerned more with the possibility of fiction tempting women away from the home or encouraging them to assert their independence within it.

It is, of course, important to see magazine fiction in the context of the magazine in which it appears. There is no space here for a sociological or feminist analysis of the item by item content of a number of magazines.[41] However, two points must be remembered. The first is that all the material included in any particular magazine which fell outside the category of 'fiction' – that is, household hints, fashion, recipes, society gossip, features, photographs and advice columns – was also a kind of fiction. This textual medley constructed an integrated social fiction which offered, with appropriate class differentiations, the model of an ideal wife, mother and woman. The second factor, common to magazines apparently directed at different audiences, is that the stories often acted in strategic opposition to the magazine's declared ideal. They offered a number of alternative models of womanhood, located beyond the suburbs. While the magazine itself, shared, borrowed or passed round a circle of friends, created a community, and the 'factual' material drew women into a larger community of like-minded readers across the country and even the Empire, the fiction created a unique imaginative world to be entered and experienced by the individual reader alone.

Forget-Me-Not, launched by Alfred Harmsworth in 1891, included a high proportion of fiction, with at least one story and one episode of a serial in every weekly edition. Sold cheaply at 1d, it claimed that its readers included men as well as women, while its A5 format made it a convenient purchase for railway travel or holiday reading. There is something of a mismatch between the material in the magazine, its cheap paper and dirty ink (which still marks the reader's fingers a hundred years later), and the claims that it made for itself as 'The Pictorial Journal For Ladies' (1893) or a 'High-Class Journal for Home Reading' (1902), and later, 'A Dainty Journal for Ladies' (1915). *Forget-Me-Not* demonstrates the plasticity of class groupings by siting itself at the edge of respectable popular reading but identifying with its readers' social aspirations. In 1901, it claims to have fostered 'men and women whose names are now linked with all that is best in literature and art, people whose works are known and welcomed in every English-speaking home'.[42] Its fiction plays constantly with these trans-class identities.

Forget-Me-Not's fiction is almost entirely romantic – deep passions and love intrigues are the imperatives of living. Historical, geographical and class locations are blurred and generalised, and the plots are vestigial or manipulated, serving only as hooks to attach the timeless passions of the central characters to a recognisable reality, and as means to enhance the importance and depth of their feelings by association with the aristocratic, the strange and the wild. 'The realm of love', which *Punch* so enjoyed mocking, is the landscape of these stories, which detach themselves from the contemporary moment as determinedly as the mid-century sensation stories from which they descend. Their common themes also hark back to the mid-nineteenth century. There is the invisible cord that binds wealth and virtue, even though it is occasionally endangered, and the instant love that both affirms and transcends class. There are fortunes lost and won, identities disguised and revealed. Love throughout is 'the blissful condition' which, once attained, is metamorphosed by the plot into moral, financial and class rewards that are confirmed by marriage. The images of women are also familiar. Female beauty is characterised by traits that are almost obsessively repeated: small hands, abundant golden hair and a naturalness that speaks of innocence and moral purity in contrast to the artificial and actressy beauty of the bad woman. Passion is conveyed by the conventions of the blush, the heaving bosom and straining embrace. Male virtue is similarly generalised as frank, honest and simple manliness.

Against this backdrop individualised elements do assert themselves. 'Banjo and I' by Hugh Tuite is a story about a strong-willed young middle-class woman who wants to amuse herself by playing the banjo, a notoriously working-class instrument and the latest fad, much loved in the music hall but deplored by the cultured.[43] In the music shop, an affluent and titled army officer falls instantly in love with her, and poses as a banjo tutor. This is a love story where the woman, aware of her admirer's disguise and enjoying the joke, constantly evades her chaperone to spend time with him, goes ice-skating, and laughs heartily. This is a model of femininity which poaches safely but tellingly from the attributes of the New Woman. Does the footer running under this story, declaring that *Forget-Me-Not* is 'the only Ladies' paper read by Men', give it an added piquancy?

In 'Lord Dovedale's Daughter' the New Woman takes a rather different form.[44] In this story, the wicked stepmother is revamped as an American woman whose brashness, self-centredness and vulgarity threaten to overcome the aristocratic order, and trigger Lady Lucia's memory of her natural mother's delicate beauty. Lucia demonstrates that the true nature of the New Woman is intrinsically the same as that of any other woman. Driven from her father's house after his marriage, she becomes simple Mary Dainton and goes to London to work and support herself. Her two identities, long-suffering and patient lady of the manor and resourceful, independent working woman, are reconciled through love in the form of Captain Howard, who 'finds the beautiful *everywhere!*' and whom she feels is 'a *good* man!' – the emphases and the exclamations are shorthand for passionate conviction.[45] 'The Rose Room', by Ravenswood, is a Gothic tale of castles, ghosts and islands transformed in a similar way to highlight women's independence and physical bravery.[46] Daphne, the heroine, is blessed with 'a head of long curling bronze-brown locks with golden strands, as if sunbeams had got enmeshed therein'.[47] By 1901 the phrasing and vocabulary, and the crude suggestion of milk-maid-like sensuousness, must have seemed archaic. Nevertheless, Daphne and Roger, the man with whom she has fallen in love, travel without a chaperone, and much is made of the fact that she is the one who rows out alone to rescue him. This is clearly seen as an act that demonstrates the independence of the modern woman, but it must also have recalled Grace Darling who became synonymous with female bravery when, in 1838, she rowed out to sea in a small boat to rescue sailors from a sinking ship. The exploration of what independence means for women in the context of traditional values is an important strand in the fiction. Meanwhile the parallel domestic material continues to celebrate the traditional woman, as an article from 1902, entitled 'Why the "New Woman" was a Failure', makes clear. The childlike woman, 'with nice fluffy hair, and ribbons and fallals', is the woman men fall in love with, the reader is told, and that kind of woman 'doesn't want to be a "new woman," she wants only to be a simple, generous, loving girl'.[48]

The outbreak of the First World War did not lessen *Forget-Me-Not*'s popularity but it did change its editorial line and its fiction. In fact, war gave even greater scope to the fiction writers as the war effort revolutionised all women's lives. Domestic servants were called up for war service, middle-class women took to the kitchen buoyed up by a sense of working for the cause, and many upper-middle-class, educated women volunteered for service at home and abroad and/or joined any number of voluntary associations. As Margaret Cooper acknowledged in *Forget-Me-Not* in 1916:

> Barely eighteen months of grim and ghastly warfare. And yet in those eighteen months changes have been wrought in things and people that could not have been accomplished in *centuries* under ordinary conditions.
>
> First and foremost, the war has helped women considerably, and put them high in the world of work, where they will soon climb higher still. Since August, 1914, a new class of women has sprung into existence, a class of which we may well be proud.

She concludes with a clarion call for solidarity: 'Never again will we permit the barriers of mere caste and social conventionality to make us strangers to one another ... We are sisters, indeed, and for always.'[49]

These transformations opened up the fictional world of *Forget-Me-Not*, as a story such as 'The Man, the Girl and the Dog' (unattributed) exemplifies.[50] Cecilia Love, the central figure, has three identities. Her public role, with which the story opens, is of an office slave 'in the cellar of a City of London office building', with long days and half an hour for lunch 'at the nearest bun shop' if she is lucky – an identity which would have been familiar to many of *Forget-Me-Not*'s target readers on their commuter journeys.[51] She is impressively competent, but the real world of figures and columns occupies only a fraction of her mind. Her inner identity is that of 'princess', a woman whose daily existence has not complemented her sense of her own potential or her aspiration to a better life. What that better life is, is made clear by her name, which suggests to the reader a third – as yet unexplored – identity, as a woman capable of love.

As the result of a bequest, Cecilia is able to abandon her working-woman mask and be a real 'princess' in a remote country house in Devonshire, where the fertility and beauty of nature in her garden – 'now a blooming blaze of colour crowned by the purple and blue of the summer sea' – prepare her to discover her passionate nature.[52] This moment is delayed by the war. Cecilia volunteers to do nursing and finds herself caught up in the retreat from Mons. Here she discovers the limits of her independence, as *Forget-Me-Not* pays homage to the re-masculinisation of men through war.[53] While the British soldiers are 'unbeatable ... fighting the greatest rearguard action that the world has ever seen', she is 'like a straw on this tide of horror', and the merest bruise destroys her self-possession completely.[54] Now she is 'blank with fear' as her previous suitor turns up and rescues her, pushing her in a wheelbarrow to a safe retreat. The story concludes with her recognition that the apparently lazy man of peacetime is at home in this world of war, while she has touched the boundaries of her independence. In this story, Cecilia's interwoven identities allow women to experience the worlds of work, of economics, of war, and of love without denigrating their roles in the world they know.

By 1925, the long outdated codes embodied by the Victorian romantic heroine had finally fallen away and the modern woman, who was always threatening to get out, had emerged. In *Forget-Me-Not*'s stories, she is a practical and unfussy woman who wears simple, functional clothes and short hair, 'with its varying shades of red and brown, curled into little rounded tendrils', and who has a quick cup of tea in the 'nearest ABC'.[55] This extract comes from the first of six instalments of a series in a format that had become very popular, in which each story was self-contained but related – a format that is still familiar today.[56] 'Cathie Sullivan – Stewardess', by Violet Methley, still sees love as a woman's major objective and fulfilment, but now the heroine's horizon has expanded as she travels the world working on a sea-going liner. The romance-myth gains rather than loses power when its context is modernised. Reading such stories in the aftermath of war, women were able to recognise two worlds: one of freedom, possibility, travel and equality, and another where love for a man, passion and marriage ruled supreme. In the real world two such different situations, with their conflicting demands, invariably posed a choice for women. In the world of the magazine, they could be reconciled by the imagination; and even in her suburban home, the reader was arguably empowered by the clear existence of a choice that lay before women, and, implicitly, before herself.

Home Notes, founded by Pearson in 1894, is, like *Forget-Me-Not*, a child of its times, directing its editorial at those who have put a first toe on the ladder of upward mobility. Typical readers would be a sedate, respectable married couple with 'a hundred and fifty a year, residing in a suburban semi-detached villa', and the focus is the woman at home.[57] *Home Notes* acknowledges all the hard work that young wives have in running a well-managed home on a small income, and it is full of advice on thriftiness, bargain offers, useful patterns and recipes. Full of mild 'battle of the sexes' jokes, *Home Notes* aims for light-hearted entertainment, while its small size and woodcut or cartoonish illustrations give it a childlike style. Distinctive about its editorial approach is the underlying recognition that the *Home Notes*'s woman works extremely hard on a small income and spends long hours on her own or with children to look after. There are frequent references to women being depressed or neglected, to their lives being given over to dull routine with little distraction, and to the conflict between outer appearances and actual income. Husbands are often exhorted to think more about their wives: 'Don't let matrimony swamp everything else; even if you are the father of a family, and the head of a household, your first duty is to the sweetheart of your youth.'[58] Whether this assumes that men read *Home Notes*, or whether such articles addressed to men were actually directed at women to give them support or raise their expectations, is hard to assess. It is certainly important to realise the social influence of a magazine such as this on young women suburbanites who might have few, if any, models of home-making to draw on.

The reading of fiction is, as we have seen, a sure escape route to alternative possibilities, so it not surprising that *Home Notes* balances its worthy advice and guidance pages with a substantial element of fiction, and gives the tired housewife the holiday that her husband might not be able or willing to provide. While marriage is the theme of the articles, love is the theme of the fiction. A short story and an episode of a serial appeared every week, with some of the serials running to as many as twelve episodes. Although the target audience is different and although the tone is less intense and more humorous than *Forget-Me-Not*'s, there are considerable similarities. The apparent importance of plot is again belied by clumsy turnarounds or sudden, unexplained events that are simply conveniences. Location is blurred, with conventional characters inhabiting stylised landscapes that might be wild, gently rural, foreign, occasionally urban but never suburban. Stories often have upper class or aristocratic characters or contexts. In a kind of sacramental relationship between the outer and the inner world, what continues to be crucially important is that character, plot and location are merely signs pointing to the larger realms of the romantic imagination. They are the entrance to the timeless world of love and adventure, which promises the opportunity to transgress class and economic barriers to claim individual worth and recognition. As Minnie Aunomier writes in her story 'Once Long Ago' (1900), there are ways to transcend the 'same grey old world': 'When the brain is tired, or the heart aching, then leave the busy, restless town, and go to that country which men call the "downs". In the sweet, fresh air, and happy, laughing sunshine, climb higher and higher away from the world, and nearer to heaven.'[59] For men such as Richard Jefferies and Edward Thomas, this was literally possible. For most suburban women, the imagination was a more accessible mode of travel.

On the whole, women are represented as sassy, independent-minded people in *Home Notes*'s fictions, but their struggle for identity always occurs within the framework of male approval, and their blows for freedom are never sufficient to topple the delicate balance of men's love, since 'gaining equal rights with man she loses all real power over him'.[60] This was a familiar feature of romantic fiction until 1914: as David Trotter comments, 'Edwardian romance of womanhood squared assertion with submission.'[61] Since 'assertion' usually took place in the realistic world of the story as a strategic flirtation or rebellion, while 'submission' was subsumed into the symbolic, inner world as 'passion', a woman would have been able to see a double victory in such stories.

Daphne Dene's short story 'Blue Blood and Red' (1890) illustrates the potential complexity of the reception of these apparently simply told, conventional romances.[62] The title sets the story's conflicts firmly among the social and political issues of the late nineteenth century. The declining aristocracy is represented by the paralysed Duke of Castletowers, whose estates are on the verge of bankruptcy, and who relies on his resourceful wife and daughter to salvage their inheritance. His daughter, Lady Amabel, however, has identified with contemporary values. Uninterested in the fate of her inheritance, she is a New Woman 'full of socialistic ideas and art fads', in a world where 'we are all socialists nowadays', as the Duchess's young solicitor proclaims.[63] Amabel's dilemma is whether she should marry for money, as her class requires of her, or whether she should marry for love, as her modern identity requires. For the reader the plot offers no real dilemma: it is simply a doorway for the imagination since it is clear that Amabel must have money *and* love. The actual dilemma is a class question (should high society become an equal society?) and

BLUE BLOOD AND RED.

By Daphne Dene.

❀❀❀

I.

A HANSOM CAB drove up to the door of Messrs. Mowbray and Mowbray, of Lincoln's Inn. From it alighted a lady, handsomely dressed, and apparently of middle-age. The pose of her head and the shape of it were remarkable, and though her features were completely disguised by a veil of elaborately embroidered lace, there was about her whole

5

'On the "throne" sat her daughter in a Portia-like robe, looking like an inspired poetess'
Illustrations from Daphne Dene, 'Blue Blood and Red', *Home Notes*

a woman question (can women have love and money on their own terms?).

The denouement of the story takes place in an artist's studio, where Amabel is discovered modelling for the artist and his student. As the Duchess sweeps into the room she sees her daughter in 'what appeared to be like a stage scene'.[64] Posed on the dais, Amabel is faced by three people, each of whom offers her a different future: the professional artist who is painting her portrait, her mother who fears that she wants to marry him, and a shabby apprentice artist whom she actually loves. Her costume for the portrait is a 'Portia-type robe', and the illustration of Amabel dressed in a legal outfit and holding a legal document in her hand both complicates her gender and empowers her to choose wisely and justly. Her eventual choice of the art student locates her supreme values in the realm of love. His background as the successor to the Castletowers's family solicitors, which he has disguised to get to know her, and which is now mediated and modernised by socialist tendencies, makes him the perfect man to receive her 'submission'. The title enhances both the romance and the realism of the story. Although I introduced this discussion by referring to 'Blue Blood and Red', the layout of the title on the page means that it could equally be read 'Blue and Red Blood'. The reader can decide for herself whether the romance lies in the tale of the aristocracy or the tale of social progress or, reconciled by the imagination, in both.

The target readership of *Hearth and Home* (1891–1914) and *Gentlewoman* (1890–1926) was middle-class and conservative, but while *Hearth and Home*, as its title might suggest, defended the front of domestic aspiration against external threat (with some persistence and venom), *Gentlewoman*'s alliance with the Establishment was comfortable and assured. Its advertisements reveal its readership's considerable consumer power, and its editorials open up a world of choice for educated women. Magazines such as these placed significantly less emphasis on fiction than *Forget-Me-Not* or *Home Notes*, and, as a result, their fictional world is more difficult to decipher. *Hearth and Home* provides a good example of the ambiguous cultural status of magazine fiction and its unpleasant suburban associations. Little space is given to fiction, which the magazine clearly sees as unhealthy reading appropriate only for the lower classes. Attacking what appears to be a collection of New Woman stories, the editorial condemns 'clever' women who 'stir up enmity between the sexes' and, in the spirit of mid-century religious fervour, it claims that the stories' effect on women 'must be pernicious'.[65] Its insistent tone of condemnation for any manifestation of the modern woman, its identification with the upper classes (each edition opened with a picture of an aristocrat), and its assumed role as the keeper of social morals leave little room for readers to waver in their dedication to maintaining class appearances, or for women to see their identity in any terms other than those of wife and mother. One of the few stories which shows a chink in *Hearth and Home*'s implacable conservatism tells how a woman dresses in knickerbockers to go walking with her husband whereupon he puts on one of her dresses and suggests they set off. She gives in and changes, but her husband realises how impractical women's clothes are and becomes more understanding of his wife's little rebellion.[66]

Hearth and Home's lack of fiction appears to be a device to signal its superiority and to distance its identity from the cultural and class ambiguities inherent in the suburbs. In a series of articles about an unspecified suburb (1895), the new developments are seen as alien territory. They have to be acknowledged, but safely ghettoised:

> Our suburb is what one might call a *country* suburb. We are beyond the reach of the tramcars, foreign meat shops, and a certain celebrated boot manufacturer's all-pervading emporiums. We possess in ourselves the elements and tradition of a village; the suburbs portion is quite a recent invention.[67]

Not only were suburbanites considered prone to inappropriate reading which might foster dangerous illusions, but they were insufficiently educated to appreciate worthwhile literature. '"Undiluted" literature', as the writer of 'Studies in the Suburbs: Our Literary Society' commented, 'would pall upon our suburbans; they require to be "educated up" to it'.[68] From today's perspective, it is amusing to note that J. M. Barrie, Stanley Weyman and Anthony Hope were writers considered too difficult for readers in the 'suburbs portion', but sophisticated fare for those who lived in the 'country suburb'.

In contrast, *Gentlewoman* gradually increased its fiction content, and in 1917 launched a series of 'The World's Best Story Tellers'. The question as to whether the reading of fiction was inappropriate during a time of national crisis, or whether it was an important aid to morale on the home front, was considered in all the magazines. *Gentlewoman*, whose pages were dominated by women's war activities, and in which any suggestion of luxurious living was tempered to set an example of patriotic thrift, must have felt that some alleviation of its sombre dignity was necessary. The introduction to the series made claims for its fiction's seriousness, and explained that the stories had been commissioned from 'distinguished' writers and would 'possess a freshness and individuality'. It then continued: 'No-one in these times has the time to read a serial story, but the hardest worked volunteer in the patriotic movements in which woman has so excelled will be the better for the hour spent in reading one short story a week, which in itself is clean and inspiring.'[69]

The series fulfilled part of its mission. Many of the stories have some kind of war theme, but in all cases the determination not to offend or to be frivolous makes them rather dull, and their formulaic conventions are rarely challenged. One exception is an amusing look at wartime austerities and the triumph of women's common sense, E. Temple Thurston's 'The Economist' (1917), in which a husband insists on economising by trapping or shooting meat for the family meals. The cost, totted up by his wife, comes to far more than that of a rabbit at the market.[70] Another is Eden Philpotts's 'A Black Sheep' (1918) (possibly a wartime version of Thomas Hardy's short story 'The Three Strangers'), in which a conman, pretending to be a soldier on leave, wins himself a free night at the pub at the expense of the gullible locals who nevertheless hear some exciting, if imaginary, stories from the front line.[71] *Gentlewoman* used fiction as part of its war effort, but the stories seem redundant for a readership which, as the remainder of the magazine copy makes clear, had the status and the opportunities to be involved in community and voluntary war work which won public recognition and admiration. It seems likely that these activities would have energised women's days, changed their lives and aspirations, and perhaps cut across class and economic divisions, more effectively than any love story. If that is so, such positive effects of war did not last. As many women returned to their homes after the upheavals of war, suburban growth entered a second phase of expansion, and the domestic myth came to dominate the world of women's magazines and fiction far more completely than it had previously.

Magazines such as *Woman* which, with some interruptions and changes of editorial policy, has been in circulation from 1890 to the present day, seem to have provided a bridge between the lively fictions of magazines targeted at working and/or single women and less affluent housewives, and the ambivalent, even hostile, attitude to fiction of those targeted at more affluent groups. In 1908 its attitude to women seemed little different from that of other magazines: women and homes were inextricable, and much of the fiction was based on the familiar conventions of exotic and vague locations, women's capacity for loyalty and devotion, and the usual misunderstandings and mistaken identities. But a different tone was emerging. Popular with educated women, *Woman* appeared in a relatively expensive weekly format, which appealed to the upwardly mobile population as well as to lower-middle-class readers.

Woman provided a context for the reading of fiction with a regular review column, 'Literary Notes and News', as well as occasional series about books. In the 1908 series 'Books which have Helped Me', for instance, contributors were invited to discuss the formative effect of a novel they had read. Titles included Olive Schreiner's *Story of an African Farm*, George Eliot's *Adam Bede* and Mrs Gaskell's *Life of Charlotte Brontë*, a list that gives a rather different picture of women's general reading aspirations from *Hearth and Home*'s. *Woman* is also notable for the number of stories that used contemporary issues, not only as a realistic hook on which to hang a narrative about the 'realm of love' but as a way of acquainting readers with the controversies and activities of the day,[72] or that showed love as complex and multifaceted.[73]

Flora Annie Steel's 'The Perfume of the Rose', announced on the front page of *Woman* on 22 January 1908 in a banner headline, is an example of this newly emergent romantic fiction.[74] Steel returned to England in 1889 after twenty-two years in India with her husband, an official in the Indian Civil Service, and she wrote several novels and many short stories drawing on her knowledge of India which are satisfyingly complicated by her 'ambiguous admiration for Indian mores'.[75] In this story, the hinterland evoked in the reader's imagination is an erotic terrain; 'The Perfume of the Rose' interrogates the dichotomy between marriage, in which religious and social ritual legitimates domestic and economic security, and spontaneous and sexual love. The passion of the spirit and the passion of the body are drawn together to suggest that, while the imagination may be the doorway to emotional richness, the material world is the way to sexual satisfaction.

Against a background of Indian civil disturbances, two lovers find privacy and sanctuary in a perfume distillery in the ruins of the king's gardens. The narrative anticipates their sexual consummation through the song of Hushmut, a crippled perfume-maker. As he watches them kiss, Hushmut sings:

> The rose-root takes earth's kisses for its
>   meat;
> The rose-leaf makes its blush from the
>   sun's heat;
> The rose-scent wakes – who knows from
>   what thing sweet?
>   who knows
> The secret of the perfume of the rose?

The intense phallic and vulvic imagery of 'rose-root', 'rose-leaf' and 'rose-scent' is sublimated into a sexual, emotional and spiritual 'secret' via the mingling of the man's and the woman's fluids, which are alchemised into 'perfume'. The second verse, which Hushmut sings to the lovers when they tell him that they are to marry, suggests that only sexual love has the power to transform the material world. The third and final verse, sung as they escape from the garden, is addressed to the future husband and helps him to understand how he and the woman he is to marry can discover an erotic abandonment through their encounter in the perfume garden:

> Dig, gardener, deep, till the Earth-lips
>   cling tight
> Prune, gardener! Keep those blushes to
>   the light.
> Then, gardener, sleep. He brings the
>   scent by night
>   who knows
> The secret of the perfume of the rose.[76]

It is interesting to ask why writing such as this did not, it seems, provoke controversy in the suburbs although novels about the New Woman did. While Steel is clearly drawing on the voice of the orient to legitimise her vision of sexual desire and satisfaction as harmlessly exotic, she also explores sexual knowledge in a way that would appear to accommodate different levels of awareness and acceptance in her readers. The lovers have no names: they are an archetypal man and woman. Their story is enacted in the tension of sexual passion before it is consummated, but their experience of what passion means differs. The man's knowingness, his response to Hushmut's innuendoes and his discomfort at his fiancée's interest in Hushmut's words and actions, reveal his (disreputable) sexual experience and inhibit him from freely enjoying the moment, which he senses is increasingly ambiguous. As the embodiment of patriarchal power, he is busy covertly observing his fiancée's responses to see if she understands what Hushmut is implying, and he is baffled by not knowing how much she knows. However, Steel suggests that masculine assumptions about a woman's sexual awareness are based simplistically on carnal knowledge: he is not able to appreciate that, regardless of her virginity, she understands more about of the nature of desire than he. In the moment of danger, she trusts Hushmut to help her escape rather than her future husband, and follows him even as her fiancé tries to break her hold on the 'dark skin' of Hushmut's hand.

Magazines regularly commissioned fiction from established writers, and writers who began working for magazines often succeeded as novelists. Nevertheless, the weekly or monthly format underpinned a policy laid down by a magazine, within which the writers contributed their individual perspectives. The intention was not to draw attention to the author's sophistication or reputation, but to provide a fictional playground for identity and emotion, where the reader could take on the role she chose. If a reader found a writer or a kind of story that she enjoyed, she would be sure to want to read more. Plot, location and character were the necessary structures to sustain a fiction but, in magazine stories, they were frequently treated with cavalier casualness. So too were different genres: sensation stories, fairy stories, historical themes, contemporary issues and colonial adventures were mixed together in hybrid forms that disregarded aesthetic completeness. The cumulative patterns, repetitions, insistences and persistences of romantic fiction within the magazine format over a period of time were central to its literary mission. They sustained the reader's interest from story to story, acting not only as a familiarising strategy but as a form of reprise that linked many separate short stories into a grand narrative of desire. The literary structures that characterise romantic fiction for women are not signs of formulaic dullness and reader passivity, but instead the surest clues that we have to the geography of women's extra-suburban territories.

Notes

1 Ros Ballaster, Margaret Beetham, Elizabeth Frazer and Sandra Hebron, *Women's Worlds: Ideology, femininity and the woman's magazine* (Basingstoke: Macmillan, 1991), 75.

2 Nicola Beauman, A Very Great Profession (London: Virago, 1989), 174.

3 Annette R. Federico, Idol of Suburbia: Marie Corelli and the late-Victorian literary culture (Charlottesville and London: Virginia University Press, 2000), 6–7.

4 Richard D. Altick, [1957] The English Common Reader: A social history of the mass reading public, 1800–1900 (Chicago: Chicago University Press, 1967), 232. For statistics on readership and library use in the London suburbs from 1890 to 1930, see the relevant tables in The New Survey.

5 Beauman, A Very Great Profession, 173 ff.

6 Kate Jackson, George Newnes and the New Journalism in Britain, 1880–1910: Culture and profit (Aldershot, Burlington USA, Singapore and Sydney: Ashgate, 2001), 30, n83; Harris, Private Lives, 33.

7 Charles Boon in Daily Citizen (3 January 1913), cited in Joseph McAleer, Passion's Fortune: The story of Mills & Boon (Oxford: Oxford University Press, 1999), 29.

8 Lyn Pykett, Engendering Fictions: The English novel in the early twentieth century (London: Edward Arnold, 1995), 33.

9 Q. D. Leavis, [1932] Fiction and the Reading Public (London: Pimlico, 2000), 54. It is interesting to compare her attitude with that of Edward Thomas in The Happy-Go-Lucky Morgans, where the names of suburban houses are not seen as ridiculous but as the bearers of history.

10 Billie Melman, Women and the Popular Imagination in the Twenties, cited in Trotter, The English Novel in History, 184.

11 Hearth and Home (28 February 1895), 568.

12 J. St John Adcock, 'Marie Corelli: a Record and Appreciation', Bookman, 26:212 (1909), 59–78, cited in Federico, Idol of Suburbia, 61.

13 Virginia Woolf, cited in Beauman, A Very Great Profession, 98.

14 Leavis, Fiction and the Reading Public, 54.

15 Altick, The English Common Reader, 110, 239.

16 R. L. Stevenson, 'A Gossip on Romance', Longman's Magazine (November 1882), 69–79, cited in Nicholas Daly, Modernism, Romance and the Fin-de-Siècle: Popular fiction and British culture, 1880–1914 (Cambridge: Cambridge University Press, 2000), 17–18.

17 Daly, Modernism, 17.

18 Letter to Bentley from Marie Corelli, 13 November 1886, cited in Federico, Idol of Suburbia, 58.

19 Leavis, Fiction and the Reading Public, 68.

20 Bertha Ruck, [1935] A Story-Teller Tells the Truth, cited in Anderson, The Purple Heart Throbs, 176.

21 See Anderson for a discussion of these romance types and Kemp, Mitchell and Trotter, Edwardian Fiction, xxiii, for a general list of Edwardian themes and genres.

22 Trotter, The English Novel in History, 183. Italics in original.

23 Jay Dixon, The Romance Fiction of Mills & Boon, 1909–1990 (London: University College London Press, 1999), 38.

24 Jonathan Rose, The Intellectual Life of the British Working Classes (New Haven and London: Yale University Press, 2001), 4.

25 Hapgood, '"The New Suburbanites"', 31–50.

26 G. M. Trevelyan, cited in Anderson, The Purple Heart Throbs, 17.

27 Anderson, *The Purple Heart Throbs*, 121.
28 Claud Cockburn, *Bestseller: The books that everyone read 1900–1939* (London: Sidgwick and Jackson, 1972), 3.
29 Leavis, *Fiction and the Reading Public*, 35, 185; Beauman, *A Very Great Profession*, 245.
30 Jackson, *George Newnes and the New Journalism*, 41.
31 Beauman, *A Very Great Profession*, 179.
32 Rose, *The Intellectual Life*, 4.
33 T. H. Green, [1888] 'An Estimate of the Value of Influence of Works of Fiction in Modern Times', cited in Cockburn, *Bestseller*, 61.
34 Antony Hope, cited in Daly, *Modernism*, 157.
35 Federico, *Idol of Suburbia*, 6.
36 Dixon, *Romance Fiction*, 27; Beauman, *A Very Great Profession*, 238.
37 Margaret Beetham, *A Magazine of Her Own? Domesticity and desire in the woman's magazine, 1800–1914* (London: Routledge, 1996), 120, 7.
38 Beetham, *A Magazine of Her Own?*, 205.
39 Altick, *The English Common Reader*, 110.
40 'The Harm Done by Hysteria', *Hearth and Home* (17 January 1895), 360.
41 Beetham, *A Magazine of Her Own?* and Cynthia White, *Women's Magazines, 1693–1968* (London: Joseph, 1970).
42 *Forget-Me-Not* (5 January 1901), editorial.
43 *Forget-Me-Not* (7 January 1893), 138–143.
44 *Forget-Me-Not* (14 January 1893), 154–159.
45 *Forget-Me-Not* (14 January 1893), 156.
46 *Forget-Me-Not* (12 January 1901), 233–238.
47 *Forget-Me-Not* (12 January 1901), 233.
48 *Forget-Me Not* (10 May 1902), 35.
49 Margaret Cooper, 'War Girls', *Forget-Me-Not* (29 January 1916), 375.
50 *Forget-Me-Not* (23 January 1915), 323–326, iii (cover).
51 *Forget-Me-Not* (23 January 1915), 323.
52 *Forget-Me-Not* (23 January 1915), 325.
53 See Jane Potter, '"A Great Purifier": The Great War in women's romances and memoirs, 1914–1918' in Suzanne Raitt and Trudi Tate (eds), *Women's Fiction in the Great War* (Oxford: Oxford University Press, 1997), 85–106.
54 *Forget-Me-Not* (23 January 1915), 326.
55 *Forget-Me-Not* (17 April 1925), 539.
56 A. Conan Doyle claims to have initiated the series, as opposed to the serial, with his work for the *Strand* – a publication strategy that was adopted as an ingenious way of encouraging readers to buy regularly and not to give up because they had missed an issue (Jackson, *George Newnes and the New Journalism*, 93).
57 *Home Notes* (10 February 1900), 163.
58 'How to Treat your Wife', *Home Notes* (10 February 1900), 164.
59 Minnie Aunomier, 'Once Long Ago', *Home Notes* (27 January 1900), 103.
60 *Home Notes* (3 March 1900), 298.
61 Kemp et al., *Edwardian Fiction*, 410.
62 Daphne Dene, 'Blue Blood and Red', *Home Notes* (20 January 1900), 45–48.

63 *Home Notes* (20 January 1900), 46.
64 *Home Notes* (20 January 1900), 47.
65 'The Harm Done by Hysteria', 360.
66 Eden Philpotts, 'A Sartorial Comedy', *Hearth and Home* (28 November 1895), 94–98.
67 'Studies in the Suburbs I – The Vicar', *Hearth and Home* (7 February 1895), 462.
68 *Hearth and Home* (28 February 1895), 568.
69 *Gentlewoman* (6 January 1917), 2.
70 *Gentlewoman* (16 June 1917), 62.
71 Eden Philpotts, 'A Black Sheep', *Gentlewoman* (12 January 1918), 46.
72 See Spencer Leigh Hughes, 'A Parliamentary Proposal', which examines women's exclusion from parliamentary politics, in *Woman* (29 January 1908), 10–12, and Edith Rickert, 'The Power of the Past', which deals with issues of heredity, in *Woman* (1 January 1908), 10–12.
73 Helen Porter, 'Amaranth', *Woman* (27 May 1908), 40, tells the story of two elderly people getting married, in the narrative voice of a young stranger who begins a conversation with the old woman. See also A. St John Adcock, 'An Old Maid's Tragedy', *Woman* (15 July 1908), 11–12.
74 Flora Annie Steel, 'The Perfume of the Rose', *Woman* (22 January 1908), 10–12.
75 Kemp, *Edwardian Fiction*, 372/373. Beauman, *A Very Great Profession*, 238, claims that Steel's fiction set a trend that was followed by writers such as Maud Diver, 'Sydney C. Grier' and Alice Perrin.
76 'The Perfume of the Rose', 11.

6

THE FEMININE SUBURB/2

Sophie Cole
Alice Askew
Louise Gerard
Mary Hamilton

'**N**OWADAYS books are so cheap that every house has a nice little library of its own, sometimes in a room set apart for the purpose, but more often scattered in different rooms of the house', *Home Notes* cheerfully and proudly announced to its readers early in 1900.[1] The sheer volume of romantic fiction published in this period poses the same problems of selection as magazine fiction. Grouping large numbers of texts into some kind of taxonomy of romantic fiction would have the benefit of clarifying those cumulative patterns of structure and emphasis that we have seen in magazine fiction. Yet I feel that such an approach would only serve to consolidate the anonymity of romantic fiction and reinforce its identity as a formulaic mass commodity. Worse, it would return to the literary critic the power to categorise and label.

Instead I have decided to risk a narrower focus, and to select a sample of novels which might well have been among those bought and placed on the shelves of suburban bookcases, and which were certainly borrowed from libraries and read by many women. The virtue of this approach is that it values the reading experience, and the differences between individual novels rather than the similarities of many. It also directs attention towards the processes of authorship rather than of production, and opens out rather than closes down textual possibilities. In the previous chapter, I noted some interesting and valuable studies of those women writers who succeeded in gaining fame and/or notoriety. What I want to investigate now is the 'in-between' literature. Just as the suburbs are 'in-between' terrain, sandwiched between the drama of the city and the lost domain of the countryside, the daily reading matter of thousands of women lies in the interstices of literary development, barely acknowledged by debates about the art of fiction at the turn of the twentieth century and irrelevant to the struggle between realism and modernism as literary modes.

I have chosen to discuss the novels of Sophie Cole, Alice Askew, Louise Gerard and Mary Hamilton. To some extent this is a random choice made deliberately. In other words, in terms of selection, my encounter with them is not very different from the experience of any woman a hundred years ago who chose a cheap edition from a book-shop, who dropped into her local library to return the books she had finished and choose another, or who read a book recommended by an enthusiastic friend. These authors wrote some of the books I have read and enjoyed. However, I did also select these particular writers according to other criteria: they published romantic fiction frequently over a long period of time, their popularity was confirmed by sales, and they differ in important ways from each other so that their novels suggest a variety of different possibilities for reader response.

In magazine fiction, as we have seen, what I term 'persistence' manifested itself in the title of the magazine, in its familiar formats, in the series and serial fiction, and in its recurring themes and concerns. The shortness of a magazine's shelf life as a commodity (although not necessarily as reading material) required a certain level of repetition to construct and confirm the magazine's identity. For the novel reader, the importance of the title of the magazine appears to have been replaced by the name of the writer. The well-known phrase, 'a new novel by', became a feature of publicity campaigns and ensured that each novel would be an opportunity to re-enter a world already experienced as a landscape of desire. Writers needed to be prolific to sustain such familiarity and engagement – and indeed these writers were. Gerard published twenty-three novels between 1910 and 1936; Cole published sixty-three novels between 1908 and 1944; Askew published over ninety novels in collaboration with her husband in the fourteen years before their deaths in 1917. Hamilton wrote at what, in comparison, seems a niggardly rate, publishing a novel every two years between 1894 and 1928. Even for the most prolific, however, book production was much slower than magazine production, allowing a contract between reader and writer to evolve more gradually, and enabling a higher level of intervention from the readers as sales went up or down and publishers were informed of their likes and dislikes, their enthusiasms and disappointments. Over the years, these writers were successful in sustaining their popularity with readers and, for this reason, their novels provide evidence of the imaginative territories both desired and mediated over time by readers – territories which offer distinctive and contrasting versions of the emotional landscapes of femininity.

Sophie Cole was born in the London suburbs to an affluent middle-class family. She was well educated, and her novels are full of evidence of her interest in literature and history – the history of London in particular. Unmarried, she devoted her life to writing, and her close association with Mills & Boon was cemented by her becoming a shareholder in the firm.[2] She had an extraordinarily long, prolific and successful career, publishing her last novel the year before she died in her eighties. Her female public was clearly satisfied over several generations by the world she created for them. Yet her novels, consistently popular over so many years, do not conform to any easy stereotype of women's romance fiction on two counts – her representations of women and her choice of location. Her central female characters are usually mature, educated and independent women who have realistic expectations about emotional fulfilment and who do not seek the opportunity to love and be loved, considering it as a bonus not a right. Her favourite location is London itself – not the slums or the seats of power, but the ancient city where its history began.

In *A Wardour Street Idyll* (1910) and *A London Posy* (1917), the central female characters are both single and economically self-sufficient.[3] Isobel Norden is a thirty-year-old single woman who works for her living in an antique shop and travels daily to work by bus from Bromley, and Ann Constant is forty-two, the curator of a historical house, and lives with her brother across the street from her place of work. Another version of the single life is seen in the alienation of a wife from her husband in *Daffodil Alley* (1926), where the heroine Delia's childlessness compounds her separateness.[4] Cole may well have been drawing on personal experience, but her astute portraits of such women appear to refer back to late nineteenth-century debates about the social status of single women. There would have been many women among her readers who recognised the particular difficulties of the characters' situations and, in reading about them, celebrated their own escape. There would inevitably have been others who would have appreciated the independence and opportunities that a single life could offer. But these are not social problem novels, and this context is never specifically signalled. Cole prefers to concentrate on how women cope with the lives that society and history have dealt them, and the decisions that they make. She writes more in the spirit of Esmé Stuart, another popular novelist with sixty novels for children and young women to her credit, who wrote in 1895:

> In writing novels, one must study life, though live life has little to do with live art. Where so many writers err is that they copy life too closely or select badly. If we are too minute we lose force; if we are too forcible at the expense of truth, we lose reality. At present the public cares only for the exciting plot or exaggerated photography [realism]. It is very difficult to go against the stream but if possible it is best to stick to one's personal ideas.[5]

Cole consciously picked her way through the contemporary minefield of women's issues, acknowledging their existence only through the nature of her characters' dilemmas and choices, and, by adopting the romance genre, she subverted the realism of issue-led fiction.

Cole then, takes an alternative approach to the question of what it meant to be a woman from both the New Woman writers, such as Mona Caird, George Egerton and Rebecca West, and from male writers, such as George Gissing and H. G. Wells, who took up this theme and for whom singleness became a statement about social and sexual agency.[6] For Cole, singleness is less a social problem than a private state of consciousness: her heroines neither seek singleness nor reject it, as they neither seek nor reject love and marriage. Singleness and love are private matters of identity and integrity as women deal with life's opportunities and setbacks. Sophie Cole makes no reference to other writers' work on this topic or to the ideas that they express. She avoids challenging or placating her readers, offering them instead a gradualist picture of women's development as they live from day to day.

Cole's use of location also marks her out from other writers in the romance genre and from conventional realists. Most unusually for women's romance fiction of her period, her location is often London itself – the city that the suburb-dwellers have done their best to leave behind. In suburban idylls discussed earlier, London was treated as the 'other' – a symbol of ugliness and corruption, and a threat to domestic values which is only distanced and mitigated by suburban love. Elsewhere, in the vast majority of romances, London is remarkable only for its absence, a place to be rapidly escaped into the expanding global suburb of the imagination. Sophie Cole's London sidesteps these contemporary representations. Her locations are both in and out of history, neither symbolic nor concrete. Contemporary London provides the realistic location; the characters walk down familiar streets; but they really inhabit a timeless city. The histories of individuals are woven into a tapestry as each life contributes to the sum of human experience. Through its inhabitants, London has seen and known everything, and so it embodies a collective unconscious of thought and feeling which invests those whose lives might appear unexceptional with significance.

A London Posy brings these elements cleverly together. Ann Constant is in love with London and deeply satisfied with her job as curator of Dr Johnson's house in Fleet Street. When the novel opens, she has just realised in a moment of melancholy that, 'It wasn't to be expected that life had any more surprises to offer a woman of her age'.[7] She is right: there are no surprises, but there are new experiences. The reader witnesses the gradual enriching of Ann's imagination, which strengthens her identity and increases her emotional fulfilment. Initially, her imagination is sustained by the past, by the group of portraits hanging in Dr Johnson's house (the 'Posy' of the title), which have become like Roman household gods, benign spirits who advise and counsel her, and give her wisdom through her participation in the history of humanity. A copy of Dr Johnson's Dictionary is on display in the library, and to the amusement of her brother she uses it like the I-Ching, opening pages at random and then interpreting the words she finds there in the light of her own situation. In this way she is guided by a great mind from the past, but also by her own intuition, to a greater understanding of the present.

Daffodil Alley makes the connection between London, history and the richness of human experience even more explicit. The marriage of Delia and Clement is being undermined by her realisation that she cannot have children, and by his involvement with his work as a professor of comparative anatomy, a position which emphasises his ability to dissect human beings rather than care for them. London, the city which 'has a myriad weird old secrets up its sleeve' acts, as Johnson's Dictionary does in A London Posy, as an almost mystical guide towards emotional truths.[8] The actual London of 1926 is a densely populated city, apparently driven forward by technology and by the labour of its citizens, but in the novel London is an essentially transformative power which opens the imagination, as we see in this passage:

> London Bridge, with the view of the Pool beyond, was at this hour a scene of enchantment, and the three would stand there sometimes for half an hour watching those strange, half-human things, the monster cranes . . . to behold from above the ant-like activities of the bargemen and sailors, the silent coming out of the red, green and golden lights along the shore and river, to see Tower Bridge open its portals to let some stately ship through into the world of smoky sunset beyond.[9]

Clement is persuaded by this peculiar urban beauty to cross London Bridge and explore further. Expecting to encounter slums, he stumbles across fragmentary clues to the story of the Great Plague which awaken his imaginative and emotional powers to humanity's suffering through history.

Sophie Cole's plots are not page-turners. The stories of the main protagonists unfold slowly and the momentous events take place in a character's inner world. Initially, what is happening to them is only important to themselves, but events gain in significance as Cole shows even the simplest life to be confusing and open-ended, both as an individual experience and as part of humanity's larger story. In *A London Posy*, Dr Johnson's house, the portraits in his collection and the words in his dictionary represent the bedrock of London's history and culture, but the interaction of past and present in Ann's consciousness shows the continuity of human thought and endeavour. Ann's brother, George, spends an idyllic day in the country with his beloved Iris, accompanied by little Thomas, a city boy who has never seen the countryside. As they walk they are surrounded by echoes of Goldsmith's 'The Deserted Village' and Gray's 'Elegy in a Country Churchyard', a reminder that such scenes are always changing and taking on new meanings. In an earlier episode, while they talk to one another on the Embankment, 'In between a lull in the roar of the trams came two or three bars of Dvorak's "Humoresque" and a little breeze rustled sadly in the young green of the trees over-head'.[10] The feelings of the two lovers, while unique to them at that moment, are also part of a culture, a season, a moment in history, a series of beginnings but also of endings.

Johnson's *Dictionary* provides the raw materials, but the stirrings of imagination prompt the telling of stories – the binding of words into a shaped coherence and a personal meaning. George, who is exempted from service in the First World War because of his weak heart, is struggling to progress with his novel. His meeting with Iris 'had set in motion that part of his brain which created a world to his own liking. He had been stuck for the next chapter of his novel, but now he longed to get a pen in his hand to put down the ideas that tumbled over each other in their eagerness for a hearing.'[11] The emotions and the imagination work together to expand human creativity and to encourage optimism for the future. Stories can also be retrospective. Denis Laurie, who is an established novelist and whose friendship with Ann forms one of the romantic possibilities of the novel, writes in order to understand his life. At the end of *A London Posy*, when George takes Iris to see his finished book being printed, they also see Denis's novel stacked up waiting to be distributed. Its title, *The Rest is Silence*, suggests that it is the culminating imaginative feat of a middle-aged man in uncertain health. Ann and Denis part, but later the reader learns that they have agreed to correspond while he is travelling, and the implication is that the letters will provide other stories.

Daffodil Alley is similarly constructed in narrative layers. The first story-within-a story, 'The Story of the Golden Heart', is found in an old manuscript in a hidden drawer discovered by Delia and Clement. It is:

> a curious narrative ringing the changes of poignancy and tenderness, at one time gay, at another reflecting something grim and sinister from the atmosphere of these rude old times. A revelation of the long buried secrets of hearts in no respect very different from the hearts of men and women today.[12]

Inspired by this contact with the past, Clement abandons his scientific work and withdraws to a rented room in a poor quarter of London, Daffodil Alley. At first he tries to write a novel set in the seventeenth century, but his struggle to create a historical tale ends when he learns the story of John Purdy, who survived the plague. His growing empathy with this long-dead man inspires him to visualise a realistic picture of seventeenth-century London and to write a story through which he learns about the power of human feeling.

The happiness of the central characters is grounded in the wisdom of their choices rather than in the outcomes of particular events, but in Sophie Cole's novels happiness and sadness are nevertheless finely balanced. In *A London Posy*, there are fleeting, almost inconsequential references to the young men away at the war; and the two heroes, left behind because of ill health, provide a subdued and debilitated version of male passion. At the end of the novel, Ann's situation has not materially changed, although her openness to experience has enabled her to live a changing and fulfilling life. She has gained in emotional strength so that she feels able to allow those whom she loves – a possible husband, Denis Laurie, and her brother, George – to move on and find their own fulfilment. *Daffodil Alley*, perhaps because of its greater distance from the war, is less muted, but the reconciliation of husband and wife at the end of the novel is tentative. Delia is still infertile, and her own and Clement's brush with the past has been too close, as she acknowledges when she says to Clement, 'those old ghosts on the other side of the curtain have no right to make holes in it'.[13] The imagination can reach into the past and put individual lives into perspective, but the knowledge gained is bitter-sweet, since it also releases an awareness of death and change into the present. The 'haunting sweetness' but 'melancholy lilt' of the song of the lavender seller makes this clear:

> I am poor and my friends are all dead
> Nor mother nor father have I;
> Cold charity finds me in bread,
> And thus as I wander, I cry
>
> . . .
>
> Lavender, sweet blooming lavender
> Six bunches for a penny today.[14]

In *A Wardour Street Idyll*, *A London Posy* and *Daffodil Alley*, women's lives are Cole's main focus. She offers a realistic narrative of the daily and the familiar, enhanced and retextured by the individual's place in her own history and in the wider, older history of London's vast community. By downplaying the drama of events and moments of passion in individual lives but reinterpreting human experience through the cycle of human fortunes, Cole's perspective points up the enduring nature of women's values and the timelessness and commonality of human feeling. Men are rarely cast as the villains in women's stories, although they may be thoughtless or, as in *A London Posy*, weakened or even demasculinised. Jay Dixon's argument, that the submission of the male to the profounder emotional values of women is characteristic of the way romantic fiction empowers women, is pertinent here.[15] Yet it does not wholly account for Cole's women characters, who gain an inner strength and self-respect beyond men's love and the world's attention.

Cole gives momentary but fascinating glimpses into what she thinks some of her readers may take away from her books. In *A Wardour Street Idyll* Isobel passes fellow travellers 'of all sorts and conditions' on her way to work; later she remarks to her boss, 'It seems to me that when one spends one's life dodging things that hurt, sentimental woes are an escape from real ones.'[16] The claim that is being made here is interesting and goes to the very heart of fiction. Readers know that fiction is not 'real', however much it might work on their imaginations, and however much they may draw on it to measure their own lives. The stories that the past offers, or that the imagination conjures up, are dangerous as well as enlightening. In *A London Posy*, for instance, George falls in love with the heroine in his own novel. She becomes so real to him that he buys her a silk rose he spots in a shop window. But Cole's stories ultimately endorse the known and familiar: George's relationship with Iris teaches him that 'dreams were but poor stuff'.[17] As Bertha Ruck claims, the conclusion of a novel is not the end of a dream but the entrance into reality.

The novels I have selected for discussion from the prolific output of Alice Askew make no pretence to being representative. While many writers maintained a consistency of theme and mood, encouraging their readers to turn again and again to a familiar experience, choosing a particular author as they would choose their favourite magazine, Askew varied her themes, from emotional dramas in far-flung places to family stories and career romances. It seems that she was sensitive enough to the marketplace to respond to different readers' needs, and astute enough to identify and make use of popular trends and contemporary circumstances. *Anna of the Plains* (1906) fed the fascination of the time with travel and adventure; *The House Next Door* (1911) was published on the wave of early twentieth-century domestic fiction; while *Nurse* (1917) and *The Telephone Girl* (1918), looked to wartime changes in women's work, and their contribution to the growing communications industry, for the frameworks of their plots. Perhaps readers enjoyed the variety, but Askew's work suggests that it was likely that readers selected types of stories as much as they did authors, since her authorial identity appears to submerge itself completely in reader-led demand. Another interesting feature of her career is that she did not write until she was married, and then wrote all her novels in partnership with her husband, Claude Askew. Although there is no knowing exactly how their collaboration worked, the novels they produced were all directed at a female readership, and the foreign adventures that figure prominently in their novels were a reflection of their own lives.[18]

In *The Baxter Family* (1911), foreign lands are merely fantasies.[19] The fictional location is a respectable small house in Parsons Green where Lydia, a clerk in a City office, lives with her aunt. The novel spans a number of familiar themes, mixing up realism and romance, drama and practicality, in equal measures. Lydia despises the suburb where she lives as heartily as Ann Veronica despises Morningside Park. When the novel opens, the reader learns that Lydia's fiancé has been killed in Argentina, where they had planned to emigrate after their marriage. Her dream of an adventurous and glamorous life is suddenly snatched away and she finds herself condemned to what she perceives as suburban mediocrity. Although she earns a good salary, she can only see her future through marriage: she has lost 'her one chance of getting out of the rut', and sees herself doomed to marry that epitome of mediocrity, a clerk – 'once a clerk always a City clerk'.[20]

In Lydia's eyes, the suburbs represent everything that is stifling. They reduce nice people, like her 'comfortable, motherly' aunt and her loyal admirer James whose 'very socks . . . spoke of the City and cheap houses and money paid across the counter', to anonymous types. She is unable to recognise that the parlour's oppressive furnishings and its abundance of brightly coloured decoration constitute 'the tale the parlour told of honest endeavour'.[21] The 'smallness' of suburban living – the 'cramped' rooms and 'cramped' life – are contrasted with the primitive and passionate within Lydia which cannot be measured.[22] It is not a social critique that questions the suburbs here but a sexual critique: sex in Askew's novels is always a factor that complicates the realistic location and situations. It also questions the difference between generations. For Harriet Baxter, who remembers the struggles of an earlier generation, the house in Parsons Green is the answer to her dreams, but for Lydia, such an attitude is history. What Lydia wants is 'real space', sexual space in which she can respond, not to worthiness, but to 'a man . . . no mere tailor's dummy but a man'.[23]

The novel concludes with a moral dilemma. This is a familiar mode of conclusion in women's romance fiction, a device which turns the narrative back towards the reader, enabling her to find her own answer and to write the final stages of the story. When John Grant, her fiancé's closest friend, who had accompanied him on his travels, arrives to bring Lydia the last messages from her dead fiancé, she falls in love with him and he with her. His dilemma is whether he should be true to his promise never to marry again after his wife's death. Lydia's dilemma – whether to sacrifice historically specific suburban respectability to timeless passion – is expressed in terms of the primitive versus the conventional: 'she might have been the first woman facing the first man, she had got so far away from prejudice and convention – from all social laws'.[24] Lydia never has to make her decision, however, because John Grant decides that he must be true to his promise and leaves. Agatha, Lydia's friend, is the one to move the story on, by reminding Lydia that work still remains. Lydia, who in the opening pages faced the loss of romance with bitterness and with a rejection of her surroundings, concludes the story by recognising that external events cannot take away from her the right to live her own life.

The irrefutable demands of passion are also the theme of *Anna of the Plains* (1906), whose erotic opening in London's high society fixes the reader's attention.[25] The opening sequence describes a ball at which Michael, the hero of the story, has decided he will ask the beautiful socialite Helen, whom he is sure loves him, to marry him. During the evening the reader witnesses the change in Helen from the woman Michael was about to marry to a woman determined not to sacrifice security to emotions. From Michael's point of view she is the 'perfumed queen of love', a 'dainty creature' with soft delicate flesh: that is, the stereotype of a desirable woman. From the narrator's perspective she is 'one of those women who are fond of wearing plumage in their hats; sparing neither the seagull nor dove' and with a heart like 'a peach-stone'. As if in proof that her womanhood is divorced from nature, when she rejects Michael's love she systematically pulls the feathers of her fan to pieces – 'slowly and quietly spoiling it'. By contrast, his natural physicality is recognised by other women with whom he dances, who 'told each other afterwards that he was a partner who would never be forgotten'. This incident confronts the reader with a set of questions about sexual values: can a man recognise the honesty of his own passions when social relations are so bound by convention? Can a woman afford feelings when the exploitation of her sexual desirability promises financial reward? Is love a possibility in a corrupt society?

The novel's questions are answered when Michael meets Anna, whose innocence is contrasted with Helen's knowingness. He meets her in South Africa, where he has moved to put his London life behind him and where he is able to inhale 'a deep breath of the pure air'.[26] Askew can safely give Anna's sexuality full rein because Anna is innocent of its significance, and she can respond spontaneously. Were suburban readers shocked by the suggestion that Anna 'had come to that ripe second of a girl's life – that wonderful moment when the virgin parts her breasts to receive the shaft of love'?[27] The metaphor appears to be deliberately confused, to read either as an explicit reference to sexual intercourse or to be obscured by the familiar formulae of heaving breasts and cupid's dart.

Again the novel ends with a dilemma the solution of which is left for the reader to decide. Anna is seduced by Piet, a stranger who had arrived ill at her parents' farm and had been taken in to be looked after. When Piet finally overcomes her scruples, Anna is 'helpless' and full of 'stupor', and she later muses on the loss of her virginity by her mother's grave, which has 'Pure in Heart' engraved on it; but it is Michael and not Anna herself who murders Piet. The reader is left to decide on the relative values of 'civilised' London and 'primitive' South Africa, on the nature of passion and on what conclusion Michael's and Anna's story should eventually have.

Although the locations of *The Baxter Family* and *Anna of the Plains* are quite different, and while the first is an example of suburban realism and the second of sensation, the fundamental response elicited from readers is the same. When passion and convention are pitted against one another, what means do women have of reconciling them in a way that is socially acceptable and personally satisfying? In *The Baxter Family*, Alice Askew, like Sophie Cole, is careful to indicate the limitations of romantic fiction as a means of reconciliation. When Lydia first hears that her fiancé is dead:

> She could no longer cheat herself to wonderful day-dreams. For there was no chance now of any rich man coming home to marry her. She must work hard all her life at her typing, or marry a young clerk and live in a meaningless little house; and the bitterness of such thoughts used to move Lydia strangely at times.[28]

Stories can interrogate, challenge, provoke and entertain, but the writers of romantic fiction seem to agree that it should never cross over the boundaries of imagination and provide answers to real life.

Louise Gerard produced her first novel in 1910 when she was thirty-two and went on to publish at a rate of one a year until 1936. Although never achieving one-off spectacular sales figures, in 1938 she was still listed as one of the sixty-eight 'Most Popular Twopenny Library Authors' of romance; and her novels, publicised by Mills & Boon as 'lavish romance, exotic background and high adventure', ran to multiple editions.[29] Educated privately at Nottingham High School for Girls, and an enthusiastic world traveller, Gerard is representative of the many educated and resourceful women who chose to make their living through writing during this period. Her novels were published in Scandinavia, Holland, France and as far afield as Hungary, and her popularity increased through magazine and film rights. The context for her early novels was the contemporary fascination with the colonies, which had grown steadily throughout the 1880s and 1890s, fostered by the work of writers such as H. Rider Haggard and Rudyard Kipling, whose tales of India took London by storm. Louise Gerard joined the Mills & Boon list within a year of Sophie Cole, and both authors were the darlings of the circulating libraries, and often linked in Mills & Boon's publicity campaigns. Their locations and their emotional orientation, however, were entirely different.

The British Empire provided an unparalleled imaginative playground for all those who were unable to join the ever-increasing numbers of tourists, colonial officials and emigrants on their journeys to the colonies. As Paula Krebs's fascinating analysis of the press and the Boer War argues: 'imagination was of necessity an important ingredient in British public perception of imperialism' because support for imperialism relied on 'the British public imagining both faraway places and a prosperous future'.[30] But even stuck at home in Britain, the average newspaper reader at the turn of the twentieth century was probably considerably more knowledgeable about far-flung countries of the world than people are today. Flights of imagination were fuelled by events like Queen Victoria's Golden Jubilee, when displays from all the countries of the Empire paraded through London. The New Journalism borrowed the techniques of fiction to arouse readers' interest in the latest military events abroad,[31] while magazines like the *National Geographic* (launched in the United States in 1888) and *The Wide World Magazine* (launched 1898) which published maps and photographs to accompany the personal accounts of adventurers, travellers, scientists and explorers to every part of the globe, fed people's appetite for information and adventure.[32]

Gerard enters this masculine world of action and conquest, of dominance and spectacle, to capture it for women's imagination with all the 'magnificent vitality' noted by Q. D. Leavis as characteristic of her genre (an insult I have co-opted as a compliment since Leavis herself invariably associated such literary energy with 'bad writing, false sentiment, sheer silliness, and a preposterous narrative').[33] Although the framework of her plots superficially acknowledges the colonial structures of West Africa, her textual territory is the exotic. The textual energy of her most popular novels comes from the dangerous tensions generated by the polarities of race, colour and gender which threaten instability in locations where imperial power (for whatever reason) is weakened. Gerard's novels are part of that nineteenth-century discourse noted by Lyn Pykett in which Africa is the testing ground of 'civilisation', 'a space in which the primitive might be civilised, or in which the civilised might regress or degenerate'.[34] The aspect of 'civilisation' that Gerard delightedly put to the test was the imperial construction of gender and of women's sexuality.

The Hyena of Kullu (1910), Gerard's first novel, and *A Tropical Tangle* (1911), both demonstrate that the great civilisation of the western world has already failed the test, particularly in relation to women's lives.[35] In the earlier novel, Molly Seaton, an 'ordinary kind of London girl clerk' and, therefore, a representative of the fluctuating fortunes of the aspiring working- and lower-middle classes, is ill with tuberculosis and struggling to keep afloat economically.[36] She is supported by her friend Leslie Graham, a talented and energetic young woman who has put ambition on hold rather than desert her friend. Their future, living a narrow and thrifty life as they hang on to economic survival and battle against ill health, is changed by a chance meeting with two West Africans, Horton Cooper and Essel Lebrassa, who are visiting England. Molly marries Cooper and later, Leslie travels to Africa to visit her. *A Tropical Tangle* opens in the heart of the Empire, in a rain-swept, windy London of dark and dangerous streets through which the heroine, Dorothy Gale, a nurse, has to battle on her way to and from work. Later in the year, as she surveys an urban cage as desperately sterile and deformed as T. S. Eliot's visions in 'Preludes' and 'The Love Song of J. Alfred Prufrock', she rejects the 'vista of civilisation' to which she is chained:

It was a hot, stifling August day, with a heated, dusty wind. In the street below a smutty plane tree stood, cased round with iron railings, on its branches a group of grimy sparrows quarrelled; at its roots was a collection of dirty papers; beyond, a hoarding covered with advertisements, above, a fringe of chimneys of all shapes and at all angles . . . belching out smoke from some factory; in the sky, a network of telegraph and telephone wires.[37]

This moment of revelation helps her to decide to apply for a nursing job in Africa which she had seen advertised, and to start a new life. *A Wreath of Stars* (1923) provides another example of how so-called civilisation has only further suppressed women's aspirations. The heroine, Norah Deane, dreams of becoming a painter but, when her sister dies, she has no choice but to look after her four motherless children until they grow up. During her domestic life in the suburbs, in the 'row upon row of small, semi-detached houses', she feels that all ambition and creativity have been drained from her. It is only when, as a middle-aged woman, she is finally released from domestic servitude to the family that she is able to leave London and travel to Venice where she rediscovers her capacity to paint.[38]

A failure of English masculinity is further evidence of the Empire's decline. It is Leslie's anger at the behaviour of two Englishmen in their casual and ignorant racism against Lebrassa at the beginning of *The Hyena of Kullu* which initially spurs her to defend him. Later, she is irritated when one of the men, Fletcher, introduces himself and then attempts to protect her when they coincidentally travel on the same boat to Africa. Although Fletcher grows in the course of the novel to appreciate her independence of mind and action, he is not rewarded with the marriage he desires. Leslie returns alone to London to build a career as a writer and journalist. Similarly, in *A Tropical Tangle*, while working in a small African medical centre Dorothy Gale discovers that the Commissioner, Frank Ashby, with whom she has begun to fall in love, is a liar who was prepared to kill an innocent black man to cover his own crime of domestic violence. The only time that her physical safety is threatened is when Dr Brookes, the white doctor who runs the hospital, drunkenly attempts to rape her. As these examples show, imperial values have become ambivalent as white masculinity stands accused of the abuse of power.

The ambiguity of masculine whiteness permeates other, more subtle, judgements in these novels. Leslie Graham, for instance, is attracted by Lebrassa's 'cultured voice and well-bred ease of manner', but the reader learns later that this is the bequest of a treacherous white father who abandoned him and his black mother, leaving him with a surface polish that obscures the inner pain of his inter-racial status.[39] Dorothy Gale, taken in by Ashby's social sophistication which marks him out as a member of the 'superior' races, fails to value the less socially presentable Mark Harrison. Mark Harrison is an English civil engineer working in the Kullu region. She marries Mark without loving him in exchange for information about Frank Ashby, whom she had hoped to marry. However, she finally recognises that her responses are conditioned, 'the result of generations of forebears of gentle birth and breeding that made her instinctively shrink from all who were not smooth and polished on the surface',[40] and she learns to love Mark for his honesty and directness.

Just as men's superficial social polish – their imperial whiteness – is no guide to their integrity, so the femininity constructed by a masculinised society throws up misreadings of a different kind. Leslie Graham is tiny, blonde and with hands frequently referred to as 'butterflies', but at all times she is confident enough to prefer 'her own immature judgement' to that of the men who surround her.[41] Once in Africa, she traverses the African bush to collect interviews and photographs, and discovers the secret behind the so-called Hyena of Kullu. She resists her own femininity by changing her name from Sylvia: 'I like Leslie better; it sounds more capable of looking after itself. Sylvia has such a frail sound, as if it ought to be kept at home with someone to look after it.'[42] In the London hospital where she works, Dorothy Gale finds that her nursing role is misunderstood by a man who deludes himself that her caring for him is a sign of infatuation; and in Africa, as we have seen, Dr Brookes expects a nurse to render service in more ways than one. Although the women's actions are motivated by appropriately womanly feelings (Leslie's by wanting to visit her friend and Dorothy's by wanting to care for the sick), the actions themselves demonstrate a loyalty, resourcefulness, fairness and independence more usually attributed to men.

There is a productive confusion or relativisation of values in the novels located in Africa. Once they arrive, Gerard's women characters operate at the centre of a series of polarised magnetic fields: black/white, man/woman, civilisation/barbarism. Of the white races, only women (although not all women) can sustain without damage the force of their conflicting attractions and repulsions: white men all succumb to moral weaknesses of one kind or another. The letter from

Molly Seaton to Leslie telling of her sudden marriage to Cooper and her life in Africa, which first persuades Leslie to make the journey herself, makes this clear. Her letter brings out the difference between the evocation of Africa in the imagination (Cooper wooed her with Othello-like tales of 'the wild, brilliant glories of the tropics'), and the reality of Cooper's sexual passion affirmed and intensified by the wilderness.[43] Molly herself, already weakened by difficult living conditions and by the sickness endemic to the western world, is drained of life by the energy of Cooper's passion. He finally kills her weakened body rather than allow the Hyena to carry her off. The delicate English roses which adorn the balconies of the colonial houses are symbolic of the fate of those who cannot cope. They are reduced to mimicking the sounds of the jungle; 'the soft, fleshy tapping of sodden roses on the balcony rail' seems to beg for them to be let in, leaving the jungle to 'flowers of a carnivorous variety . . . [with a] way of coiling round anything flesh and blood'.[44] British men are emasculated and belittled by their ownership of an empty power, and they are as incapable of understanding the meaning of their environment as the British visitors to the Marabar caves in E. M. Forster's *A Passage to India* (1924). Had Gerard been writing a hundred years later, Lebrassa could have been the bridge between cultures, but he falls foul of the consequences of miscegenation: envious of the education and privileges of his 'white side', from which he can never benefit, he betrays his 'black side' and comes to hate Africa as 'the abode of wickedness'.[45]

From the perspective of those reduced or exposed by the effects of Africa's wilderness, it is a terrifying and inchoate space, dehumanised and dehumanising, the 'Heart of Darkness' that drew in and then destroyed Kurtz in Conrad's novella. But Gerard's descriptions of the jungle as observed by her heroines are shaped by sensuous harmonies of colour, fragrance and sound which create emotional and spiritual meaning through the imagination. At one remove from conquest, women are able to participate in the atmosphere of Africa rather than to try to control it. Dorothy Gale evokes an African sublime in which 'The incense of a cathedral filled the air; the constant hum of a myriad of insects had a sound like the faint notes of some distant organ',[46] while images of the moon allow Molly in *The Hyena of Kullu* to see simultaneously the darkness of the night-time jungle ('black – black with an utter everlasting blackness') and its transformation ('It is white – white with a perfect whiteness').[47]

The plots of these novels are straightforward. Readers are able to follow easily the stages of love, adventure, danger, survival, conflict and resolution which the heroines experience; and Gerard's style, which has all the fluency and ease of a first person narrative, moves swiftly from event to event with an attractive immediacy. Despite uncomfortable evidence of what Anne McClintock calls 'commodity racism'[48] – that is, the use of a widely recognised pictorial and verbal shorthand of white cultural supremacy – the plots of both *The Hyena of Kullu* and *A Tropical Tangle* are far from being anchored in absolutes of race, gender and colour. They float on a sea of perspectives and possibilities – racial, sexual and moral – where the symbols 'white' and 'black', while never totally detached from their racial connotations, interrogate contemporary assumptions about masculinity, femininity, sexuality and cultural superiority.[49] Women readers have full scope to accept or reject, consciously or unconsciously, any number of variables relating to the role of women and their sexual and/or emotional capacities.

Flower-of-the-Moon: A romance of the forest (1914) is probably more ambitious, but less successful as an entertaining reading experience, than *A Tropical Tangle* or *The Hyena of Kullu*.[50] What is particularly interesting about it for my discussion is the way in which possibilities are not only obliquely suggested but structured around alternative stories – a British imperial narrative of supremacy and conquest and an African story of love, aspiration and the imagination – through which the love plot centring on Carlyon and Flower-of-the-Moon is threaded. The plot borrows elements from both stories. If stories are, indeed, 'the basis for the negotiation of power relations' as Edward Said argues in relation to imperial writing, then Gerard utilises them in this novel to negotiate the relation between British order and rationality (coded as masculine) and African passion and imagination (coded as feminine).[51]

The novel opens with Uhoo, an old African storyteller who travels the country with his collection of ancient stories. He is finally persuaded to tell the story of 'The Mango Blossom' to a group of bored English officers, who mildly threaten the 'old heathen' into entertaining them because they are 'tired of our own tales'.[52] The pagan tale of undying passion, unconsummated desire and hopeless aspiration unsettles his Christian listeners, but most of them dismiss its elements of rape and metamorphosis as a 'negro muddle of Diana and Daphne'.[53] The irony is that they fail to recognise the collective unconscious of human emotions which produced similar stories in pagan Greece, Rome and West Africa, and that their weariness with their 'own stories' intimates a hunger to rediscover those emotions. One officer is unable to forget the story he has been told and, as a result, his own role in the English imperial narrative is changed from a masculine one based on military action to a feminine one based on love. He struggles throughout the novel to find a way of entering a fully feminised sphere of feeling.

Like Sophie Cole and Alice Askew, Gerard blends together a number of popular elements – in her case, adventure, the exotic, the erotic and the thrilling – as innocent women find themselves alone and unprotected in unknown and dangerous situations. In the African novels, she plays to great effect with the different meanings of white and black, but the pace of the novels is so urgent that the reader is distracted from conceptualising. The attempt to break those meanings down (or sort them out) ends nowhere. Again like other women romance writers, she is more concerned with the different and the specific than with an authorial position. The most powerful impression that these novels leave is of a narrative about women surviving on their own, combating inner fears to pursue their own ideals, and being clear-sighted about the difference between men's code of behaviour and their power to feel rightly.

Mary Hamilton is the only writer I discuss in this chapter whose own life was circumscribed by conventions of class and race. She had written at least four novels before her marriage to an officer in the Indian Army in 1898, but the majority of her writing was done in India where she and her husband lived for some twenty years. She was one of a number of educated women (among them Flora Annie Steel, one of whose short stories I discussed in the previous chapter) who wrote about the difficulties of colonial life for women, and challenged the culture which created them.[54] The mismatch between social institutions and conventions and the emotional and sexual needs of individuals is Mary Hamilton's chief concern. In a series of novels located in India, she powerfully and relentlessly exposes how the failure to confront this mismatch allows dishonesty, distortion, absurdity and tragedy to worm their way into human relationships. The path of each novel is marked by a succession of moral and emotional dilemmas or crises as the conformist outer world of pre-scribed manners and morals threatens to overwhelm the desires and aspirations of the individual's inner world. Both men and women are caught in the social trap, but Hamilton focuses on women's relative powerlessness to change the status quo, on their vulnerability if they try and on their strategies for survival.

India as a physical place, a people and a culture is invisible in these novels. Hamilton employs none of Gerard's colourful landscapes and exotic descriptions to evoke strangeness and a clash of cultures. A desire to 'get to know India', such as Adela Quested shows in *A Passage to India*, would be an irrelevance. The significance of India in Hamilton's novels is rather in its power to turn the spotlight onto Englishness. Living in compounds, cut off from their home country as well as from the people whom they govern, the military and civilian servants of the British Empire experience the essence of their own culture in a kind of *huis clos* 'where everybody knows everybody else'.[55] Surrounded by servants and with their children at school in England, the women are doubly bereft. Stripped of even their traditional roles as homemaker and mother, they have no public identity or function aside from their husbands. Yet in the world's eyes, they are privileged women. In the cooler weather, social routines shape the day: polo matches, drinks at the club, dinner parties and tea parties. And during the hot summer months women and children retreat to the hills, to be visited as and when their husbands wish. In this context, where the public role is the rationale of existence and behaviour is ruled by the hand of colonial convention, Hamilton explores what it means to love, to desire and to achieve (or fail to achieve) emotional and sexual independence. She turns the reader's gaze inwards to consider the question: what kind of woman is it possible to be in this repressed upper-class colonial culture, by implication, in this 'English purdah'?

The failure to find a balance between form (marriage, promotion, social convention) and content (emotion, shared meaning, community) drives the plot of *Poor Elisabeth* (1901).[56] At the beginning of the novel, Elisabeth's emotional energy and sensuous physicality mark out her potential for passion. However, her innocent, natural womanhood is rendered dangerous by her aversion to learning and her lack of interest in the niceties of social convention, which deprive her of the means to understand and control her feelings. Although she is outwardly secure because of her white father's position in colonial administration, her mixed race inheritance renders her social position ambiguous. Elisabeth is a kind of *lusus naturae*, whose powerful and uncontrolled emotions, once triggered, gradually engulf her family, friends, husband and child, and finally her own reason. But *Poor Elisabeth* is not a judgemental moral fable about the dangers of excessive emotion or a patronizing assertion of racial inferiority. Quite the reverse: Elisabeth's life critiques the emotional ignorance of the society in which she grows up.

One of the characteristics of Hamilton's writing is the moral tightrope that she walks, drawing the reader step by tiny step into understanding the most extreme of moral dilemmas or ruptures of social convention and then withdrawing, leaving the moral and social dilemmas raised by the text for the reader to consider. She differs in this from Sophie Cole, Louise Gerard and Alice Askew, who all resist the intrusion of psychology into their emotional terrains: Hamilton's questions challenge and tease the reader. In *Poor Elisabeth* the question is, unusually, explicitly articulated, after Elisabeth has murdered her baby to prevent her husband from seeing that it is black. 'It would be curious', the authorial voice unexpectedly and quietly muses, 'to speculate if the generations on her mother's side who had held the lives of girl babies cheaply and dealt death to them as to so many kittens, had in some way handed down their point of view to Elisabeth'.[57] The possibility of such a judgement being appropriate to Elisabeth's situation is shocking. It briefly checks the reader's emotional empathy with Elisabeth's situation, and formulates the unspoken question: if madness, murderousness and emotional greed are not characteristics inherited from an inferior native race, then how can Elisabeth's fate be understood?

The novel suggests that the promising raw material of Elisabeth's sexual and emotional identity is shaped, not by a flawed inheritance, but by the ignorance of British society concentrated in the microcosm of colonial life. At first the reader encounters the false femininity of women who unintentionally delude themselves to avoid facing the social reality of Elisabeth's position. Elisabeth's acceptance at school, where she was very popular with pupils and teachers; the kindness of the ladies at the British compound who 'came to see her, with much friendly conversation and advice' when she was ill; the patient support of her stepmother; and the sympathy of Mrs Maude, who tries to cheer her up during her pregnancy; are all premised on pity – hence the title, *Poor Elisabeth*.[58] This pity is inspired by the secret but unalterable 'fact' of her mixed race status, a 'fact' about which none of the kind people has got around to informing Elisabeth, although the men, in the privacy of their club, openly talk about 'a lethal chamber badly wanted for children like that'.[59] The creeping realisation of the horror she embodies for the people around her is diffused in madness as she tries to destroy blackness by cutting off her hair and, finally, murdering her black baby.

The second way of understanding Elisabeth is framed by a familiar failure of masculinity. Robert Kennedy, an aspiring colonialist, is attracted despite himself by her vivacity and spontaneity; he abandons his white fiancée to marry her. He does not know whether he is being true to his inner desire for love, or false to his social conception of himself as an ambitious servant of the Empire and a man strictly in control of his appetites. Full of self-disgust, he draws Elisabeth into his own uncertainties and then, unable to respond to her demands, punishes her by withdrawing his love. The more he withdraws, the more she tries to please him and the further she moves from the possibility of emotional independence. The alienation of their emotional lives is brilliantly evoked when, after a long journey from the mountains where the women had retreated from the summer heat, during which she has imagined him in danger, she 'threw herself sobbing and laughing hysterically into his arms', to his uncomprehending embarrassment.[60]

Mrs Brett (1913), which is also set in a British colonial community in India, is pitched at the other end of the emotional spectrum from *Poor Elisabeth*. Quiet and restrained, it plots the changing relationships of Mr and Mrs Brett, their daughter, Judy, and her fiancé, Peter Dampier, through a series of subtly nuanced conversations as each in turn tries to reach out to or confront the others. By the end of the novel, everyone has changed partners: Mr Brett retreats to his mistress, Mrs Trotter; Judy elopes with a married man, Major Wynyard; and Mrs Brett leaves her husband for her daughter's fiancé, a man eighteen years younger than herself. Each character seems deserving of both praise and blame, and each decision seems inevitable as the reader witnesses the daily dramas that are the catalyst for the changing sets of relations. Readers of this novel in 1913 must have been surprised to find themselves endorsing Mrs Brett's extraordinary decision to abandon her social position in India for what the novel suggests might be only a short-lived happiness.

The mature resignation and deep self-knowledge of Mrs Brett exemplifies a particular kind of woman's strength against which each of the other characters is measured. Her husband sees only someone he has power over – power to forgive her a youthful affair while using his forgiveness as an excuse to remind her of his tolerance, power to humiliate her and spend time with his mistress, power to criticise her as a mother but to take no criticism in return. At home, the external façade of his prestigious position as a judge falls away to reveal a self-important, insensitive and sometimes ridiculous ranter. Judy, their daughter, feels at twenty-five that she has grown beyond her mother. Though occasionally warm towards her, Judy is more likely to presume on her mother's support, to override her wishes, to ignore her advice and, in a passion of selfishness, to resent her. This is a perceptive picture of a mother/daughter relationship. Many mothers reading this novel must have winced with pain more than once as they were caught up in its web. When Peter Dampier, her daughter's fiancé, has a serious riding accident, he is brought to live with them where he can be near Judy and be properly looked after. Confined to his bed on the veranda, he observes the family dynamics, and learns to value the inner sense of worth that has kept Margaret Brett open to love although locked in a loveless marriage.

In common with other romance novelists, Hamilton offers several stories for readers to muse over. The overarching story of Margaret's growth to wisdom and independence within a sterile marriage is told in three narratives. The first is the story of her youthful infidelity. Her husband uses this story against her, for his own self-gratification and to bring her to heel when there is conflict between them. In a painful exchange, her daughter also uses this history to insult her. Although the event happened in the early years of her married life, Margaret knows that it is still unfinished. The second story is about her growing pleasure in Peter Dampier's company, and the development of their love in the context of his injury and her nursing. His removal from the masculine world of the army allows him to enter the female world of reflection and feeling. This time the story is completed (and possibly also completes the first story) as she decides to return to England with him. The third story is that of her painting, which runs almost incidentally through the novel as an activity for which she rarely has time. Margaret begins painting to occupy herself when her daughter is growing up, but painting becomes her way of seeing, and of being in, India. At the beginning of the novel, the reader learns that her reputation as an artist has been established in England, and that she has become financially

independent. Creativity and self-sufficiency are a frequent requirement for the ability to love in romance fiction.

Of course, my discussion here brings us no nearer to knowing why
individual women readers bought or borrowed these books, what
they took away from them, or whether women read some novels by
all of these writers, or all the novels by some them. It is frustrating
that no critical acumen, however acute, can 'neatly match up text
and audience'.[61] We cannot know whether reading a Sophie Cole
novel sent readers rushing off to the library to research London's
history, or whether they saw their environment with fresh eyes on
their visits from the suburbs or on their way to work. Can we be any
more sure whether the profound dilemmas in Mary Hamilton's
novels persuaded readers to be reconciled to their lot or encouraged
them to take a stand? Did Gerard's readers identify with the courage
of her heroines or cuddle more deeply into their chairs to read about
them? Did readers of these last two authors feel that they knew India
or Africa better as a result or did they simply relate the emotional situations to their own lives? Probably there were all of these responses,
possibly all at the same time. Women writers such as Gerard, Cole,
Askew and Hamilton could be considered the forgotten colleagues
of the male romance writers, such as H. Rider Haggard, R. L.
Stevenson, G. Henty, Rudyard Kipling and H. G. Wells, who won
such acclaim during the same period and whose novels were popular
but were also considered of greater literary value. Certainly, Nicholas
Daly's argument about the importance of adventure stories is true of
romance fiction, that it offered 'a species of popular theory of social
change in narrative form' despite the fact that 'criticism perceived
this as a marginal and even juvenile literature, rather than culturally
central'.[62] It would also be valid to claim women's romance fiction as
part of the longer romance tradition defined by Northrop Frye. His
emphasis on romance as a 'process of transforming reality' which 'will
still contain that reality' has much to say about how these novels
work.[63] But, of course, neither of these definitions presume to take
issues of gender into account.

What emerges from this discussion of popular magazine stories
and novels is the subordination of the common coordinates by which
we map fictional worlds. The reference-points of a masculine literary
structure – plot, location, history and character – are displaced in
a radical feminine literary form that privileges women's growing

self-determination, endorsing a democracy of desire and the power of the female voice. The plasticity of romance fiction effectively removes it from the author's hands and places it firmly in those of the reader. An aesthetic of authorial control is replaced by the endlessly diverse and familiar, problematic and pleasurable, challenging and compensating territories of the suburban imagination. As a result, critical assumptions about the response of the reader need to be put aside in favour of an attempt to understand the possibilities of the text. I have chosen to ask questions in this chapter rather than hazard answers in order to emphasise this important point. The association of fiction, imaginative space and self-discovery is still very much a feature of modern popular novels. 'Be a mum, be a daughter, be a wife, be a sister, be a lover, but once in a while, just be you!' exhorted a hoarding advertising the new Danielle Steel novel at my local railway station recently. The picture, like so many images of the 1890s New Woman, was of a woman with her legs curled under her, engrossed in a book.

Notes

1 *Home Notes* (3 March 1900), 315.
2 McAleer, *Passion's Fortune*, 56.
3 Sophie Cole, *A Wardour Street Idyll* (London: Mills & Boon, 1910) and Sophie Cole, *A London Posy* (London: Mills & Boon, 1917).
4 Sophie Cole, *Daffodil Alley* (London: Mills & Boon, 1926).
5 Archer P. Crouch, 'Lady Novelists and their Views of Literature', *Hearth and Home* (5 January 1895), 306–307.
6 See Sally Ledger, *The New Woman: Fiction and feminism at the fin-de-siècle* (Manchester: Manchester University Press, 1997); Ann Ardis, *New Woman, New Novels: Feminism and early modernism* (New Brunswick, NJ and London: Rutgers University Press, 1990).
7 *A London Posy*, 18.
8 *Daffodil Alley*, 22.
9 *Daffodil Alley*, 53.
10 *A London Posy*, 88.
11 *A London Posy*, 52.
12 *Daffodil Alley*, 21.
13 *Daffodil Alley*, 215.
14 *A London Posy*, 188.
15 Dixon, *Romance Fiction*, 32.
16 *A Wardour Street Idyll*, 183.
17 *A London Posy*, 21.
18 Kemp et al., *Edwardian Fiction*, 10.
19 Alice and Claude Askew, *The Baxter Family* (London: F. V. White and Co., 1907).
20 *The Baxter Family*, 11, 4.

21 *The Baxter Family*, 15.
22 *The Baxter Family*, 30.
23 *The Baxter Family*, 17.
24 *The Baxter Family*, 296.
25 Alice and Claude Askew, *Anna of the Plains* (London: F. V. White and Co., 1906), 6–12.
26 *Anna of the Plains*, 54.
27 *Anna of the Plains*, 41.
28 *The Baxter Family*, 11–12.
29 McAleer, *Passion's Fortune*, 74, 47.
30 Krebs, *Gender, Race and the Writing of Empire*, 144–145.
31 Krebs, *Gender, Race and the Writing of Empire*, 14.
32 See Jackson, *George Newnes and the New Journalism*, chapter 4, 'Expanding Human Consciousness across the Globe', 163–200.
33 Leavis, *Fiction and the Reading Public*, 62.
34 Pykett, *Engendering Fictions*, 27.
35 Louise Gerard, *The Hyena of Kullu* (London: Methuen, 1910) and *A Tropical Tangle* (London: Mills & Boon, 1911).
36 *The Hyena*, 16.
37 *A Tropical Tangle*, 46.
38 Louise Gerard, *A Wreath of Stars: A romance of Venice* (London: Mills & Boon, 1923), 49. In *A Wreath of Stars*, the dreariness of Britain is only equalled by the ugliness of Venice, whose cultural pretensions are undermined by a cityscape of canals that 'might be the offshoot of the Styx' (123). In fact, Gerard sees this malaise as a European phenomenon.
39 *The Hyena*, 16.
40 *A Tropical Tangle*, 240.
41 *The Hyena*, 46.
42 *The Hyena*, 79.
43 *The Hyena*, 40.
44 *The Hyena*, 122, 117.
45 *The Hyena*, 77.
46 *A Tropical Tangle*, 154–155 (155).
47 *The Hyena*, 41.
48 Anne McClintock, *Imperial Leather: Race, gender and sexuality in the colonial contest*, cited in McLaughlin, *Writing the Urban Jungle*, 17.
49 See Dixon, *Romance Fiction*, 51 ff. for discussion of racism and symbolism in Gerard's work.
50 Louise Gerard, *Flower-of-the-Moon: A romance of the forest* (London: Mills & Boon, 1914).
51 Edward Said, *Culture and Imperialism* (London: Vintage, 1994), 9.
52 *Flower-of-the-Moon*, 2.
53 *Flower-of-the-Moon*, 14.
54 See Nancy L. Paxton, *Writing under the Raj: Gender, race, and rape in the British colonial imagination, 1830–1947* (New Brunswick, NJ and London: Rutgers University Press, 1999) for discussions of Anglo-Indian novelists from 1880–1914.
55 Mary Hamilton, *Mrs Brett* (London: Stanley Paul and Co., 1913), 168.
56 Mary Hamilton, *Poor Elisabeth* (London: Hurst and Blackett, 1901).

57 Hamilton, *Poor Elisabeth*, 26.
58 *Poor Elisabeth*, 281.
59 *Poor Elisabeth*, 230.
60 *Poor Elisabeth*, 257.
61 Rose, *The Intellectual Life*, 367.
62 Daly, *Modernism*, 117.
63 Northrope Frye, cited in Fredric Jameson, *The Political Unconscious: Narrative as a socially symbolic act* (London: Methuen, 1981), 110.

Part III

SUBURBAN REALITIES

7

✳

THE WORKING-CLASS SUBURB
Edwin Pugh
William Pett Ridge
Shan Bullock
George and Weedon Grossmith

THE working-class suburb was the hub of the suburban revolution and its most original aspect. It was here – in the in-filling developments of the inner suburbs, in the new railway suburbs of North and East London and in speculative developments in the outer suburbs – that new class identities evolved and the 'masses' of the inner city became individuals struggling towards self-determination. Topographically, the working-class suburb was everywhere but, from a middle-class perspective, it was the marginal suburb – on the margins of social status, of the aesthetic environment and of culture. It was discussions about the perceived ugliness, monotony, cultural limitations and small-mindedness of working-class suburbs that most galvanised public opinion. The upper and middle classes were happy to sell their land to speculative builders, swell their bank balances and move out to desirable suburbs themselves. They were less happy to be faced with the consequences of rapid, unplanned development and with an upwardly mobile population bent on seeking for themselves the material comforts that they saw around them.

By the turn of the twentieth century, the suburbs had begun to be identified as 'more and more the abode of working London', 'the residence of the clerk and the thriving artisan' and of 'the family of small means'.[1] Clear social classifications such as 'working class' still held good, as municipal housing, third class rail travel, and differences in employment categories and wage levels made clear. Patterns of immigration rapidly invested particular suburbs with a class identity and, within these suburbs, the distance between the houses and the railway station was another rough indicator of class status. Although all classes caught the same train in the morning, wealthy merchants travelled first class and their clerks and assistants travelled third class. It is for these reasons that I have called this chapter 'The working-class suburb' although, in fact, 'suburbia', as Edwin Pugh named it, is more usually understood as a conceptual territory. Those who had edged themselves onto the lowest level of the suburban ladder, who had aspired to the dreary streets described by Pugh in his idiosyncratic survey of London, *The City of the World*, trod closely on the heels of the lower-middle classes who, in their turn, were busy keeping one step ahead by consolidating their own class credentials.[2] Suburban mobility appears to have changed people's awareness of the possibilities of class mobility, 'namely, that where such ownership was attainable, the preferences and aspirations of many working people were remarkably similar to those in the class above them'.[3] It is hardly surprising that this should have been the case. Young women managing their own homes for the first time, families seeking greater stability and comfort and young men wanting to build a career looked to middle-class practices as their role models.

In discussing the work of novelists who chose the working-class suburbs as their location and theme, I finally leave the suburban romance behind and pick up versions of late Victorian realism. The difference from the romance genre, despite its demonstrable diversity, is striking, and it lies almost entirely in the writers' predominant interest in observable realities. However, there are also distinct differences from the realism of the social problem novels of the 1880s and 1890s. The closely structured plot, character development and moral seriousness associated with the realistic novel are usually absent. There is a lightness and transparency about the representations of working-class life in many of these novels. Although there is often an implied didacticism which encourages the reader to question the realities behind common assumptions about working-class suburban life, they cannot be seen as social critiques or, at least, this is not a helpful term. The reader is invited to smile (sometimes wryly) more often than to weep as the stories unfold. David Trotter attributes the fact that 'the portrayal of working class life became increasingly light-hearted' during this period to a resurgence in popularity of more cheerful, Dickensian perspectives.[4] But there is also an informality, a kind of artlessness, in the style of many of these books – a suggestion of thinly veiled autobiography or reminiscence, an ordinariness of content that privileges the daily and familiar rather than the dramatic or tragic – that is characteristic of the suburban literary mode.

This informality can become problematic in a working-class context, where light-heartedness can sound a false note, particularly when it is expressed through humour. Peter Keating's comment that writers who wanted to give the working classes a voice rejected 'humour based on working-class ignorance and eccentricity' is true, but he fails to address the nature of the humour evident in many of these works, which always signals a distance between author and material.[5] The humour of many suburban working-class novels is qualitatively different from the laughter that we associate with Jerome K. Jerome's *Three Men in a Boat*, where happiness is a political act of community and equality and suburban living is unequivocally celebrated. Edwin Pugh and William Pett Ridge, both popular writers of novels about a working-class and lower-middle-class life that they knew from their own experience, show respect and affection for suburb-dwellers; but both writers often appear to be mere observers of the comedy of suburban manners. The same could also be said about H. G. Wells in his social comedies, which I will consider in more detail in the next chapter. At the other end of the spectrum, the Grossmiths' *The Diary of a Nobody* (1892) cleverly exploits this sense of distance. Initially a fortnightly entertainment for the middle-class purchasers of *Punch*, *The Diary of a Nobody* exemplifies the relentless debunking which was levelled at working-class aspirations. Its popularity with middle-class readers parallels the popularity of *Three Men in a Boat* with the working class, but it focuses on the absurdity of working-class suburban claims to better lives and finer feelings.

There were few novelists other than Arnold Bennett who were prepared to give the suburban working classes the serious literary treatment that had been given to the poor of the inner city. Shan Bullock is an exception. *Robert Thorne: The story of a London clerk* (1907) is one of the few novels of suburban working-class life to engage seriously with the impact that the instability of class and gender identities had on individuals. It explores the tension between the apparent broadening of horizons in modern life and the reality of daily struggle, and between traditional and modern social practices. Issues about education, marriage and self-improvement are dealt with in all working-class suburban novels, but Bullock's novel is closer to

Charles Kingsley's *Alton Locke* (1852) and Thomas Hardy's *Jude the Obscure* (1896) as a literary stepping-stone in the history of the working classes.

It is interesting to speculate about the extensive use of humour in writing about the working-class suburb. In *The Soul of London* (1905), Ford Madox Hueffer translates Conan Doyle's middle-class suburban visions of 'a common stage . . . where love and humour and fears and lights and shadows were so swiftly succeeding each other' into terms applicable to the working-class suburb: 'He [the observer] must only not sniff at the 'suburbs' as a place of small houses and dreary lives; he must remember that in each of these houses swells a strongly individualised human being with romantic hopes, romantic fears, and at the end, an always tragic death.'[6] The claim, not just for the intrinsic value of the ordinary, but for its almost Shakespearean grandeur seems more an intellectually articulated position than one of instinctive human sympathy. Although it is clearly informed by a positive response to the transformation of the working-classes from the 'masses' to 'individuals', the need to 'remember' indicates a conscious (socially motivated?) desire to value the suburbs and suburban lives which goes against an instinctive (personal?) desire to despise them – or, at the very least, not to be part of them. This them-and-us dialectic, with its sense of spatial distance and personal alienation, when translated into literary terms becomes narratorial distance, and also narratorial ambiguity. A reminder of Frances Wolseley's comment on suburban gardens is useful here. She acknowledges that she is glimpsing from a distance a way of life quite foreign to her privileged position, but what she observes are living manifestations of suburban life – the rows of gardens along the railway embankment with which she can identify. From what position can an author 'observe' the 'strongly individualised life' of the suburbs, or as Masterman wrote, 'reconstitute . . . the inner life of Pentonvillle or Camberwell'?[7]

William Pett Ridge and Edwin Pugh were two writers who wrote about working-class and lower-middle-class life from personal experience. Pugh, who was born in London and rose via a Board School education to be a successful writer after a short spell as a factory worker, can probably lay claim to being a working-class writer. Pett Ridge's background was lower-middle-class, but his experience as a clerk, first in the Civil Service and then for the railways, before he succeeded as a writer, gave him insight into the life of close routine and rigid commuting hours that he describes in his novels. These writers were themselves examples of the class flexibility which allowed upward mobility through self-help and determination, but also through public education and (for a writer) through the expanding possibilities in popular publishing. In none of their many novels do they invite the reader to 'sneer'; they always encourage the reader to appreciate the individuality of the apparently insignificant person. However, the fact that each writer was effectively declassed by his success had a considerable influence on their material. On the one hand, their insight into the nuances of class difference and the signs and practices of class redefinition is wonderfully revealing. On the other, there is a clear sense that they are looking back towards a world that they chose to leave. *Outside the Radius* (1899) by William Pett Ridge and *A Street in Suburbia* (1895) by Edwin Pugh both reveal the tension between their authors' personal experience of working-class life and their disengagement from it. The blend of humour, affection and compassion that characterises these novels does not suggest shared experience but rather a way of bridging their own sense of distance.

This is particularly true of Edwin Pugh's *A Street in Suburbia*, which generated a (short-lived) interest in writing about the lower-middle classes.[8] The street, as the title makes clear, is the organising principle of a collection of short stories about the residents of Marsh Street. The precise location of the street is deliberately vague. The fact that it is 'a' street argues for its representative function: it is typical of dreary building developments on drained marshland, over-shadowed by railway arches carrying the trains out to more remote and salubrious suburbs. On the other hand, once in Marsh Street, the notion of the suburbs shrinks to one street only, outside which little is relevant. The stories are confined to the one location, and those who leave, or arrive, or who might leave are only interesting in terms of their presence in Marsh Street at the present moment.

Pugh located the street in 'suburbia' in order to differentiate it from 'the suburbs', not in terms of topographical location but in terms of types of location, of building design and, significantly, of class. In naming the inner suburbs 'suburbia', Pugh articulated a growing consensus that the use of the word 'suburb' could not be allowed to stretch to include the public housing developments built in the 1890s with older suburban districts. The same word could not meaning-fully be used to describe the outlying beauties of Harrow, Richmond and Dulwich and the new estates designed for the working classes located at Wood Green, Walthamstow and beleaguered Clapham. However, while accepting the need to go along with common usage for the sake of clarity, he is careful to point out, in *The City of the World*, how words carry value judgements which can shape unintended meanings: 'Just now, we are constrained to accept them [the suburbs] at face value – or rather at the values that superior persons (mainly deriving from the suburbs) – have set upon them, in order that we may resolve some order out of the chaos of our present inquiry.'[9]

One of the meanings that suburbia evoked, but which is belied by the population of Marsh Street, is uniformity and fixity of class identity. Marsh Street contains a diversity of class elements which circle around the remnants of the traditionally defined working classes. At the lower end of the scale, there is visible poverty; wretchedly clothed schoolchildren play in 'the spaces' at the back of Marsh Place and a little girl nearly dies of exposure and starvation. The centre ground is held by the shopkeepers, the one clerk who commutes daily, and the workers at the local builders' merchant. At the higher end of the scale is Phil Evers, an educated but feckless young man who is waiting on the death of a relative to take up the economic and social status to which he feels entitled, and the narrator, who, like Phil, is in Marsh Street but not of it. The inhabitants of Marsh Street acknowledge his difference. They turn to him for advice when knowledge of the written word is required, as when he helps to explain the marriage service to Jack Cotter and when they set up the Marsh Street Hall Debating Society. Harry Cummers, the clerk, who is also an aspiring novelist, entrusts him with his unpublished manuscript. The narrator seems at one remove from Marsh Street life, observing a funeral through his 'spy-glass', playing the 'spy' on Harry and his doting mother, and sitting 'with my window open' to overhear 'the conversation of the two ladies'.[10]

The humour is largely created by the distance between the narrator, and to a lesser extent Phil Evers, and the other inhabitants of Marsh Street. The way that Jack Cotter sets about finding a wife by a process of eliminating in turn every eligible woman in the street; the rigid requirement that everyone turns out for Tony Burnett's funeral only to spend all their time criticising how little it cost; the residents' self-conscious dressing up, with 'their hair brushed down in an oily fringe over their pimply foreheads', for the occasion of the

opening night of the Marsh Street Hall Debating Society; are all
portrayed as amusing through the narrator's observing eye and the
implicit contrast that it sets up with middle-class protocols.

That the humour is affectionate but nonetheless class-based is
illustrated by Phil Evers's speech. In the funniest story of the collection, the debating society meets to debate the abolition of the House
of Lords, and the narrator is asked to propose the motion. When no
one in the audience responds, Phil Evers leaps to his feet and, in a
sustained piece of stand-up comedy, parodies the elaborate style of
public debating. In doing so he offends the audience, one of whom
protests: '"We come 'ere ter be elevated, an' a bloke gits up an' talks
a lot o' bloomin' rot."'[11] Language is a crucial signifier of class difference. In the first chapter, the narrator includes himself in the Marsh
Street community, but later, when he speaks in his own voice, it is
unaccented and educated, marked out in pronunciation and sophistication from his fellow Marsh Street inhabitants and competent in
formal usage as in the debate and the wedding service. However, the
reader is invited to laugh at the working classes when they lay claim
to social superiority by borrowing words from the class above them.
The word 'shop', for instance, is to be avoided at all costs, so the
'shops' on the street are named 'stores' and 'emporium', while the fish
and chip shop is called the Fish Supper Bar. Their way of establishing
distance from the class below them – 'the class they designated "low
people"' – is essentially no different from the middle-class strategy of
received pronunciation, but only one strategy deserves to be laughed
at.[12]

The desire to tell the story of the daily and the ordinary and to
invest with value the lives of the new suburbanites clearly posed a
moral and a literary problem. The moral problem lay with an author
who had diligently left this world behind and, while appreciating its
strengths, was all too aware of its limitations. What kind of honesty
would be appropriate? This moral dilemma had a political edge.
Celebrating working-class lives would run the risk of romanticising
them; constructing a critique would belittle what individuals had
struggled so hard to achieve. Pugh resolves this dilemma through
a humour that treads a difficult tightrope. In *The City of the World*,
he discusses some of the difficulties of finding a suitable fictional form
for suburban stories of working class life. Here his voice is centre
stage and his opinions more fully articulated. Humour gives way
entirely to passion, lyricism, and to an awareness of the place of the

new suburbanites in London's history and their role as the victims of capitalism. He argues that the apparently 'small world of suburbia' is analogous to the way the smallest pebble tells the history of the world's geological formations. Suburbia needs to be interpreted in evolutionary terms because 'these dwellers in the hinterland of London stay where chance has flung them and strike their roots into the soil', forming the basis of London's identity.[13] The smallness of suburbanites is only an illusion, fostered by their exploitation in an economy which has divested them of power, reducing them to servile and anonymous 'black-coated hordes'. In fact, it is 'the suburbs that feed the City'.[14] Humour, we discover, is a distancing technique and a survival strategy for those who know about and deplore the conditions of life of the suburban working classes. If you don't laugh, you will cry, is the message behind his explanation:

> One must learn the trick of being unaffectedly interested in their sayings and doings, their thoughts and their emotions, and genuinely but not spitefully amused by their follies and their weaknesses. Given this power, however, one has at once an easy, ready means of diversion always at hand, which will outlast a lifetime. And it is only in this spirit that one may hope to look on without one's vision being blurred by angry tears at the farcical tragedy of this travesty of life as it is not lived but wasted.[15]

Pugh's political argument concludes with the romantic vision that he shunned in his fiction. In language reminiscent of the suburban romances, he consoles the suburbanites by reinforcing their hopes of domestic bliss, for which men 'offer up their empty bodies as a sacrifice', and which women create 'out of that unfailing mint whose currency bears the magical impress of love'.[16]

William Pett Ridge's *Outside the Radius: Stories of a London suburb* (1899), like *A Street in Suburbia*, is a series of short stories linked by a common location, but it is also a more specific response to a range of contemporary class issues.[17] The title establishes the location's topographical marginality; its name – 'The Crescent' – confirms its upwardly mobile credentials, while its identity as a cul-de-sac reinforces the closedness and completeness of its world. The Crescent is the protagonist of the first story and the chief character in the book, containing, shaping and investing with meaning the lives of all the people who live in it. It is in itself a symbol of all suburbs: it is suspended somewhere between the Common and the Old Town at the

very end of the London tram-line. It is only twelve years old, but it is
'historic'.[18] It is a site of class and age diversity – its inhabitants range
from a 'shop-woman', who married well, to an up-and-coming young
doctor; crucially, it is a site of class war – between family members,
between neighbours and between families and their servants. The
class identity of 'The Crescent' is unfathomable; it is busy working
out what class it is for itself.

The prevailing tone of the opening story is amusement. The
narrator watches the daily round of the suburb's activities as if from
a window (the reader later discovers that he does indeed live in The
Crescent), and these routines are held up for our amusement. The
pattern of the day is uniform, from the 8.20 a.m. departure of 'its
grown-up male inhabitants in search of gold', to the later exodus of
'small babies . . . in their hooded carriages', to the eventual return of
'the detachment which went off in the morning to attack the City
and to loot it'.[19] The inflated language provokes laughter, but a laughter tempered at the end of the chapter by an authorial warning:
'I find that to declare life in The Crescent dull and monotonous is a
mere pretence; outwardly that may be so; in point of fact there are
romances in every house'.[20] These 'romances', framed by the absurdity of suburban rituals but legitimised by the assurance that they
will reveal the real value of suburban life, have the effect of bridging
the distance that the humour sets up, but never eliminating it. Even
the scope of tragic stories, such as 'Mrs Carthew's Son', which are
dealt with entirely seriously, is diminished by their place as part of the
suburban emotional spectrum. Suburban people may be valuable, but
ultimately that value is taken by a smaller measure.

Within the individual stories, the humour in *Outside the Radius*
invariably revolves around issues of class. The inhabitants of The
Crescent are working out whether they are all the same, or each of a
different and distinct class. One of the homogenising forces at work
on them is commuting. The relentless imperatives of transport and
office hours, and the day-time abandonment of the suburb to mothers,
widows, children and the elderly, the serenity of evenings and the
sacrosanct nature of Sunday, provide a timetable for everyone. But
Pett Ridge makes clear that the conformity enforced by economic
and social structures conceals a jostling for relative class position.
The inhabitants assume different class identities through house
names, such as The Oaks and The Beeches for some, Beau Rivage
and St Moritz for others, and Beethoven Villa for yet another. In the

evening, aspiring City bank clerks pretend to a leisured existence, emerging in 'white flannels and straw hats'.[21] All scan one another for signs of class identity such as the names on their removal vans or audible dropped aitches. Their pasts are subtly questioned for social transgressions or low birth. The reader watches, as if through a telescope, the panorama of a human habitat and its differentiating practices: its usage (always 'hall', never 'passage'); its origins ('All my people live at Kensington'); its status ('The Benschers came on promotion from a suburb less important than ours'); its sense of self-esteem ('Mrs Gascoigne found herself prevented from engaging in any domestic occupation whatever'); its economic requirements ('The Crescent's idea of disbursing £600 a year').[22]

The apparent middle-class identity of this suburb, so carefully preserved and nurtured by its inhabitants, is betrayed by their continual uncertainty and insecurity and by their failure, despite all their declarations, to come up with a definition for it that is not instantly relativised by changes, events and additional information. This identity is further complicated by the class status of the narrator who, while living in The Crescent, is never simply the 'neighbour' that he pretends to be. His omniscience, his human sympathy and his values that endorse the 'genuine', label his viewpoint as liberal middle-class. His class certainty further exposes the pretensions of those whom he observes, and shrinks the emotional scale of the stories as he questions or endorses their attitudes and behaviour. It is the narrator who educates the reader's social and emotional responses. 'I liked her [Mrs. Gregory] at once, I could see that she was genuine', he tells the reader about a young shop-woman who has married a middle-class husband, and who attends afternoon classes to improve herself.[23] On the other hand, 'The moment I observed Mrs Pulborough come out of Number Nine with an elaborate card-case in her hand, exhibited so that all The Crescent might see, I knew there would be trouble'.[24]

But it is the servants who are the living proof of the confused nature of The Crescent's middle-class identity and the measure of right feeling. Detached from class anxieties, allocated one per house in houses too small to accommodate them, and employed to prove the middle-class status of women who have only recently risen above domestic chores themselves, the servants watch, listen and compare notes with each other. They often organise their respective households, as in 'The Education of Mrs Gregory'. They identify with emotional rightness and reject convention with contempt. In their role as the voice of common sense, they intervene in the affairs of their masters and mistresses with cavalier confidence, as Miss Braithwaite's servant does in 'The Case of Dr Law'. Mrs Tempest's servant conspires with her against her husband in 'The Taming of Captain Tempest', while Mrs Gascoigne's servant, Martha, engineers her mistress's escape in 'A Dash for Freedom'. It is clear that their level-headedness is a greater virtue in the suburbs than the anxious pretension of their employers, while the equality that they tacitly claim again shows the ambiguity of class boundaries.

This class confusion also has the effect of confusing the source of Pett Ridge's humour. Just what are he and his readers amused by? The jokes, the gentle mockery, the affectionate humour all encourage the reader to laugh with the narrator at those who are struggling to forge an identity in a class-conscious society and to better their economic and domestic conditions. His central insight – that true feeling is embodied in the servant class and in those who reject social pretensions – creates a conflict both with the aspirations of the suburbanites he is portraying and with his middle-class narratorial voice. A contemporary reviewer feels no such conflict, praising Pett Ridge in terms that coincide comfortably with contemporary class values, and claiming that 'he never for an instant stands aloof from his characters to laugh at or scorn their foibles or failings . . . Mr Pett Ridge sees that even in a commonplace suburb the main levels of life are at work – Love, Ambition, Shame, Sacrifice'.[25]

In *Mord Em'ly* (1898), William Pett Ridge brings a different perspective to this complex relationship between class and humour, and he is more successful in conveying the absurdities of suburban pretensions without the ambiguity that the avuncular humour of the narrator figure can bring to his accounts of suburban life.[26] The reader sees the world through the eyes of Mord Em'ly herself. She is one of life's survivors, who was brought up in a State orphanage after her mother's death and forced to make her own way in life. This is Pett Ridge at his best. His ear for everyday, casual repartee, and his celebration of the way that her endearing mixture of practicality, sentimentality and cynicism effectively deals with her problems, exposes the thin line between Mord Em'ly's own social position and that of the family she works for in Peckham, and the different values that they espouse.

Much of the humour still arises from the clash of cultures, as Mord Em'ly learns that her function is as a status symbol as much as a servant, since visitors must not 'imagine for a moment that we don't keep a maid', and that if she cannot pronounce her own name properly ('You should say Maud, and then wait for a moment, and then say Em-ily') she will be renamed Laura – presumably because it cannot easily be translated into her dialect.[27] But this humour does not supply the dynamic of the novel, which lies in Mord Em'ly's exuberance and her pleasure in the energy and colour that is London. The uniformity of the houses, where 'No. 18 was precisely like No. 17, and like No. 19', and the claustrophobia of the tiny bedroom that she occupies in Peckham, where she has to stand on the furniture to see the sky, seem outward signs to her of a deeper malaise in the suburbs: 'That people should so carefully abstain from taking advantage with both hands of the happiness that life offers', she thinks with dismay, 'appeared . . . to be a minor form of insanity'.[28]

Mord Em'ly runs away from Peckham, lured by the forces of life and the sociability promised by images of Elephant and Castle on a Saturday night. But to return to a working-class existence in the inner city is not an option that Pett Ridge offers. Mord Em'ly, despite her passionate love of London, opts for emigration to Australia, a new kind of New World which, by implication, joins the forces of natural energy and integrity with those of social progress and middle-class aspiration. In this vision, the suburbs have succeeded in providing a means to social improvement and betterment, but, from the youthful perspective of Mord Em'ly, at a terrible cost to the simple joys of human connection and spontaneity.

Dickens's portrayals of Bob Cratchit in *A Christmas Carol* (1843), Uriah Heep in *David Copperfield* (1850) and Wemmick in *Great Expectations* (1861) made the clerk a familiar literary figure, but the emergence of the so-called clerk class during the 1890s submerged the possibility of a Dickensian individuality. Their identity was that of an anonymous mass, a strange mutation of the working classes that had been generated by industrial concentration and, in London, by the City's international role as a centre of commerce. The clerk has already made several appearances in novels discussed in this book, but few writers attempted to pluck a single individual from the clerk class and to place such a sorry figure at the centre of their work. Shan Bullock, in *Robert Thorne: The story of a London clerk* (1907), and Edwin Pugh, in *The Broken Honeymoon* (1908), were two writers who took up the challenge.[29]

In *Robert Thorne*, the figure of the clerk holds the key to the future of British civilisation. In his history of Robert Thorne, from his decision to study for a job in the Civil Service to his decision to emigrate to New Zealand, Shan Bullock raises the question as to whether the apparently ordinary and predictable lives of Thorne, his friends and his colleagues are a sign of mediocrity and of the decline of civilisation into mechanistic and emasculated conformity, or whether such characters are the true nurturers of civilised values and the hope of the future in a world distorted by unregulated capitalism. This novel constructs its authenticity and its link with traditional realism through the narrator's claim that he is simply making public the story that Robert Thorne had told him. The occasional explanatory footnote reminds the reader of the veracity of the account during its progress, and the wealth of realistic detail in the descriptions of office and suburban life substantiates it.

Domestic life in the suburbs is contrasted with life in the City, and each is shown to carry both positive and negative connotations. The suburbs offer the possibility of domesticity, personal value and self-betterment, but at the cost of public conformity and anonymity and, worse, of a commitment to the economic treadmill. The personal values cultivated in the suburb – honesty, hard work and domestic stability – are commendable public virtues, but also ones on which capitalism is able to build a compliant workforce. In the office Robert finds companions and friends, and through his determination to succeed, the impetus to pursue his education and explore his cultural heritage. The social interactions of workplace and home ultimately give him a level of experience and self-awareness that enables him to make a decision about his own future at the end of the novel.

Two familiar issues encircle the clerk's identity: class and gender. At first success as a clerk promises Robert worldly advancement and the hope of a career. The hard work and self-sacrifice that studying for his Civil Service examinations requires seem in themselves a promise of some future reward, while going to London and taking up a position at Somerset House seem to be a first step on the ladder. His experience at work rapidly proves the opposite: there is no way forward. Only the slimmest chance of promotion beckons at the end of long years of unquestioning service. Frustrated at work, his desire for knowledge becomes privatised as a personal pleasure. He visits the National Gallery and British Museum. After he is married, his

wife Nell and he read to each other from Dickens, Jane Austen and
Walter Scott as 'lighter reading', and 'otherwise Carlyle, Shakespeare,
Tennyson', while Robert includes Arnold, Huxley, Darwin and Virgil
in his own reading.[30]

In the office, his colleague Mr Cherry's obsessive rituals (reminiscent of an earlier clerk in Herman Melville's short story 'Bartleby
the Scrivener') daily remind Robert of the possibility of mental
illness. This pathological response to office work is absent from
Dickens's portrayal of Wemmick in *Great Expectations*, perhaps
because of the domestic fortifications he erects to keep the office out
and the personal in, but it is characteristic of writing from the 1890s
onwards. One of the earliest glimpses of what was to come is Mark
Rutherford's conscious annihilation of personality in the workplace
in *Autobiography and Deliverance* (1885) and his adoption of 'two
selves' so that 'my true self was not stained by contact with my other
self'.[31] Perhaps even more shocking is the statement in *Robert Thorne*
that Oliver, Robert's colleague and friend, makes about his situation:
'I was born to be a fossil', he tells Robert, acknowledging that he is
an evolutionary cul-de-sac. For the same reason, however, he sees
himself as a necessary provider of more clerks: 'Clerks are made to get
married and keep up the population', he adds.[32] Undeterred by this
pessimism, Robert determines to write an alternative evolutionary
history; after each experience, he notches up more mental 'rings', like
a maturing tree.

While being fixed in his class identity, the gender identity of a
clerk is problematic. The accusation of unmanliness, thrown at
Robert when he first tells his father of his desire to train for the Civil
Service, carries with it the weight of the contemporary debate about
the crisis of masculinity and the future of Empire. To work with a pen
while physically cooped up in an office was seen as an insult to manhood, and indeed one of Robert's earliest sensations at work is of
being 'small', while simultaneously unnerved by the masculine ethos
of the office, where drinking, joking and stratagems for avoiding work
are expressions of frustrated energies. As he becomes more familiar
with the routines of the working day, it is leaving the workplace that
returns him to his manhood as 'the self that at four o'clock flung
off its office coat and strode manfully out'.[33] Paradoxically, then,
his manhood is rediscovered in the suburbs where friendships, love
and marriage, free time and the security of home are found in the
feminised domestic realm.

Their delight in the companionship of marriage is further evidence of the clerk's feminisation. Robert's friend Oliver, 'branded' by
his misery at work, is 'fully content' at his rented home in Peckham.
Mr Hope, an office paragon who is later jettisoned by his employers,
is a different man at home with his devoted and creative wife. After
their marriage, for Robert and Nell 'Each day was a great thing . . .
we were the centre of our own little world. Home. Ourselves.'[34] Later,
in a passage which strikes a remarkably modern note, Robert passes
a group of his friends as he pushes the pram across the park, but
although he is uncomfortably aware that they will find him ridiculous, his pleasure in his first child rapidly reasserts itself. The corollary of the crushing dehumanisation of the workplace is the feminised
man, glad to be home, glad to be married, glad to be a father – a type
we have already met in the suburban romances of Doyle and Howard
– but a phenomenon revealed as part of a process of social transformation by Shan Bullock.

Again we find that society's future is inscribed in the suburbs,
even if, in *Robert Thorne*, that future has several versions. In the first
and most obvious version, the suburbs are the geography of class
mobility. Robert begins his London career in a rented room in
Kennington; he moves to a small rented flat in Dulwich, looking
'over a garden on a railway embankment', and later to a house at
Denmark Hill. Mr Hope, at the peak (and, as it turns out, at the end)
of his career at Somerset House, lives in his own house in Brixton
with attractive gardens at the front and rear; while Mr Willard, Nell's
wealthy father, lives in a splendid villa set in its own grounds at
Camberwell. The layout of this class geography is described in a long
passage worth quoting in full:

> It interested us [Robert and Nell] greatly, for instance, to explore the
> various, residential zones of our neighbourhood, passing from the hum-
> ble little roads of our own particular zone, each with its two rows of
> grey-brick houses, all precisely alike, all narrow, crowded, ugly, yet
> every one of them a home; to pass from these out into the brighter zone
> where the houses had brass knockers and letter boxes, and flower beds
> in front, and small gardens behind, and attics in the roof where the ser-
> vants slept. Thence into the genteel air of the red-brick villa region,
> some detached and screened from the vulgar gaze by privet hedges or
> high oak fences, some only semi-detached and protected by no more
> than a metal-work fence and what Mrs Hope called a bed-quilt lawn, so
> at last reaching the impressive district, where, behind high brick walls
> or amidst sheltering trees, stood the residences of the great.[35]

This description is not materially different from many others in sub-urban literature, but its interest in *Robert Thorne* is that Robert's and Nell's hobby is to walk the class map and to dream about occupying favourable spaces on it.

Of course, the class map is also an economic map. The positive aspect of class mobility is overshadowed by the economic realities at its foundations. 'It was a goodly way, we knew, from an attic in Kennington to a villa in Surbiton', Robert recognises soon after his arrival in London – and he isn't talking about travelling time.[36] Mov-ing upwards usually means two things: more work and/or more debt, and moral compromise and/or moral conformity. Oliver works in the evening to supplement his wages and to pay for his two-room flat in Peckham. When Robert and Nell marry, they have to buy all their furniture on hire purchase, and they are in debt for the first ten years of their marriage, tying Robert irrevocably to his clerk's desk. Even the better-off are not exempt. Mr Willard and his family live in relat-ive affluence in Camberwell until the failure of his business, followed shortly afterwards by his death, leads to the sale of their home, while Mr and Mrs Hope have to leave for the country when he is made unexpectedly redundant. Inasmuch as the design and occupation of the suburbs is an economic exercise, the suburbs offer no escape from the structural forces that destroy the inner city and send people to them for refuge. If the promise of the suburbs fails, where next?

Like Mord Em'ly, Robert and Nell decide to emigrate, after Robert has realised that the clerk is caught in what he calls a 'heroic pretence'. The realisation comes gradually through his own experi-ences, and through listening to and watching others. This is not the pretence of the 'pretentious'. Robert believes that each individual knows what is happening – the members of the clerk class know that 'our houses are jerry-built, our clothes shoddy, our food adulterated, ourselves not what we are', but they see this as the sacrifice they accept for 'civilisation'.[37] Like the soldiers who would fight the First World War only seven years later, they are heroic, because they endure this knowledge. They step 'valiantly to work through all the hazards of London winter weather'; they 'walk steadily on' whatever diversion offers itself on either side; they are 'to be respected'. What helps them to endure is that entirely suburbanised, feminised ideal, 'that ennobling thing, the love of a good woman'; the soldiers likewise would later sing 'Keep the Home Fires Burning' while they dreamed of 'Homes Fit for Heroes'.[38]

6

'the humble little roads of our particular zone, with its two rows of grey-brick houses, all precisely alike, all narrow, crowded, ugly, yet every one of them a home'

Markhouse Avenue, Walthamstow (1905)

It seems surprising that C. F. G. Masterman, who must have been reading *Robert Thorne* even as he was writing his chapter on 'The Suburbans' for *The Condition of England*, thought that there was 'humour in the struggles of Robert Thorne' and that Robert 'could yet be content'.[39] There are certainly humorous incidents, and Robert is certainly a survivor; but Masterman failed to recognise that his character is constructed as a 'thorn' in the side of the system, and that Bullock's vision is a radical one. Back in the late 1880s and the early 1890s, it was possible to envision the suburbs as the location of the future. In his novel Bullock shows how that dream has been subverted by the forces of the market and, inadvertently, by the virtues of the clerk class who share it. Thorne's decision to emigrate transfers his hopes and dreams to the new world of New Zealand.

Edwin Pugh's *The Broken Honeymoon* was published a year after *Robert Thorne*, in 1908, but despite strong similarities between the two novels Pugh's focus is on the personal rather than the political. Framed by the imperatives of life as a clerk, and by the restraint that the exigencies of such a life demand, the narrative tells the story of Ferdinand and Rosetta. It explores the nature of love, and the possibility that love may provide an alternative version of self-definition from that of the workplace in a suburban situation. Ferdinand's view of marriage is initially coloured by romanticised assumptions about what love is. When he first sets out to convince the sceptical Rosetta that love and marriage are valuable and enduring, he deploys conventional images. Marriage, he declares, 'will be a long winding road . . . There will be storm and shine, darkness and light, bitter cold and angry blasts . . . [but] we may drive home at last, hand in hand, with all our sorrows forgotten.'[40] As they walk in the moonlight, 'the aspect of the jerry-built streets was magically transformed into the semblance of some city of enchantments'.[41] How difficult it is to apply this attitude to daily realities is something that he discovers in the course of the novel. The reader, however, is immediately aware of the particular dangers that he faces. Ferdinand proposes to Rosetta in a suburban park, where 'Nature' is 'trimmed and clipped and garnished' and confined 'within the circumscribed bounds of that neat green London park'.[42] The familiar link between suburban home and marriage, and the conflation of being in love and love itself are both interrogated in the context of a suburban nature that has lost its naturalness.

Ferdinand's and Rosetta's 'ordinary six-roomed habitation in a part of Kentish Town that called itself, with a colourable show of reason, South Hampstead' turns out to be a site of gender conflict and of sexual disappointment.[43] Brought up by a maiden aunt after the death of his parents, sent to boarding school from the age of eight and employed as a solicitor's clerk in his uncle's office before moving to London, Ferdinand is emotionally sensitive but sexually inexperienced. His marriage freezes his desire for Rosetta and his first sexual experience, on his wedding night, fills him with self-disgust. Ashamed at discovering what he experiences as his animal nature, he feels he has shattered the 'sex-illusion' he had believed in.[44] What is interesting about Pugh's treatment of this episode is that, in this case, his focus is not on the tension between the public and private person (the City clerk and the suburban husband) but on the conflict between Ferdinand's image of himself as a man and the masculine self he has not yet discovered (between suburban conventions and suburban possibilities).

The resolution of the conflict is facilitated by Ella Candlish, a friend of Rosetta's, and explained in gender terms:

> There is a great deal of the woman in you, Ferdinand. It is just because there is so much of the woman in you that you are not so successful with women as men of a coarser fibre are, usually. And whilst I am on that subject I would like to say that the two sexes do very often get mixed up in the same body, far more than is commonly supposed. There are lots of great bearded giants with gruff voices striding about whose flesh and blood is the only masculine part of them. And there are just as many fair, fluffy, clinging young damsels whose femininity goes no deeper than the skin.[45]

Ferdinand's 'feminised' masculinity is shown to be the truth of his sexuality: Rosetta's scepticism about romance, on the other hand, her practicality over the details of finding a home and her refusal to accept Ferdinand's sexual alienation argue a 'masculine' rationality. Through this realisation comes a mature love based on understanding and tolerance; and it is this hard-won knowledge, rather than the moonlight and romantic fantasies, that tips the novel's balance in favour of the suburbs and legitimises the lives of those whom society ignores or despises.

It is interesting to read *The Broken Honeymoon* in the light of Pugh's political position on birth control as he outlined it in *The Great Unborn* (1918).[46] Inspired by a collection of letters received in

1915 by the Women's Co-operative Guild in response to a request for information about pregnancy and childbirth, and horrified by the number of young men who were dying in the war, Pugh argues that women must gain control of their own fertility so that children can reach their individual potential rather than be casually produced according to a masculine agenda to be used as cannon fodder in war or surplus labour in peacetime. Pugh's clearly articulated feminist argument, written out of conviction rather than in hope of financial gain (as he claims himself in the introduction, it is an unlikely publishing prospect), reinforces the ethos of The Broken Honeymoon – that civilisation consists in an affirmation of the domestic realm which is supported and shared by the feminised man. Michael Wilding's argument for a fresh reading of classic authors of this period, 'resituating them in the context of specific thinking on society and politics', applies equally to novels that have been relegated to obscurity. When read through 'specific thinking' about class and location in early twentieth-century England, both The Broken Honeymoon and Robert Thorne reveal 'the repressed radical components of their fiction' which confront and rebut portrayals of the romantic and the ridiculous in working class life.[47]

The Diary of a Nobody (1892), by George and Weedon Grossmith, brings together the theme of the clerk class and the issue of humour in representations of the working class. Ironically (although not surprisingly), The Diary of a Nobody is the most famous piece of writing about the suburbs of this period. If Three Men in a Boat is the most complete piece of suburban literature, combining in energetic zest a suburban vision, a suburban voice and a suburban readership, then The Diary of a Nobody is its polar opposite, a suburban anti-vision articulated in a middle-class voice for a middle-class readership.[48] A summary of its story also shows its adversarial relationship with other clerk fiction such as the novels of Shan Bullock and Edwin Pugh. Charles Pooter, a middle-aged and hard-working clerk, moves to a house in a railway suburb that embodies his dreams of social advancement. His social life and his household management are derived from middle-class models, and his hope for future promotion is dependent on middle-class power. Devoted to his wife, Carrie, and the very soul of integrity and hard work, he finally wins his promotion and, with it, the deeds to his house. Versions of such a plot (with diverse resolutions) can be found in any of the novels discussed in this chapter and in many others besides: but in *The Diary of Nobody* it is the source of a brilliant satire on the aspirations of the lower classes. The humour in *The Diary of a Nobody* is not generated simply by funny incidents, such as Pooter's painting the bath red in Bohemian style, nor by an authorial stance such as Pett Ridge's or Pugh's attitude of humanist social observation. The humour lies in the mismatch between Pooter's own (suburban working-class) assessment of his life and the thoughts and activities he considers worth recording in his diary, and the author's (urban middle-class) view of the inherent absurdity of his displays of self-value.

Because 'Pooter' has become synonymous with modern definitions of suburban identity – boring, respectable, full of inflated self-importance and a social climber obsessed with outward show – it is almost impossible to criticise the class orientation of *The Diary of a Nobody* without seeming to be unable to get the joke, being overly serious, or simply exchanging one prejudice for another. On the other hand, it is impossible to laugh at Pooter's endless struggles (and it is almost impossible not to) without unconsciously assuming a position of middle-class superiority. All critics encounter the same difficulty without necessarily realising it. For instance, when W. E. Williams confidently identified the English as a nation whose disarming idiosyncrasy is to recognise 'that we are as absurd as we are depicted', in his introduction to a 1945 edition, he clearly felt that his comment was unproblematically inclusive.[49] Yet how could he be so sure that every reader would agree? Surely 'we' are much readier to acknowledge our neighbour's absurdity than our own. More recently Kate Flint claimed that *The Diary of a Nobody* was 'at one and the same time a celebration and a gentle critique', but she fails to address the question of what exactly the readers are being invited to celebrate, other than their deeply relieved personal conviction that they are not Pooter.[50] I would argue that the pleasure and the laughter for readers does not lie in a recognition of the delightful absurdities of human behaviour, but in the certain knowledge that Pooter is different from, and less than, themselves.

The popularity of *The Diary of a Nobody* when it was published lay in the subtlety with which it identified the class insecurities of its period, and empowered those who felt threatened by suburban growth and class change. The simple practice of applying different criteria to the same activities according to the class identity of those involved provided a social safety-valve that has become a part of modern culture. Reading a book, taking a holiday, moving to a new home, gardening, entertaining friends or seeking promotion at work (to list just a few examples) were suitable, even sophisticated activities for the middle class. But when Pooter does them, they become the presumptuous, imitative, vulgar and ridiculous pretensions of the working class. This is nowhere so cruelly apparent as in the Grossmith brothers' treatment of the middle classes' own prized values – love, marriage and domesticity. Pooter is loyal and loving to his wife, Carrie; he is endlessly concerned with the well-being of his son, Lupin; and he spends much of his time gardening and decorating. He is the feminised suburban man so frequently celebrated both in romantic and in realist novels. But in *The Diary of a Nobody*, the reader is under no illusion: Pooter's suburban values simply prove that the working classes have been fooled.

It is a form of critical cheating to measure fiction by fact, but the claims to realism made by Pett Ridge, Edwin Pugh and Shan Bullock, and the satirical social commentary of *The Diary of a Nobody* deserve examination. One measurement can be taken from rare accounts of the lives of railway clerks gathered by the *New Survey* team in the late 1920s and early 1930s in a farsighted attempt to record the daily lives of those 'members of a class that is generally inarticulate'.[51] These railway clerks and their families wrote in their own words about their lives in suburbs such as Willesden, Hornsey and Chadwell Heath, usually in London County Council public housing. One clerk had succeeded in becoming a homeowner, and he felt that he and his family were 'fortunate in having a house to ourselves'.[52] Tucked away at the back of the volume, these accounts provide a moving insight into the level of thriftiness and hard work demanded of working men and their families. Survival depended on a steady, responsible and hard-working husband, and a wife who was a competent house-keeper, a good mother and a loyal companion. There was no room for illness at one end of the scale or extravagance at the other. For those who aspired to something better, time had to be squeezed out of evenings and weekends for educational classes, union activities, reading and the family.

When these accounts were written, they arguably represented the zenith of clerkly achievement, a distinctive stage in working-class upward mobility. Freed from the narratorial uncertainty of declassed writers such as William Pett Ridge and Edwin Pugh and, therefore, from the humorous perspective which, however affectionate or self-protective, consolidated their class identity rather than their individual identity, these men emerge into suburban history as Robert Thornes, rather than Leonard Basts, Harry Cummers and Charles Pooters. Their accounts show them to be reflective, educated and hard-working, with a strong focus on family activities and a lively political awareness. Although still officially categorised as working-class by *The New Survey*, these men and their families had already redefined what that meant. It is likely their children were among those who benefited from the inception of the welfare state and the access that it gave to grammar school and university education as the working classes continued to press for better opportunities after the Second World War.

Notes

1 'The Formation of London Suburbs', *The Times* (25 June 1904), 8.
2 Edwin Pugh, [1908] *The City of the World: A book about London and the Londoner* (London: Nelson and Sons, 1912), 30–33.
3 Harris, *Private Lives*, Lady Bell, cited in 115.
4 Trotter, *The English Novel in History*, 128–130.
5 P. J. Keating, *Working-class stories of the 1890s* (London: Routledge and Kegan Paul, 1971), xi.
6 Ford Madox Hueffer, *The Soul of London* (London: Duckworth and Co., 1905), xv.
7 C. F. G. Masterman, [1902] *From the Abyss*, extract in P. J. Keating, *Into Unknown England, 1866–1913: Selections from the social explorers* (Manchester: Manchester University Press, 1976), 26.
8 Edwin Pugh, *A Street in Suburbia* (London: Heinemann, 1895).
9 Pugh, *The City of the World*, 65.
10 *A Street in Suburbia*, 104, 71, 108.
11 *A Street in Suburbia*, 66.
12 *A Street in Suburbia*, 89.
13 *The City of the World*, 64, 65.
14 *The City of the World*, 123, 127.
15 *The City of the World*, 124.
16 *The City of the World*, 127.
17 William Pett Ridge, *Outside the Radius: Stories of a London suburb* (London: Hodder and Stoughton, 1899).
18 *Outside the Radius*, 3.
19 *Outside the Radius*, 8, 10, 16.
20 *Outside the Radius*, 20.
21 *Outside the Radius*, 16.
22 *Outside the Radius*, 25, 28, 215, 196, 237.
23 *Outside the Radius*, 31.
24 *Outside the Radius*, 313.

25 Review of *Outside the Radius* in *Bookman*, 17 (February 1900), 153.
26 William Pett Ridge, *Mord Em'ly* (London: C. Arthur Pearson, 1901).
27 *Mord Em'ly*, 35, 33.
28 *Mord Em'ly*, 42.
29 Shan Bullock, *Robert Thorne: The story of a London clerk* (London: T. Werner Laurie, 1907); Edwin Pugh, *The Broken Honeymoon* (London: John Milne, 1908).
30 *Robert Thorne*, 180.
31 Mark Rutherford, [1885] *Autobiography and Deliverance* (Leicester: Leicester University Press, 1969), 250. In fact Bartleby, in Herman Melville's short story, predates this, but in an American context.
32 *Robert Thorne*, 41.
33 *Robert Thorne*, 73.
34 *Robert Thorne*, 173.
35 *Robert Thorne*, 207.
36 *Robert Thorne*, 30.
37 *Robert Thorne*, 249.
38 *Robert Thorne*, 137.
39 Masterman, *The Condition of England*, 78.
40 *The Broken Honeymoon*, 92.
41 *The Broken Honeymoon*, 94.
42 *The Broken Honeymoon*, 92.
43 *The Broken Honeymoon*, 146. Searching for a home and its attendant conflicts are considered in detail by Shan Bullock and Edwin Pugh. For a tragic ending to this particular theme, see W. J. Dawson, 'The Transformation of John Loxley', in *London Idylls* (London: Hodder and Stoughton, 1895), 145–178.
44 *The Broken Honeymoon*, 191.
45 *The Broken Honeymoon*, 309–310.
46 Edwin Pugh, *The Great Unborn: A dream of tomorrow* (London: C. Palmer and Hayward, 1918).
47 Michael Wilding, *Social Visions* (Sydney: Sydney University Press, 1993), 2.
48 For a full discussion of *Punch*'s anti-suburban campaign, see Hapgood '"The New Suburbanites"', 36–40.
49 George and Weedon Grossmith, [1892] *The Diary of a Nobody* (Harmondsworth: Penguin, 1945). Editor's Note, 11.
50 Kate Flint, 'Introduction' in George and Weedon Grossmith, *The Diary of a Nobody* (New York and Oxford: Oxford University Press, 1995), vii. Overall this is a highly informative introduction to the novel.
51 'A Worker's Family Life from the Inside', *The New Survey*, vol. 9, part 4, 391–431 (393).
52 'A Worker's Family Life', 395.

8

THE SUBURBAN CUL-DE-SAC

George Gissing

H. G. Wells

I N my two concluding chapters I want to discuss a group of four writers who demonstrated in their work both the coincidences and the antagonisms of literary representations of the suburbs. My sense of them as a group comes partly from their position in the literary marketplace in the 1890s. George Gissing, H. G. Wells, Arnold Bennett and G. K. Chesterton, though educated, intelligent and talented, were not university men (although H. G. Wells aspired to be) or members of the London literary establishment. Each of them had to establish his reputation and earn his living on his own merits under rapidly changing literary conditions. Wells was a crucial part of the group. He was a lifelong friend of Gissing, of Bennett and, despite considerable differences and ideological quarrels, of Chesterton. The bond that held Chesterton and him together, Wells claimed, was that they both hated equally 'the spectacle of human beings blown up with windy wealth and irresponsible power . . . [and detested] the complex causes that dwarf and cripple lives from the moment of birth, and starve and debase great masses of mankind'.[1] This was a view that the whole group more or less shared, but which each understood in a fundamentally different way.

These writers drew on similar material, and they were all concerned with the same contemporary issues: the new reading public and the fragmenting cultural environment, the nature of London's expansion and its new populations, and the changing relations, particularly sexual relations, between men and women. All of them, to a greater or lesser degree, focused on the suburbs and on the lives of the new suburbanites as a crucial element in understanding the future direction of their culture and civilisation. All of them grappled with the idea of the 'ordinary', and with the problem of writing about a social identity that had no history of individuation and yet appeared to mark a turning point in a thousand years of western culture, and even to hold the fate of that history and culture in its hands. Their political, moral and social perspectives on this overwhelming issue were inevitably mediated by their personal histories and individual temperaments, which, in turn, shaped a dazzling spectrum of literary responses. I begin with George Gissing and H. G. Wells, both of whom explored the failure of the suburban vision; and I continue with Arnold Bennett and G. K. Chesterton, whose faith in the extraordinary nature of the ordinary was never diminished.

George Gissing was the suburbs' severest and most effective critic, drawing a line under the possibilities of the suburbs even as many of his intellectual contemporaries were envisioning the future in a suburban image. Several of the novels that he wrote during the 1890s are remarkable for the way in which they raised criticism of the suburban way of life above the level of self-interested complaint or anxious social commentary to make a powerful literary and political statement. Focusing on the same issues that concerned all critics of the suburbs – the debasement of traditional culture and its implications for domestic life and gender identity – Gissing mapped out a bleak and disturbing suburban terrain. He exposed as an illusion the apparent openness of the suburbs which was suggested by notions of territorial expansion, aesthetic space and the social future in many contemporary writings. In contrast, he produced fictions characterised by a brutal delimitation of spatial and social vision and a narrowing of social choice. Gissing certainly recognised the suburbs as the cradle of a new civilisation, but he did not like what he saw. In striking contrast to the idylls created by Conan Doyle and Pett Ridge, and to the social equilibrium envisaged by Booth, Howard, Morris and Jerome, he perceived a profound instability of purpose and identity characterised by a shifting of intellectual, moral and sexual values. In a series of brilliant social critiques, he exposed the plots and strategies of a suburban shadow world which constructed what characters could know and what there was to know. The realistic surface of the novels is the manifestation of invisible but determining political and economic structures which produce, not only the concrete world of the suburbs, but its narratives and psychology.

In *New Grub Street* (1891), *The Odd Women* (1893), *In the Year of Jubilee* (1894) and *The Whirlpool* (1897), Gissing establishes a multi-perspective sequel to the social and psychological determinism he had explored in his slum novels of the 1880s. In *New Grub Street*, for instance, the London of Bloomsbury and Chelsea is a literary manufactory where the rising middle classes' aspirations to intellectual richness and social betterment repress and obscure their awareness of an unchanged working-class identity defined by the old economic criteria. In *The Odd Women* (1893), Greater London is constructed as a modern and liberating system of rail and road grids connecting centre and suburbs – an orderly, timetabled space across which the characters try, but fail to travel;[2] while in *In the Year of Jubilee* (1894), London and its cluster of suburbs in Camberwell, Brixton and Denmark Hill are organised as a cultural map. The drama of the title *The Whirlpool* (1897) belies its portrayal of the insidious power of suburban culture as it submerges previous cultural norms and delivers up a new mode of consciousness defined by consumerism, gratification and covert anti-intellectualism. Together these novels portray a city whose history, cultural inheritance and identity are hostage to the proliferation and fragmentation of suburban development and to an overwhelming alliance of consumerism, universal education and women. Over a period of time, these elements merge and are internalised as 'a state of mind', a version of the suburban psychology which Gissing and others so feared.[3]

In *New Grub Street*, Gissing begins to explore how the war on the outward signs of urban deprivation has not transformed the intractable urban structures of slum London, but only concealed them.[4] The realistic surface of London and its inner suburbs is submerged in a symbolic fog and rarely described. The reader is told that London is the novel's location, but an acceptance of this fact is paralleled by an awareness that the external world is barely visible; the fog that envelops London closes down the reader's focus to small, claustrophobic, atomistic units. Names such as Gloucester Gate, Camden Town and Great Portland Street, for all their authenticity, provide only an illusory familiarity, like a Monopoly board. The actual location is 'New Grub Street' – itself invisible, no more than a concept. Once upon a time a reality, Grub Street is now metamorphosed. The novel's value-laden concept-city encompasses city and suburb alike, and blurs topographical boundaries and social definitions.

Inevitably, an important aspect of this confusing social reality is class definition. Within the novel, the outward social distinctions between middle class and working class are as inflexible as ever, and are recorded with Gissing's usual sense of referential authenticity. It is to these social rules that the characters conform. However, for the new middle-class, educated suburb-dwellers to be able to define themselves as such, they have had to repress (or have had concealed from them) the knowledge of their unchanged working-class identity. Despite the outward signs of social improvement and the changed nature of their work, they are still members of the classes who sell their labour for money on an open market.

This is made plain in the well-known episode from *New Grub Street* when Marian, who researches and writes the journal articles that are published under her father's name, is working in the British Museum Reading Room. Occurring early in the novel and soon after its transfer of location to London, the episode highlights the true nature of supposed class mobility. Playing on the reader's assumption of the implicit value of the Reading Room, which is more usually discussed in terms of culture than of class, Gissing investigates the nature of the relationship of the intellectual to that environment, and to the activities that take place there, by exploiting its effect on Marian's consciousness. She hovers uneasily between 'fact' and 'fantasy'. The fantasy is her intellectual aspiration and her desire to contribute to contemporary culture. The facts are her exhaustion, her recognition of the parasitical nature of her work, the 'need for earning money' and 'the work of literary manufacture'. Viewed from the perspective of these facts the Reading Room becomes merely a centralised warehouse of raw materials, organised and powered by an invisible energy that maintains a 'ceaseless hum', a phrase evocative of Herman Melville's 'The Tartarus of Maids', where physical and sexual energy is also diverted to power the 'ceaseless hum' that produces acres of blank paper. The Reading Room is as surely Marian's destination each morning as the dock gate is for the docker; she 'made her usual way to the Museum' and 'toiled there among the other toilers'.

The infiltration of London's contemporary value systems into the construction of personal identity produces a conflict in individuals between the dominant model (in this case, that of capitalist society), and the internalised values drawn from the cultural and social histories with which they grew up.[5] The apparently ahistorical, observable public world of *New Grub Street* is the world of the educated, the cultured and the new middle classes. However, Gissing shows us the unarticulated and barely comprehended layering of history that exists behind the imperatives of the present in the individual consciousness. He singles out two particular concepts – poverty and love – which point to a nexus of culturally inherited images, emotions and relative meanings with which the characters have to engage.

From the socially constructed repression of the characters' awareness of the forces that shape their society and their sense of self, comes the 'dream'.[6] The tension between an individual's unexpressed needs and desires (often experienced as personal conviction, even though they may merely be fragments of an earlier acculturisation), and the construction of their identity in the present, fosters a retreat into an imaginary vision. The palliative for loss of meaning and control is fiction-making or 'dreaming' – which is initially therapeutic but ultimately destructive. Reardon, the novel's tragic hero, who is struggling to make a living as a novelist, hangs on to his dream of Italy, of the beauty and the rich cultural heritage that it embodies, but he appears tragically out of touch with his own culture. For Marian the dream is romantic love, and it is this dream, despite her rational recognition of Jasper's self-serving greed, that makes her tell him that she loves him. When he kisses her, she takes the opportunity to grasp a moment of oblivion from her daily reality: 'Marian closed her eyes and abandoned herself to the luxury of the dream.'[7]

The danger of individuals' alienation from their society is in the power that it surrenders to capitalist commodification to provide a socially sanctioned dream in which cultural forms (romantic fiction) and social classes (the lower classes) are identified with each other. This is one of Gissing's bitterest responses to what he perceived as cultural dilution and manipulation. The 'dream' gives an opportunity for further control to a society which pre-empts dissatisfaction by diverting it into a compensatory pleasure-world such as those provided by Conan Doyle and Pett Ridge. 'Nothing', Sykes, a failed novelist, complains to Reardon, 'can induce working class men or women to read stories that treat of their own world. They are the most consumed idealists in creation, especially the women.'[8] For those like Reardon, Biffen (another failed novelist) and Sykes who recognise their alienation but who fail to penetrate, decode and internalise the meanings of daily existence as consciousness, the dream fractures their identity. Such fracturing, Gissing shows us, leads to despair and self-destruction. It is interesting to relate Gissing's analysis of personal imaginative worlds to the quite different dream of William Morris in *News From Nowhere*, and to the dream-come-true of Jerome K. Jerome in *Three Men in a Boat*, but also to juxtapose his understanding of the compensatory nature of popular fiction with conflicting contemporary responses to it discussed in earlier chapters.

In *The Odd Women*, Gissing's treatment of London foregrounds the illusory nature of individual freedom by counterpointing the ease of communication and transport across the widening terrain of suburban and urban London with the actual frustration of individual movement.[9] A surface realism is carefully established as Monica catches a bus from one end of Kennington Road to the other, Rhoda loiters in Chelsea Gardens and Virginia hesitates, confused by the vortex of Charing Cross station. The novel establishes a similar sociological authenticity. The addresses that Gissing chooses for his triangle of couples define precisely the characters' existing relationship to the class structure.[10] Virginia and Alice rot quietly in the declining gentility of Lavender Hill, beleaguered by Clapham Junction and encroaching working-class housing developments. Monica and her husband, Widdowson, are isolated in their respectable suburban villa retreat at Herne Hill. Rhoda and Mary, intellectual and forward looking, reside amid the growing distinction of Chelsea. Initially, these addresses are linked by an overview in which space seems unproblematic. Not only do the locations of the novel move to Jersey, Clevedon, Cheddar, France and elsewhere, but within London itself there is the possibility of crossing boundaries and defining personal areas in a way that seems to defy excitingly the restrictiveness of the slums and the invisible constraints of New Grub Street. The centrality of women as the active characters emphasises this point. They walk the streets and travel freely as independent individuals who are neither sexually exploited nor dispossessed.[11]

Yet the spatial freedom evoked early in the novel becomes an illusion which represses awareness of a very different existential reality. The physical distance between Lavender Hill and Chelsea, for instance, is easily negotiable by foot, train or hansom, but the ideological distance is far harder to negotiate, as Robert Thorne also discovered in Shan Bullock's novel. Virginia and Alice cling to their tiny room and make the journey to Chelsea only once. Widdowson seeks stillness and isolation as a means of maintaining his dream. Like Soames in *The Man of Property*, he tries to recreate a Ruskinian family in a suburban idyll at his villa in Herne Hill, but although he wants Monica to take the road out of the City, he does not want her to take it back again. Monica, however, who is part of the younger generation, sees the streets and freedom of movement through them as full of promise. At the beginning of the novel she revels in 'free wandering about London', but her increasingly frenetic travel finds no haven for her consciousness, no justification for her sense of independence.[12] She is ill at ease at Chelsea, panic stricken at Bayswater and enervated at Lavender Hill. Later, she acknowledges her situation as only a 'semblance of freedom'.[13]

Ease of urban movement in *The Odd Women*, then, actually creates physical and emotional exhaustion and claustrophobia. In *In the Year of Jubilee*, which is set largely in the Camberwell and Denmark Hill districts, Gissing develops this idea and uses it to explore the transformation of the notion of culture.[14] Urban mobility is still a central figure, but it expresses ideas of transitoriness and of superficiality in relationships, manners and learning. The event of the Queen's jubilee becomes the signifier of cultural change. The movement of the masses which throng to witness the jubilee procession makes up part of the slippery surface of a scene too diverse, too colourful, too noisy and too fluid to be understood. Almost as if they had not existed before this moment, the crowds emerge as the new population of Britain, conquering the streets, shops, monuments and restaurants for their own use, and turning the bastions of privilege, such as gentlemen's clubs, into targets for sightseeing. That the crowds recognise the essential lack of meaning in the event – or, in today's vernacular, the victory of spin over substance – is shown by the fact that so many people who have been released from work for the day do not bother to watch the procession: the crowds only accumulate in the afternoon and evening. If surface and spectacle are all that matter, then people are free to choose where they go and what they wish to see, and most of what they wish to see is themselves, multiplied thousands of times in the urban crowd.

In the Year of Jubilee is set in respectable, self-important, homeowner suburbs, with Falmouth and Teignmouth annexed as outposts on London's cultural periphery, where the leisure time afforded by regular work or small inheritances tests people's capacity to occupy their time constructively. Reading, the key to culture, is a favourite activity which, in Gissing's perception of the suburbs, has become a cause of intellectual paralysis. The Peacheys' suburban house in Camberwell, with which the novel opens, is an example of domesticity already ravaged by such debasement:

> The only books in the room were a few show-volumes, which belonged to Arthur Peachey, and half-a-dozen novels of the meaner kind, wherewith Ada beguiled her infinite leisure. But on tables and chairs lay scattered a multitude of papers: illustrated weeklies, journals of society, cheap miscellanies, penny novelettes, and the like.[15]

'Show-volumes', like the false books in urban pubs today, are simply a form of interior decoration, a world away from the humble but proud beginnings of a family library described as typical of the suburban home in *Home Notes*. The diversity of the Peacheys' actual reading matter, its broken-up, easy-to-read formats and its narrow concern with the matters of the day, are depicted as fragmenting the attention, destroying perspective and encouraging superficiality. Samuel Barmby, who repeatedly recites extraordinary facts that he read 'in the paper' simply because they are extraordinary, is another example of how context fails to inform meaning. Yet Gissing allows his own polemic to register ambiguity. However smug Barmby is, wreathed with the 'smile of a suburban deity', the reader cannot entirely condemn him for his genuine attempts to better himself and to learn about his world.[16]

Nancy Lord, the novel's central character, is offered as one of several models of suburban culture. Her opinions are unformulated and her response to society is uncritical. She is portrayed as one of a new breed of economically independent and educated young women with no specific role in life. Gissing's summary of Nancy is that: 'Miss Lord represented a type; to study her as a sample of pretentious half-educated class was interesting; this sort of girl was turned out in thousands every year, from so-called High Schools'.[17]

She drops a reference to *Nineteenth Century* magazine, which she does not read, simply to impress Tarrant, an educated man of independent means who later becomes her lover. She borrows a book on evolution from the circulating library – again to impress – but becomes bored with the subject and uncomfortable with her own 'insincerity'. Nancy only knows what she thinks she is supposed know and disguises her superficial attention to the issues of the day as intellectual sophistication. Such an attitude to knowledge, Gissing implies, leads to directionless egotism: Nancy felt that 'she was the mid point of the universe'.[18]

Despite these first impressions, Gissing's portrayal of Nancy is intriguing in the way that it raises questions about the overall validity of the attacks that he makes on the impact of universal education and consumerism on the consciousness of the individual. It is true that her first show of independence occurs only because she wants to join the jubilee crowds, excited by the throng, the noise and the colours; and on social occasions she relies on a sense of self-worth which she makes little attempt to deserve. However, Nancy's passions and affections have not been co-opted by materialism and self-gratification as those of members of the Peachey family, and of her own mother, had been. She escapes the worst influences of contemporary culture because her suburban existence is untypical. Her father, an embittered self-made working man, is determined to enforce traditional values, with the result that she has not been encouraged to measure herself by the criteria of modern culture.

Nancy's uninhibited sexuality seems to be her most positive characteristic in defying the falsity and hypocrisy of suburban life. Her relationship with Tarrant confronts her with the tension between her desires and society's conventions, and she is forced to take an unprecedented responsibility for herself. Her early meetings with Tarrant have a kind of Darcy/Elizabeth frisson, and their fencing with each other, in which each recognises the games that they are playing, arouses real passion in her. Although in social terms she is seduced, since Tarrant clearly sets up his opportunity and overcomes her scruples, she has already responded to the 'impulse of lawless imagination' that he inspires. Her feelings are deeply rooted in a spontaneous eroticism which begins to find expression away from her suburban home, as, 'With luxurious heedlessness she cast aside every thought that might have sobered her; even as she at length cast off all her garments, and lay in the warm midnight naked upon her bed'.[19] The following day, as she walks with Tarrant, she secretly enjoys seeing their shadows overlap in a moment of playful sexiness unusual in Gissing's writing. This experience of physical passion gives her the strength to maintain her love, and to support the child to which she later gives birth, in the face of economic and social adversity. It is only when her courage fails that she 'shrank back into her suburban home.'[20] In learning to know her own nature, she is able to continue to live in the suburbs and be free of the worst of their insidious effects.

In *The Whirlpool*, the stakes are even higher.[21] 'Civilisation' and 'culture' become contested words – words that echo through the novel, prompting memories of a canon of behaviour, texts and geography which has lost its authority over the modern imagination, becoming no more than a regret in the minds of the few men who would formerly have been responsible for its perpetuation. Overlong and over-plotted, *The Whirlpool* is still the novel which conveys most powerfully Gissing's notion of the battle for a cultural future, and his growing recognition that the battle has been lost and that those who have lost it no longer have any answers. While *New Grub Street* ends in tragedy, *The Whirlpool* ends in tragic resignation. The suburban terrain which encircles London and which extends ever outwards under the pressure of population movement, becomes a metaphor for a society and culture which are stretched thin, distressed and brittle, broken up into atomistic individuals acting out forms of social intercourse.

The title of the book holds a double-edged threat. The 'whirlpool' is not a metaphor for the layout of the suburbs, but for the cultural vacuum that swallows up intellectual judgement and social tradition. In a paradox that brings this cultural whirlpool and suburban expansion together, the further out you are, the deeper in you are, as is exemplified by Cyrus Redgrave, whose fashionable bungalow in the grounds of a Wimbledon house is the site of his illicit liaisons. People are drawn in, then spat out like flotsam and jetsam to float on the restlessness of suburban growth and change. As in Gissing's other novels, each suburb is carefully individualised and travel between them is scrupulously described. The reader follows routes through Brixton, Pinner, Wimbledon, Bayswater, Gunnersbury – but these are never more than temporary stopping places. The constant movement that paradoxically became the hallmark of the seemingly placid suburbs is partly caused by the imperative of upward mobility, as we have seen. But it is also a result of the desire for change which led to the nomadic life that Rolfe refers to in *The Whirlpool* and that Forster focuses on in *Howards End*. The temporary nature of library loans, the ephemeral pleasures of the daily and weekly entertainment papers, the delights of fashion which relied on newness for their success, the 'simple' life which disposed of inherited possessions, the ease of movement from place to place, all encouraged Gissing to anticipate a Yeatsian vision of culture as a 'riderless horse' and civilisation as people who 'shift about – all that great glory spent'.[22]

The Whirlpool also sees men finally surrendering the development of modern culture to women. The gendered conflict which was
apparent in the earlier novels culminates in The Whirlpool, in which
the feminisation of the suburbs is complete. Gissing sees the suburbs
as connected with a generation of women which has been given the
chance, by domesticity, economic stability and leisure, to seize advantages of education, greater physical freedom and sexual knowledge
and forge a new identity. In Gissing's eyes, the suburbs and women
were made for each other and by each other. While it is true that the
women in The Whirlpool are often anxious, afraid, under duress or
highly stressed, this is indisputably their world. The wealthy Cyrus
Redgrave temporarily exerts sexual power over several women at his
home in Wimbledon, but he is finally outwitted by the women he
seeks to exploit. Hugh Carnaby, an English gentleman, apparently
stays true to his values and, when he ventures into business manu-
facturing bicycles, he seems to have achieved success. The reader,
however, knows that he has succumbed to his wife's domination and
that his bicycles will simply contribute to the suburban dream and
women's freedom. Harvey Rolfe, whose story is ostensibly the central
narrative, is nevertheless sidelined as an anachronistic figure with
no purpose or direction, who walks off into the sunset as many lone
heroes with nowhere to go are accustomed to. His learning dwindles
away once its logic is exposed to the criteria of modernity: at the end
of the novel he no longer even makes a pretence of reading and considers selling his books. Masculinity is no match for the subtle alchemy
of women. In conversations which rival Henry James's writing for
their intricacy of inflection, Gissing shows women dissolving familiar
social protocols and values into a vortex of nuanced words beyond
men's comprehensions. The cultural decay and the feminisation of
cultural values later expounded at length by Wyndham Lewis began,
for Gissing, in the suburbs.[23]

Gissing associates this process of feminisation with the related
cultural concern about 'over-refinement' and its evolutionary implications, which is also explored by H. G. Wells in The Time Machine,
published two years before The Whirlpool, in his depiction of the dangerously parasitical, pale and attenuated Eloi. In The Whirlpool, the
suburban emphasis on domestic comforts and amenities, on drawing
room activities and leisure, is seen to distort the mind and damage
the physique. Alma's and Rolfe's life in Wales and the Mortons' life
in Kent are compared with the effete and pointless days of suburban

living. The *raison d'être* of town planning in the suburbs – space, fresh air, good housing – is fleetingly mocked. Carnaby is more concerned with the profit from his bicycles than with their health-giving qualities; the fresh air of the outer suburbs never penetrates the drawing rooms, or peoples' thoughts. New houses are liable to be damp (Rolfe's house in Pinner) or endangered by faulty plumbing (Harriet Winter's drains).

The women who are drawn towards the whirlpool, and whose historical moment has given them the power to challenge male values, have no precedents or guides. And, in any case, their choice is ultimately determined by the extent of their compliance with the second god of the suburbs – consumerism, the public face of capitalism. Consumerism is at the heart of Alma's dilemma as to whether she should stay an amateur musician or turn professional. She is on particularly ambiguous ground since she has no economic need driving her decision. On one level Alma's skill as a violinist is in a familiar tradition of women's accomplishments. Such a skill could formerly only be nurtured in the middle-class context of leisured time and social intercourse. As soon as there is a possibility of Alma's using her talent professionally, it becomes a commodity and she enters the marketplace and is up for sale. Her music is only one element in her market value and her market usefulness – after all Dymes, who acts as her agent, charges her £150 for his services.

The conclusion of *The Whirlpool* reveals the logic of the text. Rolfe has apparently retreated from the modern territory of the suburbs, with their gardens, fresh air and places to walk, into the equally modern compensatory dream of Empire, primitive manliness and the tough physical life: his key text is Rudyard Kipling's *Barrack-Room Ballads* (published some five years before *The Whirlpool* to instant popular success). The point is that although *Barrack-Room Ballads* is a contemporary talking point, it is demonstrably no more or less relevant to contemporary concerns than his friend Morton's reading matter. 'By God! We are the British Empire, and we'll just show 'em what *that* means!' Rolfe announces. Morton's reply, 'I'm reading the campaigns of Belisarius', is a deliberate non sequitur, but what the conversation reveals is that both men have disengaged themselves from the present to find refuge in dreams of masculine military heroism.[24]

Gissing's analysis of suburban values and psychology completely jettisons any *rus in urbe* Romanticism or Ruskinian domestic ideal.

The suburban psychology that Gissing explores is shaped solely by the processes of urbanisation and represented another stage in the evolution of contemporary consciousness. What Gissing suggests is that the process of urban development is progressive in chronological and physical terms, but represents a downward spiral in cultural, intellectual and moral terms. The suburbs moved outwards promising a new freedom and new possibilities, but their actual reinstatement of inner city class and economic structures threatened a psychological retreat from moral and cultural clarity in direct proportion to their distance from the immediacy of urban experience.

Gissing's last novel, *The Private Papers of Henry Ryecroft*, published just before his death in 1903, provides an interesting gloss on his earlier work.[25] When Ryecroft receives a small inheritance he chooses to give up work and leave London, deliberately rejecting his lifelong urban experience for suburban comfort. The suburb as *rus in urbe*, as retreat, as an ordered and leisured counterbalance to the stress and freneticism of the city, becomes the realisation of Ryecroft's 'dream'. There, he can read, think and write at will, he can learn and observe the signs and movements of the seasons and the elements, and tend his garden. However, *The Private Papers of Henry Ryecroft* is not a companion volume to Doyle's and Pett Ridge's suburban romances. Ryecroft's decision is far from a romantic fantasy based on the repression of economic and political realities. Nor does it represent Gissing's final capitulation to the blandishments of the suburbanised city which he so ruthlessly exposed in the novels of the 1890s.

In honest acknowledgement that, at the turn of the twentieth century, the way of life he values is made possible only by money, Ryecroft uses his inheritance to take advantage of the suburb's potential for the invention of a desired self. His carefully nurtured creation of his own intellectual and anti-social or anti-urban version of the suburban ideal is represented as a deliberate act of and for self. Perhaps, as the twentieth century opened, Ryecroft's satisfaction may have seemed plausible and acceptable as an appropriate reward for a hard-working and poverty-stricken life. Similarly, today's readers, who are well versed in the individualism of the 1980s and the related ideology of convenience of the early twenty-first century, might well congratulate Ryecroft on his good fortune. But I would argue that *The Private Papers of Henry Ryecroft* offers a chilling commentary on any hopes that Gissing may have harboured for collective and civilised sub/urban life in the future. Ryecroft's acceptance of personal satisfaction within a personally constructed world as the only remaining logic for living appears to recognise the connivance of others (however unconscious) in the continuing repression of a publicly shared intellectual, moral and emotional community. Ryecroft effectively 'privatises' the civilised aspirations of urban development as a suburban garden.

Gissing's sophisticated depiction of the determining structures rather than the surfaces of urban change, and his uncompromising recognition of their human and cultural cost, were probably, as with so much of his writing, ahead of his time. It is Gissing's insight into cultural development as he explored it in the novels of the 1890s which still seems to offer a valid and disturbing meaning for the sub/urban experience of the twenty-first century.

In chapter one, I discussed Wells's vision of the suburban future as it was laid out in *Anticipations* (1902) and *A Modern Utopia* (1905) – a planned environment which would mitigate the problems of urban congestion, and integrate into the city the beauty and healthiness of the rural. In the three social comedy novels he wrote between 1900 and 1910, his treatment of the suburban reflects the ideas that he was formulating for his social vision. In *Love and Mr Lewisham* (1900), *Kipps* (1905) and *The History of Mr Polly* (1910), we witness the lives of members of the expanding lower-middle class as they make decisions about the future. Newly empowered by education, improved economic security and broadening social horizons, these people must make decisions that are momentous, not just for the individual concerned, but because of their potential contribution to humanity's push forward towards a more enlightened state.[26] The suburban location includes, not only the environs of London, but any population centre within reach of London which is touched by the forces of urbanisation and therefore drawn into Wells's vision of a society in a state of change.

The social structures that Wells depicts are, in fact, as constraining as those depicted in Gissing's novels, but his sense of their influence on the history of society is entirely different because Wells placed a higher value on individual agency and its power to effect change at every level. These novels explore what happens when an individual claims for himself what society does not officially allow him. At such crucial moments come epiphanic insights. In the small hours of the night, the middle-aged Mr Polly, for instance, suddenly 'understood there was no inevitable any more'. The narrator explains that:

> When a man has once broken through the paper walls of everyday cir-
> cumstance, those unsubstantial walls that hold so many of us securely
> prisoned from the cradle to the grave, he has made the discovery. If the
> world does not please you, *you can change it* . . . There is only one sort
> of man who is absolutely to blame for his own misery, and that is the
> man who finds life dull and dreary.[27]

Mr Polly rises to the occasion, and decides to 'clear out'. The unexpected spaces in life which are extracted from their allotted destiny
by an individual's desire do not necessarily, however, turn out to
be a way out of suburbia, or even out of a suburban frame of mind.
Evolutionary processes are mysterious. Mr Polly's gamble on happiness is successful. He builds a new life working in a pub on the
Thames, finding peace in the country-side and the undemanding
structures of his daily life. When he does venture back and briefly
glimpses his wife, he knows he has made the right decision. Kipps is,
on the whole, glad to go back to his roots; while Mr Lewisham ends
up exactly where he had planned not to be. What these spaces seem
to become for individuals are crucibles in which the chemistry of
the whole social mix, of contemporary consciousness and of social
attitudes is changed.

Two of the three narratives tell the story of young men on the
brink of manhood; while Mr Polly who, at thirty-seven, has entered
middle age, shows that it is never too late to claim selfhood. All three
share the same plot elements of rebellion against an allotted destiny,
adventures in new worlds, sexual discoveries, and temporary conclusions that seem little more than momentary breathing spaces. Such
are the vivacity and credibility of Wells's portrayals that we never forget the individuals he creates – Mr Polly, Kipps, and Lewisham – even
if we forget the details of his novels' unexceptional plots. The tension
between their inner dreams and desires and the actualities of daily life
eventually forces all of these characters to make a series of choices,
each of which shapes their evolving identities. There is something of
the child in these characters, and Wells is careful to emphasise their
simplicity. They are blank slates who have the opportunity to write
their own stories: they are society's new beginnings.

Part of the importance of Mr Polly, Mr Lewisham and Kipps is
that their individuality is a historically recent possibility. Wells shows

them emerging from the anonymity of the masses into their social, sexual and moral selves, in the belief that the vigour of individuality will further the processes of twentieth-century civilisation for better or worse. He threads their narratives of individual escape in and out of the dangerous Darwinian themes of taxonomic destiny, suitable habitat, the struggle for survival and the imperatives of sex and reproduction. Kipps, Mr Polly and Mr Lewisham each have to find a way of productively reconciling in themselves their ahistorical Darwinian nature and their historically specific social nature, and in doing so, to extend the process of evolution from the animal to the human realm. As John S. Partington argues, using Wells's terminology from 'Bio-Optimism' (1895), 'The battle is no longer humanity against nature but rather the moral battle of adapting the "artificial process" to the "natural process"'.[28]

This is well illustrated by the series of dilemmas Lewisham faces in *Love and Mr Lewisham*, and his eventual reconciliation of their complexities. It starts simply enough. Lewisham is set on getting a good education and building a 'Career' for himself. Even within the limited opportunities of late Victorian society, there is no reason why he should not succeed. He is clever, personable, determined and energetic, and he is generally accepted to be capable of winning a scholarship to study science in London. He falls at the first fence, however, when he is taken completely by surprise by his own sexual nature and finds himself so fascinated with Ethel, a young woman whom he accidentally meets when she is on a visit from London that he returns too late to fulfil his duties as a schoolmaster, and loses his chance to be entered for the exam.

The chapter named 'The Scandalous Ramble', in which Lewisham spends the day with Ethel, cannot be bettered for its evocation of a young love which has not yet distinguished between sexual needs, romantic games and the social framework of marriage and children. Both lose all sense of time, social duty or personal consequences as they seize the felicitous Darwinian moment. In a world that seems transformed by their heightened perceptions, they see 'that spring was wonderful, young leaves beautiful, bud scales astonishing things . . . with an air of supreme originality', unaware that they too are part of the spring cycle. Their talk is 'curiously inconsecutive' but their state 'highly electrical' until as the sun goes down, they become 'figures of flame'.[29] The moment is then taken over by social convention until, little by little, Lewisham finds himself moving inexorably towards a marriage which his intellectual ambition resists but his sexual desire demands.

The novel concludes with his integration into suburban life in Clapham, in a road 'of little yellow houses with sunk basements and tawdry decorations of stone' near the 'vague spaces of Clapham Common'.[30] It is here he fulfils his biological and social destiny, declaring that he will be a better husband, that 'The future is the Child', and that being a father is 'the most important career in the world'.[31] Is this a victory for the repressive suburb, as domestic life subsumes other ambitions? Or a victory for the liberating suburb which raises Lewisham above selfish concerns to recognise the needs of others and the value of domestic life? A defeat or a triumph for Lewisham? Wells emphasises that Lewisham experiences his situation as his personal choice and willing contribution to the world, but the dynamic of the narrative has taught the reader that a decision rarely signals an ending but simply the next stage in an individual's evolution.

As the conclusion to *Love and Mr Lewisham* demonstrates, Wells's vision of the suburbs is intriguingly chameleon, setting the dreary routine and dingy lives of the actual contemporary suburb against his vision of a possible sub/urban future, and using this contrast to interrogate the choices of the central characters. Consequently, his stories of simple souls are never as simple as they so cleverly appear. They are not only comedies of manners or fashionable tales of lower-middle-class life, even if at times they are reminiscent of Pett Ridge's work, with their informality of style, light-hearted mood and intimate and affectionate knowledge of a way of life that has been left behind. They are never simply moral fables, although the moral transparency of the central characters informs their every decision and action and we love Mr Polly, Kipps and Mr Lewisham for not seeing the deceptions, hypocrisies and futility which the reader sees all too clearly. Wells never pursues overt social critique to its logical conclusion as Gissing would do. He is happy to diffuse fictional dilemmas into amusing caricatures, as with the 'dodgy' Mr Chaffery, Ethel's stepfather, who finances an apparently respectable suburban life with a number of dubious schemes including séances, and who maintains that 'Lies are the mortar that binds the savage individual man into the social masonry'.[32] Alternatively, he will switch to satire, focusing condemnation on individuals such as 'a certain high browed gentleman' who is concerned with 'social problems' but has no idea how to 'dam that

stream of human failure'.[33] Although the suburb as a domestic
and feminised realm provides a kind of answer for Kipps and
Mr Lewisham, this idea has none of the comprehensive force that it
has in the suburban romances or in the work of Edwin Pugh and
Shan Bullock.

The reason why no one general perspective is allowed to dominate is that Wells believed that the answer to life's dilemmas lies in
self-realisation, a faith in the inner knowledge accumulated through
experience and mediated by reflection. 'One seems to start in life',
Mr Polly tries to explain to his companion at the end of the novel,
'expecting something. One starts with ideas that things are good
and things are bad – and it hasn't much relation to what *is* good and
what *is* bad.'[34] Lewisham, baffled at the anger and resentment in
his marriage, experiences 'a sense of extraordinary contradiction, of
infinite perplexity', and asks 'How the devil did we get to this?'[35]
Kipps, who has the greatest struggle with language, comes up with
'I was thinking jest what a Rum Go everything is'.[36] For these 'simple
souls', simplicity is the driving force in the search for understanding.
The negative side of simplicity is limitation – the short cut to suburban monotony. 'I shall do nothing unless I simplify my life', declares
Lewisham to Miss Heydigger, a fellow student. 'Only people who are
well off can be complex.'[37]

Wells's success in writing accessible and enjoyable novels which
ensured his popularity with suburban readers must surely owe much
to his belief that the modern novel should capture the flow of life's
activities and feelings. The novels are written with the immediacy of
a personal diary. The rush of insight, of repulsion, of affection or of
engagement which permeates each episode enlivens the dialogue and
shifts the style effortlessly from comedy to satire to romance and back
again. Even references to his narratorial role – as when he requests
the reader not to tell Kipps 'That I have put him in this book' – serve
to reinforce the intimacy of his story.[38] Later, he was to claim that the
novel was an inadequate tool for conveying social visions, but in these
novels, his life, more or less in the guise of Mr Polly, Mr Lewisham
and Kipps, is the source of his vision. This is not to underestimate his
art: the individual episodes which sparkle with remembered feelings
serve a larger social and aesthetic mission. Indeed, Wells himself saw
Love and Mr Lewisham, the earliest of the social comedies, as something of a mission, 'a more serious undertaking than anything I have
ever done before'.[39] With unusual modesty, he confessed to Edward

Garnett that he felt he had failed to achieve what he had set out to do. However, the geometrical image that he uses to convey Lewisham's relation to society indicates precisely what he does achieve, not only in *Love and Mr Lewisham* but also in *Kipps* and *The History of Mr Polly*: 'his little life circles [exist] within the arc of a huge circle of the common life sweeping through them & in a sort of unfavourable mysterious way locking them together in a scheme quite outside his personal schemes altogether'.[40]

Wells's intelligence, his brilliance in shaping a narrative and his determination to preach the gospel of social and personal interaction never interfered with his recognition that the significance of life for the individual lay in moments of intensity of feeling – a Wellsian version of the co-existence of the ordinary and the extraordinary. When Mr and Mrs Lewisham enter their tiny apartment in Chelsea, for instance, Wells enables us to believe in and enjoy their glorious delight and happiness, even though we know that economic realities will soon destroy it. Kipps's memory of his breathless closeness to Ann's curls as a young lad never leaves him, and Mr Polly's delight in his Thames-side visit has all the completeness of a child's. Wells is one of the few writers to capture something of Jerome's spirit of happiness in his belief that other people have 'a capacity for joy and beauty at least as keen and subtle as yours and mine'.[41]

Ann Veronica (1909), published only four years after *Kipps* and the year before *The History of Mr Polly*, marks a transition in Wells's thinking.[42] The location is specifically suburban, and the middle-class, affluent Ann Veronica's rebellion has less to do with the unarticulated dreams of a young Kipps than with the convention-ally understood repressiveness and conformity of suburban life. Morningside Park, where Ann Veronica lives with her father and aunt, is little more than a framework for Wells's exploration of male and female sexuality and a device to oppose to spontaneous feelings and intellectual autonomy. Visions of the future for Wells have moved away from urban planning and the reorganisation of com-munities to domestic and sexual transformations. The future that he explores in *Ann Veronica* lies in the hands of the woman who is both intellectually and sexually independent and who promises a new kind of union between men and women.

Even so there are two general points that are worth making. One is that *Ann Veronica* signals a change in class focus, and that it is what the middle classes have made of the suburbs, rather than the suburbs themselves, which is the object of Wells's critique. Morningside is the kingdom of the wealthy middle classes, who expect women to enjoy a life of leisure and luxury and who safeguard their own continuance with rigid social rules and regulations. Transposed into *Beyond the City*, one of Conan Doyle's sunny romances, with which *Ann Veronica* shares very similar plot elements, Veronica's play for independence would be a time-limited game. Her New Woman identity would indicate a charming modernity, her devotion to her father would help keep the memory of her mother alive, and she would marry Teddy, a young, devoted suitor from an equally moneyed family, after becoming engaged at a tennis match. But in *Ann Veronica* Wells challenges the refusal to accept the changing lives of women as anything other than a game. The science laboratory where Ann Veronica recognises her biological and sexual identity, the Alps where she experiences sexual fulfilment and London where she sets up house with Capes, are new locations whose meanings the suburbs have failed to incorporate. There is a parallel here with Robin Hill in John Galsworthy's *A Man of Property* – as we have seen, Soames Forsyte cannot find love in a rural suburban house built for social display and domestic control.

The second point reveals an uncomfortable complacency in Wells's version of the middle-class suburb. When Ann Veronica is in prison for her suffragette activities, she takes stock of her position and discovers, like Kipps and Lewisham before her, that 'life is many-sided and complex and puzzling'. Part of its complexity, she recognises, is that 'even the sort of civilisation one has at Morningside Park is held together with difficulty', and that the other side of being the 'broken-in' person she dreaded was the discipline of being a 'decent citizen'.[43] She returns home to the suburban haven provided by her father and plans her elopement from there, eventually setting up a new domestic haven, provided by Capes. The distance between the two homes is presumably measured by intensity of love and equality of gender, and it is bridged by courage in the face of social convention. But the reader may well be sceptical. There is more than a dash of pragmatism in Ann Veronica's decision to return to the physical and economic comfort of her father's home while waiting for the emotional and sexual comfort of Capes's arms.

In *Tono-Bungay* (1909) and *The New Machiavelli* (1911), Wells's vision has darkened. In these novels we glimpse a pessimism as profound as Gissing's about the way in which the current state of society has betrayed the future.[44] The belief in suburban expansion that animates *A Modern Utopia*, and the faith in human agency and potential that lights up *Kipps* and *Mr Polly*, have dwindled. The social and personal puzzles that Lewisham, Kipps and Mr Polly all encountered and tried to understand for themselves have become a depressing cultural ethos. Muddle is the keynote of these novels: 'muddle', 'chaos', 'puzzle', 'a cascade of accidents', 'planlessness', 'accumulations' are words that George Ponderevo uses in *Tono-Bungay* as he becomes progressively more closely acquainted with London.[45] In *The New Machiavelli*, Dick Remington picks up the same refrain until almost everything else is drowned out in the clamour. Business, education, housing, politics and human relations are all infected, 'entangled' in a web of failed social organisation, beyond comprehension and almost beyond hope.

In these novels, the suburbs become the symptom of this terrible social malaise. The bricks that are given to Dick Remington to play with as a little boy at the beginning of *The New Machiavelli* represent creativity and progress. Sawn from local timber, planed and polished, they are beautiful in themselves. Beauty, engineering and creativity come together as Dick builds his childish landscapes. However, when he begins to register the environment outside his playroom, in the streets of the suburb of Bromstead, he realises that exactly the opposite is the case and that 'building was the enemy'.[46] Between a boy's imaginative vision of progress and the potential of the world in which he lives lies the history of urban sprawl, the disastrous consequence of the failing 'ordered structures' of the past being finally overwhelmed by 'great new forces, blind forces of invasion, of growth'.[47]

Both *Tono-Bungay* and *The New Machiavelli* give the reader a version of this history. In both novels, sub/urban sprawl is a fictional location and a concrete manifestation of the failure of civilisation. The suburbs' greatest crime is to set the environment against humanity, in an evolutionary regression that drains away human energy through an 'irresoluble complexity of reality' – a response that sets up a scenario that can usefully be set against Thomas's account of the suburbs in *The Heart of England*.[48] Soon after his arrival in London, George Ponderevo sees the 'oddity' and 'essential absurdity' of 'solvent, decent people living in a habitations so clearly neither designed nor adapted for their needs', and he condemns as 'foolish' a society that can 'house whole classes, useful and helpful, honest and loyal classes, in such squalidly unsuitable dwellings'.[49] The consequences of doing so are profound. An 'irresponsive' London – uncaring about its citizens – forces a rupture between the community and the individual, and accidentally constructs a suburban terrain of 'undistinguished houses, undistinguished industries, shabby families', populated by 'inexplicable people' who were once the hope of democratisation but whose meaning for society has been lost.

In *The New Machiavelli*, the history of suburban sprawl appears incomprehensible through the eyes of a small boy:

> All my childish memories are of digging and wheeling, of woods invaded by building, roads gashed open and littered with iron pipes amidst a fearful smell of gas . . . of hedges broken down and replaced by planks, of wheel-barrows and builders' sheds, of rivulets overtaken and swallowed up by drain-pipes.[50]

The suburban garden is no comfort here, but merely repeats a series of social ills. Flowers and vegetables only flourish if they are pampered like aristocrats and everything that could threaten them is destroyed. Like the Eloi of *The Time Machine*, the suburban flower and the suburban vegetable become weak and artificial life forms. On the other hand, weeds flourish without any care or attention, reducing the gardener to a primitive creature, grubbing in the earth in the relentless pursuit of their destruction. Perhaps some of the energetic humour in his account of Dick's father and his unsatisfactory garden was inspired by Wells's new friendship with Elizabeth von Arnim and by his reading of her garden books.[51] It is the garden which provides the appropriate image for an organic growth gone mad: 'It was a sort of progress that had bolted', Dick tells the reader, 'it was change out of hand, and going at an unprecedented pace nowhere in particular'.[52] And if Wells mixes his metaphors, this is no more than complexity requires.

The lives of George Ponderevo and Dick Remington are distorted by their world as they struggle to tell their stories, to find the link between their lives and the society in which they live, and to 'simplify' in the hope of finding meaning. There is no more powerful indicator of the failure of community in these novels than the movement from the third person of the social comedies to the first person of *Tono-Bungay* and *The New Machiavelli*. As if talking aloud, seeking explanations for themselves as much as for the reader, both George Ponderevo and Dick Remington look for coherence through a medley of ideas, impressions, events, conversations, reflections and relationships. Like detectives looking for clues, they can dismiss nothing as irrelevant until they know its place in the whole story. The very shape of the novels mimics sub/urban sprawl, with its complexity and uncertainty of purpose. Yet artistically Wells is very much in control – the form of his novels, like the spirit of the age, resists 'a single, concentrated impression' and aims instead for an equality of many impressions.[53]

Both Gissing and Wells use the changes brought about by suburban growth as a way of interrogating the society in which they lived and the direction of its future. Gissing's vision is remarkably consistent. Each novel, whether concerned with slums or suburbs, is a profound indictment of the invisible economic structures which constrain the city, its inhabitants and its culture. His use of the material city, with its mysterious intractability and determining power, to construct an urban pathology which obscures all but the faintest glimpses of an alternative, is savagely convincing and deeply pessimistic. His faith in the individual is correspondingly weak, since even those whose values he endorses are fatally disempowered.

Wells's novels, by contrast, show a changing response to social problems. The social comedies, with their conviction that the private person and the public person are indivisible and that society can be shaped and changed by the individuals within it, allow for a sense of joy and progress despite the difficulties, repressions and constraints that the characters suffer. And there is an egalitarianism about these novels which promises a victory for society as a whole through the simple and the ordinary. Wells never lost his belief in the individual entirely, and it is probably this factor that brings relief to the unremitting shallowness of the world of *Tono-Bungay* and the hypocrisies of *The New Machiavelli*. Wells abandoned his single-minded faith in the possibilities of social organisation and divided it up between the power of science and the power of women. 'I call this reality Science, sometimes I call it Truth', states George in a rush of ill-founded optimism at the very end of *Tono-Bungay*, when he reasserts his belief in the power of humankind to progress.[54] Dick Remington chooses love, but the reader may be excused for wondering to which suburb he will return after his elopement.

Wells was a political animal, and as his fame as a writer and thinker spread he became one of the most influential figures of the early twentieth century. Yet his novels are oddly apolitical. The flow of the individual's life is the driving imaginative force and, in his suburban novels, it invariably subordinates the context of that life to the emotions. Of Gissing's work, the opposite is true. Suspicious of socialism and sceptical of egalitarianism, his novels are nevertheless among the finest examples of the critique of urbanisation in Victorian fiction, with the lives of individuals inextricably bound up with and defined by their social situation. But whether the suburbs were a lost opportunity, or evidence that an opportunity never existed, both writers agree that the future civilisation inscribed in them is a bleak one.

Notes

1 H. G. Wells, [1914] *Social Forces in England and America* cited in Foot, *H. G.*, 208.
2 See John Goode, *George Gissing: Ideology and fiction* (London: Vision Press, 1978), for a discussion of the impact of standardised clock time in *The Odd Women*.
3 Silverstone (ed.), *Visions of Suburbia*, 13.
4 George Gissing, [1891] *New Grub Street* (Harmondsworth: Penguin, 1968).
5 David Harvey, *Consciousness and the Urban Experience* (Oxford: Basil Blackwell, 1985), chapter 5, 'The Urbanization of Consciousness', 250–276. *New Grub Street* anticipates Harvey's brilliant historical materialist analysis of the production of social consciousness by nearly a hundred years.
6 Adrian Poole, *Gissing in Context* (London: Macmillan, 1975), 143.
7 *New Grub Street*, 366.
8 *New Grub Street*, 416.
9 George Gissing, [1893] *The Odd Women* (London: A. H. Bullen, 1905).
10 See the poverty maps for the South East and South West regions in the appendix to Booth, *Life and Labour*.
11 Elizabeth Wilson makes the point in *A Sphinx in the City* (London: Virago, 1991) that 'the city . . . might be a place of liberation for women' (7) and, in relation to modern times, that 'urban life . . . has emancipated women more than rural life and suburban domesticity' (10).
12 *The Odd Women*, 33.
13 *The Odd Women*, 412.
14 George Gissing, *In the Year of Jubilee* (London: Watergate Classics, 1895).
15 *In the Year of Jubilee*, 5.
16 *In the Year of Jubilee*, 311.
17 *In the Year of Jubilee*, 145.
18 *In the Year of Jubilee*, 104.
19 *In the Year of Jubilee*, 113.
20 *In the Year of Jubilee*, 297.
21 George Gissing, [1897] *The Whirlpool*, edited by William Greenslade (London: J. M. Dent, 1997).

22 Yeats, 'Coole Park and Ballylee, 1931', 276.
23 Wyndham Lewis, *The Art of Being Ruled* (London: Chatto and Windus, 1926).
24 *The Whirlpool*, 416.
25 George Gissing, *The Private Papers of Henry Ryecroft* (London: Constable, 1904).
26 H. G. Wells, A *Quartette of Comedies* (London: Ernest Benn Ltd, 1928), including [1905] *Kipps: The story of a simple soul*, 15–387, [1910] *The History of Mr Polly*, 391–623, and [1900] *Love and Mr Lewisham*, 863–1100.
27 *The History of Mr Polly*, 566.
28 John S. Partington, 'The Death of the Static: H. G. Wells and the kinetic utopia', *Utopian Studies* (2000), 96–111 (98).
29 *Love and Mr Lewisham*, 899, 903.
30 *Love and Mr Lewisham*, 956, 984.
31 *Love and Mr Lewisham*, 1099.
32 *The History of Mr Polly*, 526.
33 *Love and Mr Lewisham*, 1014.
34 *The History of Mr Polly*, 621.
35 *Love and Mr Lewisham*, 1057.
36 *Kipps*, 387.
37 *Love and Mr Lewisham*, 1094.
38 *Kipps*, 386.
39 Letter to Elizabeth Healey, 22 June 1900 in David C. Smith (ed.), *The Correspondence of H. G. Wells, vol. 1, 1880–1903* (London: Pickering and Chatto, 1998), 356.
40 Letter to Edward Garnett, 26 June 1900 in Smith (ed.), *The Correspondence of H. G. Wells*, 59.
41 *The History of Mr Polly*, 526.
42 H. G. Wells, [1909] *Ann Veronica* (London: Virago, 1980), 207.
43 *Ann Veronica*, 207.
44 H. G. Wells, [1909] *Tono-Bungay* (London: Pan Books, 1978) and H. G. Wells, [1911] *The New Machiavelli* (Harmondsworth: Penguin, 1978).
45 See *The New Machiavelli*, 110, 116, 30, 31, 32, 9.
46 *The New Machiavelli*, 38.
47 *Tono-Bungay*, 81.
48 *Tono-Bungay*, 162.
49 *Tono-Bungay*, 71, 72–73.
50 *The New Machiavelli*, 37.
51 Wells met Elizabeth von Arnim in 1910.
52 *The New Machiavelli*, 39.
53 Wells, 'The Contemporary Novel', 197.
54 *Tono-Bungay*, 329.

9

THE SUBURBAN EXTRAORDINARY
Arnold Bennett

G. K. Chesterton

GEORGE Gissing was both the complete realist and the complete artist, translating the external materiality of London into diverse symbolic suburban landscapes, and into damning critiques of Victorian capitalism and contemporary life in his novels of the 1890s. Wells, by contrast, was a realist who was also an optimist, an artist who was also a missionary. However, in his novels he found it increasingly hard to sustain his optimism and find a form that could hold these dualisms in satisfactory balance. What did Arnold Bennett and G. K. Chesterton have to add to what they all perceived as a political as well as a literary problem?

Bennett shared elements of both Gissing's and Wells's literary and social thinking. His portrayal of the British Museum Reading Room in *A Man from the North* (1898), for instance, may well have been suggested by Gissing's powerful evocation of the writing factory in *New Grub Street*, but Bennett's comparison of research to 'a cannibal feast of the living upon the dead' with 'the trucks of food . . . always moving to and fro' is even more savage.[1] Clearly, he hated the dead hand of the past on the young minds of the present and also shared some of Gissing's fears about the commercialisation of culture. However, his work is quite distinct from Gissing's. Unlike Gissing, as Linda Anderson points out, he did not see these developments 'in terms of a crisis' and was perfectly prepared to attack 'mischievously' the role of the artist which Gissing held sacrosanct.[2] Like Wells (but unlike Gissing) he preferred aspiration and curiosity.

Bennett always took a positive pleasure in observing and enjoying a variety of cultural forms – a characteristic that he shared with Chesterton. Hilda's discussion with Edwin Clayhanger in *Hilda Lessways* (1911) is characteristic of his perspective. When Clayhanger attributes the local theatre's nickname, 'The Blood Tub', to its programme of melodramas, Hilda exclaims 'Why are people like that in the Five Towns?' – to which Edwin replies, 'It's our form of poetry, I suppose'.[3] Since, earlier in the novel, Hilda had stated that she did not like poetry, Edwin is making a rather more significant point to a middle-class young woman than she realises. Bennett felt that the serious business of living should never entirely eclipse the capacity to enjoy light-hearted pleasures. In his *Journals*, he records his response to Beatrice Webb's remark that the new Labour Cabinet members worked very hard and had 'no silly pleasures': 'I hope they have; I hope they have'.[4]

Bennett did not share Gissing's dread of the crowd or his fear of the culturally diluting effect of a Board School education. Like Wells, he had no difficulty in seeing the individual within the crowd and observing, not just the type, but the differences that indelibly mark one person out from another. But unlike Wells, he was not drawn to what Alan Sillitoe (taking a different tack from David Trotter) calls 'Dickensian sickliness', or even to characters that stand out by virtue of some exceptional human quality.[5] Bennett was intrigued by what constituted the ordinary, how much of the extraordinary the ordinary contained and, no doubt, what yardstick of the ordinary made sense of his own achievement. Margaret Drabble, whose insights in her biography of Bennett owe much to her instinctive affection and respect for her subject, sees this fascination as essentially egalitarian. She takes Rebecca West to task for her failure to discern Bennett's 'passionate yearning for fraternity and joy and opportunity for all' in an article about him after his death in 1931.[6]

In Bennett's novels, the ordinary is a material fact which relates to jobs, family, location, class – all the familiar markers of social identity, and the stuff of the realist novel. What makes Bennett's characters extraordinary is their *own* sense (not Bennett's) of the uniqueness of their experience and the importance of their lives: they do not think that they are ordinary. This atmosphere hovers over them like a halo – a sign of an invisible existence, a virtual world of other identities, separate from lived reality yet deeply connected to it through their emotional and sexual needs. When Bennett tries to suggest this circumambient psychology in his realistic novels, it sometimes strikes a false note – what John Lucas calls, 'the damnable trinity of miraculous, mystical and mysterious' (one could throw in 'sublime', 'enchanted', etc.).[7] But cumulatively it works. The ordinary individual cannot be dismissed simply as a social outcome (like Alma or Rhoda or Reardon in Gissing's novels), or as the sparklingly exceptional person who takes on his society (like Kipps, Mr Polly or George Ponderevo in Wells). Each person's life is a balance of ordinary external daily realities and extraordinary internal emotional or imaginative responses. The tension of maintaining this balance creates moments of confusion and, sometimes, more or less dangerous self-delusion. Occasionally, it yields real insights: sometimes, as with Henry Earlforward in *Riceyman Steps*, it prevents consciousness from being able to change. Perhaps oddly, Bennett is closer to another, younger contemporary, James Joyce, than to Gissing or Wells in this understanding of the ordinary, as stories such as 'Clay', 'Eveline' and 'The Dead' in *Dubliners* (1914) show.

Bennett was interested in the suburbs chiefly as the habitat of the ordinary, a habitat so densely populated that the finest eye and pen were required to discern and evoke its distinctions. Given that he did not see London until he was twenty-two, and that he was a first-hand witness of the building explosion of the late 1880s and 1890s, he is remarkably willing to accept the suburbs as a material fact. Perhaps the grim industrial landscape of the Potteries was harsher on the imagination than the domesticity of the London suburbs. For whatever reason, Bennett did not share Gissing's, and eventually Wells's, sense of the suburbs as symbolic of cultural decline and symptomatic of the failure of political vision. 'People have got into a way of sneering at the suburbs. Why, the suburbs are London', Mr Aked tells Richard Larch in *A Man from the North*. Mr Aked is clearly an enthusiast – the subject of the suburbs is his hobby – but even so the suburban locations in this novel have no connection with the prophecies of doom made by social commentators. Later, with the publication of *Riceyman Steps* in 1923, Bennett's treatment of housing and domesticity as the site of the ordinary took a very different turn. It is the different perspectives of these two novels that I want to compare here.

It could be argued that a discussion of *A Man from the North*, Bennett's first novel, properly belongs in an earlier chapter, alongside the work of Shan Bullock, Edwin Pugh and other novelists who focused on the clerk as a new type on the London scene, a type inextricably involved with the identity and destiny of the suburbs. But Bennett has a habit of slipping quietly across literary boundaries, and the distinctiveness of his writing is illuminated more effectively by contrast. Richard Larch is a solicitor's clerk with aspirations to education and success, for whom clerkdom is just a step on the way to literary fame. His search for a woman to love proves tricky, but he does manage to fall in love with the two women he meets, one after another. Both of them live on the same suburban street, and both, in different ways, draw him into the conventions of suburban living.

All the themes of suburban fiction are interwoven in A Man from the North: the nature of masculinity; the need for love and its corollaries, marriage, children and domesticity; the ambition and optimism of youth; upward mobility and class redefinition. Bennett's achievement is to subordinate the familiar realist plot in which routine, drabness, convention and constraint might lead to a totalising image of failure (Gissing) or, at the very least, to an exceptional escape (Wells), to the plots imagined by the central characters themselves, which are full of promise, feeling and surprise. In this way Bennett intervenes in the suburban formula to demonstrate, within it, the distinctiveness and the interest of each individual.

In A Man from the North, we see the world exclusively through the inexperienced eyes and feelings of Richard Larch. It comes as something of a surprise at the end to realise that the image Richard has of himself as an imaginative, passionate, clever and talented young man runs parallel to a quite different social identity. Only at the end of the novel is the reader shown that Richard has, in fact, worked hard at his job, gained respect for his conscientiousness and authoritativeness, and been regularly promoted until he has a good income, financial investments and the austere demeanour to go with these achievements. It is something of a surprise to Richard too: to himself he is not a clerk but a writer. He forgets 'that he was himself a clerk' as he criticises his peers during a weekend holiday at Littlehampton.[8] When he is summoned to his boss's office, he expects the drama of dismissal rather than the affirmation of promotion, and he has no premonition that the woman he loves is acutely aware of his social status and ready to drop him when her own status rises.

A crucial element that fuels Richard's imaginative life, as it fuels Mr Lewisham's, Robert Thorne's and Ferdinand's, is sexual desire.[9] The London of A Man from the North is divided into male and female territory. Richard has to overcome the almost insurmountable problem of meeting a woman, since he has no family framework or social connections, and then he has to endure the frustration and confusion of translating sexual desire into marriage and domesticity. Whenever Richard sees a woman, even just glimpses one from a window, his imagination immediately pictures her as a wife and, by association, a sexual partner. Like Robert Thorne, his inner self recoils from the masculinity of his workplace and its 'gross and ribald atmosphere', preferring 'the feminine atmosphere' because 'he was convinced that, at the heart of him, he was essentially a woman's man'.[10] In a state of constant anticipation and heightened awareness, his imagination provides him with the numerous twists and turns of a romantic plot. It is in this spirit that Richard's appraisal of Adeline, the rather limited young woman with whom he falls in love, which is criticised by John Lucas as 'distressingly patronising, a huddle of vapid generalizations' which reveal Bennett's 'ignorance', needs to be read.[11] Richard does not see Adeline through the eyes of a clerk as an available suburban woman who might be the answer to his sexual frustration and desire for domestic security. The urgency of his imagination and the depth of his, rather than Bennett's, ignorance transform her into a womanly essence – 'a possible solution to the riddle of life', a woman who is 'intimately a part of nature'. It is easy for him to ignore her lack of intellectual powers or of a capacity for deep feeling: 'She was and that sufficed'.[12]

Richard's imagination also works its alchemy on his career. From the very beginning of the novel his rejection of his actual career as a clerk and his ambition to be a writer are, as Anderson argues, 'a kind of self-protective fantasy, justifying a refusal to come to terms with himself and with reality'.[13] But it is also much more fun and more interesting to be a budding writer, for whom every day holds new creative feats and every finished work promises fame and fortune, than to accept, as one's whole reality, the routine and predictability of a clerk's duties. Some of Richard's highest and lowest moments are experienced in relation to his inner ambition. It is an important factor in his sense of being alive, of feeling purposeful and spontaneous as well as, finally, feeling sick with despair.

Richard's parallel identity as writer also legitimates his feelings of cultural superiority and ensures (for him) his place on the social ladder above colleagues such as Jenkins. Richard studies in the British Museum, discusses literary projects with Mr Aked, reads Zola in French and privately despises Adeline (before desire takes over) for reading and enjoying Mrs Henry Wood's bestseller, *East Lynne*, and for singing popular songs rather than Schubert. When he finally relinquishes his cultural ambitions, he consoles himself by blaming his father for bequeathing him to obscurity, and by claiming that 'it would be impossible to write in the suburban doll's-house which was to be theirs'.[14] It is not long before he reinvents himself as the model suburban husband, 'dutiful towards his employers, upon whose grace he would be doubly dependent, keeping his house in repair; pottering in the garden', and 'master of his own dwelling'.[15]

Richard Larch is surely an embodiment of the kind of man so ridiculed in *The Diary of a Nobody*, and a close relative of Mr Lewisham, whose worldly ambitions are thwarted by social convention and buried in suburban domesticity. But, in fact, Bennett portrays him as neither. There is no hint of the Grossmiths' patronising humour in Bennett's portrayal of Richard Larch, or of Wells's picture of a gradual breakdown in the co-operation between modern society and a young man's wider needs and aspirations. For all his difference in perspective, Bennett's method is closer to Gissing's in the way he constructs the psychology of the ordinary. Despite the apparent simplicity of Larch's life, he actually inhabits a universe of deceptive surfaces, illusions, dreams and changing circumstances generated by the infuriating instability of his own responses. He never knows whether he loves Adeline, but devotes his time, money and energies to winning her and is devastated when she leaves him. He certainly does not know whether she is rather dull and semi-literate, entirely beautiful and fascinating or ruthlessly manipulative and materialistic. He marries Laura, a cafe waitress, in full recognition of the life that awaits him, but instantly creates an alternative picture of domestic bliss in his head. He joins in Mr Aked's literary project with gusto but does not mind that it never gets off the ground because, in his tellingly suburban terms, 'it was pleasant to dream of the dream'.[16] He never succeeds in finishing any writing but remains convinced of his essential difference from the average clerk.

This capacity for self-invention, for fluidity of impression, for recognising the possibly protean nature of even the most material of realities and the utter seriousness of life, is inherent in the suburbs, and inspires Mr Aked's manifesto on their mysteries: 'How many houses are there in Carteret Street? Say eighty. Eighty theatres of love, hate, greed, tyranny, endeavour; eighty separate dramas always unfolding, intertwining, ending, beginning, – and every drama a tragedy. No comedies, and especially no farces.'[17] Despite the fact that Adeline claims to despise the suburbs, and that Richard himself observes the signs of neglect and meanness, Aked's enthusiasm succeeds in arousing 'the latent poetry of the suburbs' in Richard's mind.[18] Mr Aked's respect for the suburbs is not an uncomplicated authorial position. What is self-defeating about his obsession is his belief that he can reduce the 'complex entirety' of the suburbs to a constant law. He tries using a social science perspective to attach a moral physiognomy to individual suburban regions, Newtonian laws of motion to explain the relationship of suburbs to the city, and metaphysical speculation to wrest meaning from the diverse phenomena of suburban life. Even so, historically speaking, his project is original. He is quite right that the only authority he is able to use in his research is Gissing, whose books he tries to consult in the British Library. Even Charles Booth had several years to go before completing his survey of the suburban districts. Gissing, whose suburban novels can be used like maps to explore his suburban districts, would not, however, have shared Mr Aked's vision of the suburbs' grandeur. Like Casaubon's 'Key to all Mythologies' in George Eliot's *Middlemarch*, the book that tried to sum up the suburbs was unlikely to be completed.

So what is the angle of repose for Richard Larch's suburban adventures? He cannot be seen as a failure, because he finds a measure of self-determination as 'master of his own dwelling' and is buoyed up by the hope that he might pass his literary potential to his child: he has, in Linda Anderson's words, made 'an important psychological adjustment'.[19] He has not escaped his ordinariness or his location as one person among many in the densely populated suburbs, but through his imaginative and emotional experiences he has fashioned it, as each individual does, in his own image. Bennett makes sure that Larch is no Reardon, starving, misunderstood, alienated by his society and finally crushed by its antagonistic values. Against all the odds, the man from the north comes to London, builds a career, finds economic security and a wife. Bennett leaves considerable responsibility for his destiny in Richard's own hands. If he makes mistakes, they are his own. His innocence (he is a slow learner), his blindness (he sees clearly enough but often prefers not to see), his masculinity (he needs sex even at the cost that society exacts) shape both his uniqueness in his own eyes and his public ordinariness.

At this point I want to include *Hilda Lessways* (1911) in the discussion, although this novel is set in the suburbs of the Five Towns
and Brighton as well as London, because in his portrait of Hilda,
Bennett moves away from the viewpoint of *A Man from the North*
(and of other novels) to consider 'the enigma of the universe' from
the perspective of women.[20] In doing this, he was, of course, joining
the trend towards novels about women's changing position in the
modern age that had developed since Thomas Hardy's *Tess of the
D'Urbervilles* (1891) and the emergence of the New Woman novel.
Hilda, like Richard Larch, sees herself as different and, with her
twenty-first birthday approaching, she imagines herself taking up the
challenge of the 'enigma'. What is interesting is that, although a
woman's daily concerns are necessarily very different from a man's,
Bennett portrays her imaginative responses as being the same as
those of the feminised man.

Hilda revolts 'against the odiousness of the whole business of
domesticity', seeing it as women's surrogate religion, and she is
baffled as to how one small house can take the combined effort of
three women (her mother, herself and the servant) all day, every day
to manage it.[21] This anti-domestic stance, and her early determination to take responsibility for her own affairs, seem at first to signal a
New Woman story, but as with Richard Larch, we find that Bennett
complicates any possible stereotyping by juxtaposing Hilda's own
perspective on events with the events themselves. Hilda, even more
than the innocent Richard Larch, is a blank slate. Though beautiful,
young and economically secure, she has no traditional feminine
accomplishments: she does not read, play the piano or embroider.
She has no need to earn money, and work for work's sake is an alien
notion to her and to the provinces of the 1880s where the novel is set.
In her own opinion her greatest asset is 'the power to feel intensely'.[22]
Her innocence, her ignorance and the licence she gives to her feelings
combine in the context of her aimless, leisured middle-class life
to create a more emotionally inflamed subjectivity than Richard,
with his daily work, had time for. To convey the unfocused power
of her feelings, Bennett's language stretches meaning into a diffuse
vagueness, reminiscent of both the formulaic passion of the popular
romance and the strained emotionalism of some of D. H. Lawrence's
writing. The smallest events are invested with special significance. When Hilda undertakes a routine visit to the solicitor on her
mother's behalf, she experiences a sense of empowerment so that 'the

whole future, seemed to be drenched in romance'. Later, at a supper party with the Clayhanger family, Clayhanger's calm assertion that religious faith should not be forced produces a moment of ecstasy: 'She wanted to exult, and to exult with all the ardour of her soul'.[23]

This strange emotional imbalance leads her relentlessly towards disaster as she makes a series of mistaken decisions. Her inflated sense of her own importance as a shorthand typist means that she refuses to leave the office early, and so fails to reach her mother before she dies. She allows the charm of the local solicitor, George Cannon, to blind her to the dull business of her finances which leads to considerable losses. As she acts the role of a woman of passion, she rushes from a bigamous marriage to George to manipulating an engagement to Edwin Clayhanger, only to find that she is pregnant with George's baby. In an instant she paints a picture of herself as a fallen woman – 'Grief! Shame! Disillusion! Hardship! Peril! Catastrophe! Exile!' – although, as the novel ends, she dimly discerns some hope of survival.[24] Like Richard Larch, she does not blame herself but retains her faith in the drama of her emotional existence.

Through an accumulation of detail, and through dialogue and characterisation which were strongly located in time and place, Bennett constructed a realistic world in both these novels – the working life of a lower-middle-class clerk in *A Man from the North*, and the domestic existence of a middle-class woman in *Hilda Lessways*. What these characters experience in the material world – the fun of theatre-going and seaside visits, the routine of days at work, duties such as helping a sick friend or organising a funeral, the gentle pleasures of an evening with friends, the milestones of marriage and children, the shock of deception and unreciprocated love – is brilliantly evoked by Bennett, and simultaneously inscribed as the ordinary texture and fabric of the human condition. Always in the foreground is the drama of the subjective life, which is in a constant state of interpretation, reinterpretation, response and reflection and which transforms the ordinary into the extraordinary individual.

In the novels he wrote before the outbreak of war in 1914, Bennett both closed the suburbs down and opened them up. He lifted the symbolic weight with which they had been invested as the location of the new future, but he dismissed with equal lack of interest the demonisation of the new suburbanite and suburban culture. For him the suburbs were a material fact that rendered utopian visions, rural dreams and class-based attacks irrelevant. Instead he elevated the close observation of this new social organisation, and sought to legitimise a suburban psychology in which subjectivity was forced to struggle for existence as never before. From a distance, the suburbanites could easily appear a 'dark torrent of human beings', but this did not prevent Bennett from recognising the intrinsic interest of the new sub/urban populations.[25]

Riceyman Steps (1923) draws a line under the suburban world of 1880 to 1914 with all the controversy it inspired. Set in 1919, the novel depicts a London traumatised by war and unable to gather itself together to envisage any future at all. Existing buildings crumble gradually away, and the brave new expanding territories have turned in on themselves. It is somehow shocking to see the concept of 'home', so carefully nurtured through the suburban years, slip back again into the concept of 'housing' as men return from the war to find themselves without anywhere to live. With London gripped by a house-famine, rents soar, houses are divided and subdivided, and gardens and parks are neglected. As the story of Henry Earlforward, a bookseller, and Mrs Arb, who runs a grocer's shop, develops, British civilisation, embodied in London's streets, seems to have lost its grip, gradually deteriorating and returning to the slums and despair of the 1880s.

Early in the novel, inspired by his ambition to marry Mrs Arb, Henry Earlforward takes her on a Sunday morning exploration of the Riceyman Steps area. He professes to know everything there is to know about Clerkenwell, but he fails to understand that Clerkenwell and those who live there are now part of a downward spiral. The garden in Riceyman Square 'seemed to have no business where it was'. The grand houses have been turned into tenements, the archery ground has disappeared beneath pavements and the little alley of Model Cottages is abandoned while grim tenements tower over them. Riceyman Steps, where both Mrs Arb's and Henry's shops are situated, is bounded by a hostel for the homeless, a large pub and the noisy and dirty King's Cross Road. In images reminiscent of 1880s slum novels, Riceyman Square is described as a place of 'squalor and foulness' where 'interiors were appalling' and 'sinister groups of young men' hang around 'doing nothing whatever'.[26]

Domesticity is also under siege. The market for second-hand cookery books is lively in Henry Earlforward's bookshop, as people try to brush up on forgotten skills to make the best of wartime supplies. For Violet Arb, with no children to constrain her movements, home had been wherever her heart was, as she followed her husband where his work dictated. After her husband's death, however, she briefly turns the confectioner's shop that she buys on Riceyman Steps into a haven of warmth, light and sweetness reminiscent of the pre-war suburban domestic ideal. Henry's shop, by contrast, is an anti-home – the dust deliberately cultivated in an obscuring film and the cold sufficient to paralyse humanity. When Mrs Arb moves in with Henry after their marriage, some superficial aspects briefly change before their shared territory becomes the arena for a battle to the death. Commerce eventually wins, as the bookshop is sold to a larger business and all traces of domestic living are obliterated. The failing potency of the domestic ideal is summed up in the shockingly appropriate image of the vacuum cleaner. The chapter title 'Vacuum' inflates the idea of the machine, which Henry had hired to clean the house in preparation for his marriage, into an emotional state.

Elsie, Henry's and Violet's servant, believes in the values of home and domesticity but, although she can make her living on the fringes of other peoples' homes, she never achieves the room of her own in the basement of a house in Riceyman Square that she saves so assiduously to rent. Her fiancé, Joe, is homeless when he returns from the war and he and Elsie are forced on to the streets for their few moments of intimacy. Their only experience of a 'home of their own' is, ironically, in the bookshop, after it has been stripped and cleared and is waiting for the new fittings to arrive. As temporary squatters in its empty rooms, Joe and Elsie 'are happy in the island of homeliness around which swirled the tide of dissolution and change'.[27] Their plight is representative of the neighbourhood, where families are crammed into tenement blocks or subdivided houses and the stories of their lives intermingle in their proximity as if the suburban revolution had never taken place. These are not the 'homes fit for heroes' so beguilingly illustrated, complete with gardens, in the government propaganda of the time.

In *Riceyman Steps*, Bennett created a profoundly pessimistic picture of a society collapsing back onto itself after the surge of energy which drove expansion and modernisation until the outbreak of war. There is no longer any room for characters to seek the 'enigma of the universe', that troubling, exciting and complicating moment of realisation that, in earlier novels linked subjectivity into universality for characters like Richard Larch and Hilda Lessways. Henry's epiphany, his realisation that 'Life was bigger, more cruel, more awful than he had imagined' is a diminishing not an energising experience and it is triggered by the discovery that Elsie has opened his safe.[28] The satin slipper which Elsie ties to Henry's and Violet's honeymoon bed is the sole indicator of 'All the enigma of the universe', but even for Elsie its meaning is undecipherable, like a fragment of Sanskrit text.[29] The newly flat, one-dimensional world, in which the ordinary is no more than ordinary, is itself threatened with collapse. Bennett threads images of disease and infection through *Riceyman Steps* in a way that again recalls the slum novels of the 1880s. The positive forces in the novel are those that drive disease back – Dr Raste, the overworked but socially conscious doctor who lives in Riceyman Square, and Elsie, who defies convention to bring health back to Joe's sick body and mind with her own physical warmth.

So does Bennett's concept of the ordinary, in its intrinsic interest and its infinite variety, survive both the assault on suburban progress and a war effort that subsumed individuality into anonymous national collectivity? The answer is both yes and no. Bennett's fascination with the nature of individual consciousness is fully satisfied by the complex psychology of Henry Earlforward, who does believe that he is ordinary, and who would be bewildered and irritated by the local assessment of him as an oddity. Bennett's depiction of Clerkenwell and its community is as powerfully convincing as the world of Anna Tellbrook in *Anna of the Five Towns* (1901). However his brilliant creation of an 'ordinary' monster in Henry Earlforward inevitably poses questions about the nature of 'ordinary' angels. In a literary sense Elsie fills this role, but she emerges so nearly as the stereotype of the good servant that the intricacies of her characterisation during the novel tend to get lost at its conclusion.[30] When she is stealing food from the kitchen, lighting the fire against house rules or sneaking Joe into her bedroom she is part of Bennett's vision of the ordinary. As the perfect servant (at a time when servants had become a troublesome luxury) – as Dr Raste notes, she 'was ready to go on living and working without any fuss from one almost impossible moment to the next' – she seems anachronistic.[31] And, of course, that is what she is. As early as 1901, in his discussion of women, servants and the changing nature of domestic management, H. G. Wells had gladly recorded that 'self-respecting inferiority is being utterly destroyed in the world'.[32] But perhaps a progressive view of history does not have all the answers. Bennett may simply have been offering more than one way of looking at the human condition, through an ahistorical acknowledgement that heroism could consist in ordinary people doing extraordinary things out of a sense of a common humanity.

Because of the Christian perspective of much of his writing and because of his eventual conversion to Catholicism in his mid-forties, G. K. Chesterton is remembered more for his differences from the deeply secular Gissing, Wells and Bennett than for his similarities. Born nearly twenty years after Gissing, and several years younger than Wells or Bennett, he was firmly located in the intellectual milieu of the early twentieth century. Unlike Gissing and Wells, who were driven by compelling, if different, ideas about the future direction of society, he shared with Bennett a sense of the peculiar importance of the ordinary in the here and now which completely bypassed anxieties about the aesthetics of the suburbs, the dreariness of the masses and cultural dilution. Again like Bennett, Chesterton had no difficulty straddling what others saw as the cultural and class divide: in his opinion, society certainly had a problem, but the problem was the educated and upper classes rather than the working and lower-middle classes, 'who have the vast, beautiful, and incontestable superiority to the rich, that they do not think their fellow creatures spoil the face of their mother earth'.[33] The consistent theme of his writing is the tragic retreat of those with political and cultural power into defensiveness and negativity, and the danger to the future of society posed by the detachment of intellectual energy and rational thought from the real circumstances of peoples' lives.

The suburbs were both the location and the inspiration for Chesterton's optimism. John Carey points out that the logic of Chesterton's worldview (in a very different way this is true of William Morris's as well) was that 'The earth itself was a suburb'.[34] For Chesterton the realisation of this notion was rooted in a love of London, of the suburbs where most Londoners lived and of the culture that was distinctively theirs.[35] Chesterton felt strongly that where people lived held an imaginative power which reached back to childhood experiences: the material world served as a constant reminder of the past, and day by day wove the tapestry of community and culture. Two of the recurring icons in Chesterton's novels – the lamp-post and the tree – reveal the psychological process by which individuals invest a familiar object with an essential identity. Chesterton's lamp-post lights up suburban streets, combining the practicalities of safety and technology harnessed to human ends with the romance of shadows and unfamiliar colours. It is very different from T. S. Eliot's neurotic lamp-post in 'Rhapsody on a Windy Night', also written in the pre-war period. In *The Napoleon of Notting Hill* (1904), a collective of humble lamp-posts is instrumental in repelling the attack of the property developers when they are switched off at a vital moment, plunging the streets into darkness; while the pool of light from a single lamp-post which 'gilded the leaves of the tree' in a suburban street in *The Man Who Was Thursday* (1908) provides a thrilling stage for the 'anarchic poet' Gregory's impressive role as a spy.[36] Chesterton recognised, as the writers of romantic fiction also did, that no outsider can unpick the complexity of an individual's psychological history when it is embodied in a particular object. Once the living connection is severed, the meaning is lost, just as the meaning of the slipper that Elsie attaches to the honeymoon bed in *Riceyman Steps* is lost. Consequently, no outsider can confidently deny the intrinsic value of someone else's psychological and actual landscape.

The recovery of the ordinary through the reconnection of words with their literal, traditional or original meanings is central to Chesterton's moral, social and imaginative purpose. Auberon Quin, who is elected King in *The Napoleon of Notting Hill*, for instance, wants to restore gardens to the heart of London and see 'a mountain of lavender ... a purple hill of incense' at Lavender Hill and 'a scheme of lemons and olives' at Southfields.[37] If people's lives are monotonous and drab, then their colour should be restored and they should be transformed (as they are in Jerome and Morris) into a colourful pageant with cloaks and robes in sumptuous colours replacing Edwardian business suits. Shops, those heartlands of the small-minded in thrall to the forces of commerce, become in Notting Hill Aladdin's caves of colours and treasures. Products are redolent of the places from which they come, and they are stored in containers that are themselves works of art. And the 'public good', so frequently cited as the irresistible reason for overriding public opinion, is restored to its rightful ownership.

A related issue is the recovery of the history of the ordinary from the seductive embrace of ideology. One of Chesterton's greatest fears was the growth of a monolithic idea that would use rational serious-ness to ignore difference and enforce an unhealthy homogeneity on existence. He objected, for instance, to the contemporary passion for applying evolutionary theory to social issues, which he felt spread impossible dreams of human perfectibility on one hand, and doom-laden scenarios of deterioration and barbarism on the other. Neither of these possibilities seemed to include a role for the majority of human beings who were having to make sense of their lives from day to day, except as a homogeneous mass necessary to the hugeness of the ideological scale. He disliked dreams of empire which subverted the human spirit of adventure, discovery and wonder in favour of narratives of conquest and exploitation. He was similarly suspicious of emergent socialism, as a mechanistic way of organising life that had forgotten the good of the people whom it was supposed to be benefiting.[38] H. G. Wells, a long-time friend of Chesterton, was held guilty of the crime of the overarching theory, although in Chesterton's eyes his goodwill exonerated him.[39] *The Napoleon of Notting Hill* was written as a counterattack against social prophecies, a rallying call to the lower classes to follow their own vision and, in doing so, to play the winning hand in the game of 'Cheat the Prophet'.

Yet Chesterton, who was one of the most committed of the writers discussed in this book to making the case for ordinary people, their culture and the suburbs in which they lived, presents an enigma to the modern reader which appears very difficult to unlock. John Carey claims that Arnold Bennett is 'the hero' of his book, *The Intellectuals and the Masses*, because 'His writings represent a systematic dismemberment of the intellectuals' case against the masses'.[40] I would not want to quibble with this assessment but I wonder why Chesterton is not equally celebrated by one of the few critics to do exactly what Chesterton tried to do – attacking mainstream thought with provocation and brio and debunking political and cultural assumptions that dismiss the masses and their trivial concerns. Instead Chesterton barely merits a mention. Is it his religious convictions which have created a barrier that modern thinkers find difficult, almost impossible, to penetrate, despite the fact that cultural embarrassment about the Edwardian era in other areas has begun to be broken down? Terry Eagleton implies that, since religious faith offers God as 'the metaperspective which unified all these others', it is a form of intellectual cheating and perhaps therefore a stumbling block to critical appreciation.[41] Religious faith certainly influences the imagination and the language of religion influences metaphor in Chesterton, and in much of the literary tradition that preceded him. But, in formal terms, it is only one thread (albeit an Ariadne's thread) among the bewildering and quixotic impressions that he marshals in the celebration of the ordinary, the suburban, the masses and their culture.

'When the chord of monotony is stretched most tight, then it breaks with a sound like a song': *The Napoleon of Notting Hill* is one such 'song'.[42] When the novel opens we are presented with a London whose energy has withered under a supposedly beneficial regime of routine, bureaucracy and belief in efficiency and rationality. Auberon Quin, a little man, a 'mechanical' government clerk, sees this but can do little about it other than play the fool and raise some laughs until he is selected as King by a newly instituted democratic procedure.[43] With the power to do what he likes, he brings the noise, colour and energy of the circus arena to his court. He replaces modern political procedures with medieval chivalry, breaks up the empire of mono-lithic London and brings self-determination and local involvement to its suburban districts. But Quin is confounded when the game gets serious. Adam Wayne, a young working-class man from Notting Hill, is inspired by Quin's call for local self-determination and revels in his suburb's new glory. When the leaders of the aristocratic Borough of Kensington threaten to drive a road through the old part of Notting Hill, he marshals the shopkeepers to defend their rights against the power of money and the bullying notion of 'public good'. Wayne and Quin both die in the defence of Notting Hill, and the concluding chapter is a ghostly conversation between them about the meaning of it all.

It is easy to extrapolate from *The Napoleon of Notting Hill* the motifs that run through the literature of the suburban lower-middle and working classes. Through Quin, Wayne and Turnbull (the curiosity-shop keeper on Pump Street) Chesterton explores how the individual who is usually hidden by the anonymity of the masses can flourish, and criticises what he calls the 'arithmetic' values of practical men which suppress such individuals. E. M. Forster's prac-tical man, Mr Wilcox, comes to mind. Mr Wilcox's power to control events, because of his grip on the material world and his sublime indifference to the fate of those his decisions affect makes him a man of a type that Chesterton deeply disliked and feared. Although in some ways the novel is a social critique in the manner of Wells and, even more, a celebration of the drama of the individual in the manner of Bennett, Chesterton is less interested in either of these

aspects than in evoking the forces of untrammelled human energy
and demonstrating its ability to connect the present to the past and
the future. Turnbull is the quiet hero of this novel. His choice of shop
and the armies of toy soldiers in his back room reveal his hatred of
the monotony of modern civilisation, his recognition of the importance of the past, a belief in heroism and a need for play, although the
modern world has reduced him to a mere shopkeeper. Just before
he dies in battle, 'The evening sunlight struck his face; it looked
like a child's', and it is in the spirit of rediscovered youth that he is
prepared to die.[44]

The suburbs get their most flamboyant, and their most affectionate, treatment in this novel. In *The Napoleon of Notting Hill*, Notting
Hill is a haven, a precious and familiar piece of London, a community, the source of a lifetime's memories, worth living in, worth dying
for, a suburban district, a landscape of self-invention and self-belief,
an adventure – and every other suburb has the same infinite potential. Chesterton achieves this effect, without sentimentality, through
the deployment of a dazzling array of literary modes, mixed and
matched, subverted and celebrated. With egalitarian ease, he moves
from one mode to another, disturbing and disorientating his readers.

One of these is the social problem novel: *The Napoleon of Notting
Hill* presents a critique of the devaluation of ordinary people's lives
and culture, and launches an attack on the kind of intellectual
imperialism that claims a right to sever people from their roots at
home and colonise other peoples' countries abroad in pursuit of an
exclusive and mechanistic ideology (there is a dig at H. G. Wells
here) founded on false science.[45] The debate over the future of Pump
Street is a good example of how the so-called rational approach (in
this case, the economic approach) is shown to be merely a point of
view. The businessmen, who assume that every thing has its price, are
baffled by Adam Wayne's refusal of their inflated compensation offer
for the demolition of Pump Street. Chesterton broadens the frame
of reference to demonstrate a contrary logic: '"That which is large
enough for the rich to covet", said Wayne . . . "is large enough for
the poor to defend."'[46] When the argument descends to bluster and
bullying, and Wayne is accused of absurdity, he asks, 'Why should
I think it absurd?' since Notting Hill is 'high ground of the common
earth, on which men have built houses to live, in which they are
born, fall in love, pray, marry, and die'.[47] Chesterton is careful not to

equate Wayne's loyalty to Notting Hill with the patriotism of imperi-alism. At the end of the novel, when he is about to die, he is asked how large the Empire of Notting Hill seems to him then, and he simply circles his sword around himself to the fullest extent of his arm. The space that the individual occupies is the only empire to which he has a right.

Of course, Wayne's statement at this point is also a heroic one in the face of death, and the story of his stand against the forces of mod-ern society is told as a medieval chivalric tale of courage and honour. The King's game of making his officials dress in medieval court clothes and observe chivalric modes of address, which initially makes everyone feel ridiculous, swells and expands through the force of Wayne's imagination into a way of expressing the values he endorses. Chivalric speech meets Chesterton's easy-going contemporary idiom somewhere in the Renaissance. When the King greets 'Our cousin of Bayswater' and bids 'Welcome, West Kensington', the shop owners assume a Shakespearean grandeur. Fantasy is never far away: the 'sacred mountain' of Notting Hill, Wayne's sword 'broken at the hilt', the gathering of a small band of honest men all echo for the reader today in the adventures of such characters as the hobbits in J. R. R. Tolkien's *The Lord of the Rings*. Wayne is a disadvantaged nineteenth-century boy living in an inner-ring suburb. But he is also Gawain, the brave knight who willingly chooses to die for his cause. He is also Adam, first man, new man, born from one state into another. And he is Christ, in a narrative that flickers into existence at Wayne's last stand, as he backs up against a tree, arms outspread in his defence, while his attackers assess their chances and acknowledge that he will die rather than submit. The climax of the novel is pure adventure, an account of the first rip-roaring battle, in which the tiny forces of Notting Hill employ courage and ingenuity to disperse the vast armies of Bayswater, South and North Kensington (there are echoes of *Stalky and Co.* here, although not of its imperial code). In the spirit of every adventure ever told, victory is seized from defeat and in the darkest moment a stroke of brilliant resourcefulness and indi-vidual courage defeats the logic of numbers and weapons to triumph. In Chesterton's wonderfully topsy-turvy world, the products of the nineteenth century are turned into the great weapons of a medieval siege. City cabs are inveigled into Notting Hill and used to block all the roads; the street lights are switched off, plunging the enemy into darkness and allowing Notting Hill's scattered army to regroup;

and surrender is finally exacted as Wayne threaten to open the water-tower on the top of the hill and flood the opposing army.

I have discussed these passages at length because I think it is important to see how Chesterton expresses his faith in the ordinary through the energy, diversity and entertainment-value of a popular culture that contradicts any sense of colourlessness and monotony and opens up the spontaneity and vividness of ordinary life. To see a suburb as simply a suburb, a space on a map, a negotiable piece of land or, worse, as something beneath contempt, is reductive of human history and experience. As Quin points out in his ghostly discussion with Wayne at the end of the novel, there are some people whom – 'nothing intoxicates', to whom all places are just 'silly suburbs'.[48] Paradoxically, 'intoxication', the scrambling of one's reason and one's senses and a heightened feeling of exuberance and excitement, is necessary if the world is to be seen with continuous freshness:

> You saw a moon from Sussex Downs
> A Sussex moon, untravelled still,
> I saw a moon that was the town's,
> The largest lamp on Camden Hill.[49]

The Man Who Was Thursday: A nightmare (1908) begins and ends in Saffron Park, a thinly disguised Bedford Park, one of the earliest purpose-built suburban communities whose place among late nineteenth-century suburban visions is discussed in chapter one. Chesterton would probably never have shared its initial dream of 'corporate happiness' but certainly, by 1908, he saw Bedford Park as an appropriate example of what was going wrong with Edwardian culture: spurious intellectualism, divorced from reality, carried away by its own cleverness and fineness of sensibility and convinced of its superiority to the culture of the masses. In this hothouse atmosphere the latest subjects for fashionable conversation were anarchism and pessimism – and art as their most sublime expression. When Gabriel Syme arrives at the party at the opening of the novel, he walks into a world of artifice, a pre-Raphaelite painting, a drama in which the actors and the audience are blind to the fact they are playing with moral and literal dynamite. Syme's nightmare begins when he exchanges vows in a Faustian pact with Gregory, the anarchist poet. To prove to Gregory that a man of honour exists in the cynical modern world, Syme promises him that he will never reveal whatever Gregory chooses to tell him. He is, of course, completely unprepared to be told that Gregory is part of a terrorist cell operating in London, and, as a result, he is plunged into a series of moral dilemmas and a terrifying adventure.

When the novel opens, Syme had already learnt that anarchism is a reality, and that anarchy and violence are inextricably linked. He describes witnessing a terrorist attack as a sudden and total oblitera-tion of consciousness in which he is 'blind and deaf for a moment' and then sees 'bleeding faces'.[50] The dreadful and destructive sud-denness of the event makes him realise the preciousness of the pre-dictable, which constitutes the necessary structure of daily life. In a different time, with different politics and a different style, Chesterton is nevertheless a direct inheritor of Burke's when he asserts that he has: 'no great opinion of that sublime abstract, metaphysic rever-sionary, contingent humanity, which in cold blood can subject the present time and those whom we daily see and converse with to immediate calamities in favour of the future and uncertain benefits of persons who exist only in idea.'[51] Syme sets in motion his own personal 'rebellion against rebellion'; the reason for his presence at the Saffron Park party is to hunt down anarchists as an undercover policeman. Fear of terrorism at the hands of anarchists was familiar during this period and London, a known gathering place for foreign exiles many of whom had become part of British organisations, was particularly vulnerable. Peter Kropotkin, for example, who had been exiled from Russia for his Communist-Anarchist activities, lived in London from 1886 until 1917, when he returned to Russia at the time of the revolution. While he was in London, he exchanged ideas with leading British socialists such as William Morris and Bernard Shaw, both of whom had considerable respect for his personality and some sympathy for his ideas. The most influential of these foreign exiles was, of course, Karl Marx, whose ideas had been influencing revolutionary thought since the publication of the *Communist Manifesto* in 1848.[52] The spy thriller was as appropriate a genre for the 1880–1914 period as it was later to become for the cold war with the novels of Ian Fleming and John le Carré. Hunting down terrorists is the central adventure of *The Man Who Was Thursday*, and it is a remarkable novel.[53]

But practical anarchism, horrible as it is, is merely an outward sign of the moral anarchism that underpins it. A moral anarchist is, of course, a contradiction in terms, since, according to Chesterton, such people refuse to acknowledge the possibility of moral distinctions having relevance to human thought or behaviour, and consider the breaking of moral codes a minor form of social rebellion. In doing so they strike at the root of individual responsibility and the possibility of action, as Syme discovers when he is temporarily overcome by moral indecision on being faced with two balanced and contradictory courses of action. The moral guide for the committed anarchist, in Chesterton's opinion, is despair, which generates the conviction that 'Every man knows in his heart . . . that nothing is worth doing'.[54] The artist who plays the anarchist's game, divorcing art from life, is little better. At the party, Gregory and Syme dispute the meaning of poetry. Gregory celebrates the artist as a kind of terrorist for whom the predictability of life is an anathema. For Syme, exactly the opposite is the case. For him, a timetable is preferable to a book of poetry. Chaos, he argues, is dull because it cannot engage the imagination in anticipation, while real magic lies in the satisfaction of expectation: the 'whole magic is in this, that he [a man] does say Victoria, and lo! It is Victoria'.[55] Whatever the reader thinks of poetry, Syme's definition of magic could have considerable appeal today.

Robert L. Caserio's essay on modernism as terrorism makes a powerful point about the integrity of Chesterton's position on art. I would like briefly to consider Chesterton's response to another aesthetic realisation of the modern, impressionism, whose popularity had swept across England at the turn of the century but whose claims about the nature of seeing had aroused his suspicions.[56] He suggests that impressionism disrupts artistic truth, creating anarchic, hallucinogenic experiences which serve only to confuse and disorientate. In the sequence from *The Man Who Was Thursday* in which Syme might be being chased by President Sunday, the head of the secret society with which he has become involved or, alternatively, might be chasing the police, he and his five fellow conspirators plunge out of bright sunshine into a wood. Desperately trying to distinguish friend from enemy, to see clearly the identity of those around him, Syme is baffled by a chiaroscuro that constantly changes the shape, the colour and the significance of what he looks at. The description is beautiful, fantastic and entirely in keeping with the atmosphere of Syme's adventure, but Chesterton cannot resist pointing out that this is 'Impressionism . . . another name for that final scepticism which can find no floor to the universe'.[57]

The story he tells, Chesterton makes clear, is a dangerous story which can only be recounted from the vantage point of survival: as the introductory poem concludes: 'And I may safely write it now / And you may safely read'.[58] Danger does not lie in the adventure itself, which has all the elements of a good thriller, nor in its night-mare elements, which are simply mysteries that the reader waits in suspense to see resolved. But the written messages that President Sunday tosses at Syme and the chasing policemen in the fantastic penultimate sequence, which seem like so much gobbledygook, have a similar effect to the random and incomprehensible nature of terrorism. Dr Bull's note with an unanswerable question ('What about Martin Tupper *now?*'), and Gogol's note with an answer to an unspecified question ('The word, I fancy, should be "pink"'), point to a hidden context which might provide an answer, if it could be found.[59] Syme's sanity is not threatened by a simple failure to under-stand, or by the possibility of a cosmic joke, or even by a universe without meaning. The terror lies in having to face the loss of what is knowable. As the friends later discover after the confusions have been explained, they all relied on 'the thing I never saw', – the voice in the dark – to support them.[60] In spy story terms, this voice gave them the mission to track down the anarchists and, in Chesterton's moral narrative of resistance to modern chaos, it was the inner voice of individual conscience which refused to abandon a belief in the beauty of order.

Syme does find a route back. The simple pleasures remain with him and recur at the darkest moments of his adventure giving him courage and consolation. They are the source of the instinct which takes him back to Saffron Park and, at the conclusion of the novel, to 'the girl with the gold-red hair, cutting lilac before breakfast, with the great unconscious gravity of a girl'.[61] The suburb which had betrayed its nature and allowed anarchy in is restored through love as a location of the ordinary.

The formal complexity of *The Man Who Was Thursday* is, para-doxically, a fitting expression of the kind of human simplicity Chesterton tried to evoke. When everything is resolved – all the deceptions, dangers and duplicities that human beings create for themselves – there still remain the important questions about the human condition. The excitement (the adventure), the comedy (the flagrant absurdities), the mystery (I defy any reader to claim that they never once wondered whether Chesterton had lost the plot), the fantasy (the arbitrary changes of seasons and weather to add twists to the plot or drama to an event), the allegory (strength through suffering) and the love story (Syme and Miss Gregory) are the extra-ordinary elements that lie behind the ordinary suburban man and woman who, most of all, want the train to be on time.

Gissing, Wells, Bennett and Chesterton all signalled the closure of the suburban theme in different ways. In Gissing's novels the sense of closure is overwhelming. Although he was the first of these novelists to make the suburbs his focus (as Arnold Bennett's Mr Aked knew) and had witnessed the horror of the inner city slums at first hand, he felt no optimism about suburban expansion. He used his material to compose a ruthless indictment of a materialistic society which he felt had betrayed Britain's cultural heritage and sacrificed its future on the altar of mediocrity. The integrity of his realist aesthetic only serves to negate any possibility of change. Characters like Nancy Tarrant in *In the Year of Jubilee*, and even the self-aware Rhoda Nunn in *The Odd Women*, seem frail in a brutal world, and human agency seems an illusion in a society where shifting surfaces disguise capital-ism's single-minded project.

H. G. Wells began at a very different point from George Gissing, but the pessimistic drift of *Tono-Bungay* and *The New Machiavelli* is barely disguised by his energetic interest in the workings of society and the place of the individual in a larger scheme. Unintentionally, he nurtured his own disillusion by his determination to search for an overarching idea that would resolve society's contradictions, and his growing sense, as a consequence, that society had run out of control. Chesterton certainly feared this aspect of Wells's thinking. John Carey argues that 'system meant the end of individuality', and as the reader moves from the delight of Wells's social comedies through the ironies of *Tono-Bungay* to the retreat of *The New Machiavelli*, the power of his vision weakens.[62] The individual is marginalised or over-whelmed by social forces variously defined as Darwinian, capitalist, (misguidedly) socialist and unscientific, while the suburbs shrink from a national vista of equality to the dingy and limiting terrain of the defeated.

Arnold Bennett never lost interest in the lives of ordinary work-ing people. His natural imaginative habitat is the suburbs, whether those of the Five Towns or the lower-middle-class suburbs of London. His ability to give the reader 'access to the realities that blaze and coruscate inside dowdy and commonplace bodies' is remarkable, even frightening, when we see its possible implications in a character like Henry Earlforward.[63] Bennett's vision is unsentimental and secular. The enigma or mystery that his central characters confront marks an inner moment when individuals become aware of a new dimension of themselves – an extra-rational intensity of living that occurs irregularly and spasmodically but is an intrinsic part of the human personality. Nevertheless *Riceyman Steps*, as I argued earlier in this chapter, marks the conclusion of one significant phase of suburban history and fiction in the aftermath of the First World War.[64]

G. K. Chesterton, the least consciously literary writer of the four whom I have considered, was arguably the most original. He effectively narrowed the distance between his identity as a middle-class author and the classes for whom and about which he wrote, by deploying the forms of popular culture that they most enjoyed. Play is important to Chesterton's vision: it is a way of relaxing, of finding enjoyment and laughter, but it is also a learning process. Playing at something, as children do, playing at being a king, or a hero, or a spy, as Quin, Wayne and Syme do, is a means of discovery. Play is also a complex form of communication. Wells, reminiscing in 1944 about his relationship with Chesterton, describes an evening of acrimonious differences which were finally resolved by playing out scenes with a toy theatre.[65]

The greatest contrasts between these four writers arose less from their political positions than from their attitudes to literary art and from their very different temperaments. Gissing exemplified everything that Chesterton, at the other end of the spectrum, detested. He was inclined to depression throughout his life, and appears to have been a man in constant struggle with himself. In addition, he was committed to an austere artistic integrity which despised journalism and the popular readership. It has to be a joke at Gissing's expense that Bennett allows Mr Aked to claim that he read Gissing's novels 'for fun'. Wells was at the opposite extreme again. A highly intelligent man who revelled in ideas, he pitched his novels and articles at a popular readership, winning the appreciation of Arnold Bennett as well as a vast, devoted readership which put his books on a par in popularity with those of Charles Dickens.[66] Bennett gives the impression that he stumbled into literature almost accidentally, but once there, his commitment was total. As a journalist he was influential in forming public opinion about books; as a popular novelist he became affluent and in a position to enjoy a convivial life; as a serious novelist and a socialist he caught the mood of the times with several realistic novels about individual men and women responding to a changing world. Virginia Woolf certainly dismissed his talents in her well-known essay 'Mr Bennett and Mrs Brown', published in 1923. However she was fighting back out of a self-interest triggered by her irritation at Bennett's review of *Jacob's Room*, in which he had criticised the weakness of her characterisation and expressed doubt about her literary future.[67] Chesterton rivalled Bennett in his commitment to journalism as a crucial contribution to, and intervention in, popular culture and opinion. For him, novel writing was perhaps simply an alternative approach to communicating his concerns about modern civilisation to his many readers; and his refashioning of traditional genres, which rivals Wells's science fiction in its originality, merged easily with the parable, myth and symbol of the religious imagination. Together, the fundamentally different approaches of these four writers mapped out the suburbs and the lives of the new aspiring suburbanites, the society that produced them and the ideologies that might explain them.

What is true of these writers is true of my discussion as a whole. At the beginning of this book, I argued that the concept of the suburban imaginary, mapped using a triangulation of location, social significance and individual desire, held apparently disparate writings in a symbiotic relationship within a suburban grand narrative. However, in the egalitarian spirit of this inquiry, 'grand' is not intended to imply a single, monolithic narrative but one comprised of many diverse and competing smaller narratives, all of which contribute to our understanding of the suburban idea. For this reason, I have avoided emphasising a chronological progression, preferring to consider the thirty-five years from 1880 to 1925 as a site of exchange in which these writings interconnect and overlap. There is no doubt that at least one of these narratives follows the drum beat of history, tracing a loss of optimism as early hopes for the suburbs gave way to the frequently grim realities of suburban living in the twentieth century. But many of them do not fit easily into models of regression or progression, and few of them are told from only one perspective. One of the most controversial elements is the class narrative; another is the empowerment of women and its corollary, the re-gendering of the domestic realm; yet another is the fading of the rural dream. A narrative of literary history might (or might not) favour the experiments with form, the sidestepping of tradition, the emergence of distinctively female voices and the changed relationship of writers and readers. Like a 'truth in mosaic', all the conflicting and diverse responses to the suburbs work together to compose a picture of historical change, of cultural, gender and class transformations, and of bewildering formal inventiveness.[68] Such a process might well be called a revolution.

Notes

1 Arnold Bennett, [1898] A Man from the North (London: Methuen, 1912), 68.
2 Linda Anderson, Bennett, Wells and Conrad: Narrative in transition (Basingstoke: Macmillan, 1988), 44, 53.
3 Arnold Bennett, [1911] Hilda Lessways (London: Methuen and Co. Ltd, 1961), 388.
4 Journal entry for 4 February 1924, in Arnold Bennett, The Journals, selected and edited by Frank Swinnerton (Harmondsworth: Penguin, 1971), 470.
5 Alan Sillitoe, 'Introduction' in Arnold Bennett, (1923) Riceyman Steps (London: Pan Books, 1964), 15. See David Trotter's comment on Dickens and portrayals of the working classes on page 171.
6 Margaret Drabble, Arnold Bennett: A biography (London: Weidenfeld and Nicolson, 1974), 351.
7 John Lucas, Arnold Bennett: A study of his fiction (London: Methuen and Co, Ltd., 1974), 195.
8 A Man from the North, 166.
9 Several critics including Lucas, Arnold Bennett (20), and Anderson, Bennett, Wells and Conrad (57), have commented on the thematic similarity of A Man from the North and Love and Mr Lewisham which was published two years later.
10 A Man from the North, 46, 249.
11 Lucas, Arnold Bennett, 23.
12 A Man from the North, 186.
13 Anderson, Bennett, Wells and Conrad, 55.
14 A Man from the North, 263.
15 A Man from the North, 186.
16 A Man from the North, 120.
17 A Man from the North, 100–101.
18 A Man From the North, 106.
19 Anderson, Bennett, Wells and Conrad, 57.
20 Riceyman Steps, 234.
21 Arnold Bennett, [1911] Hilda Lessways (London: Methuen, 1961), 38.
22 Hilda Lessways, 8.
23 Hilda Lessways, 29, 187.
24 Hilda Lessways, 407.
25 Hilda Lessways, 139.
26 Riceyman Steps, 68.
27 Riceyman Steps, 261.

28 *Riceyman Steps*, 250.
29 *Riceyman Steps*, 234.
30 See Lucas, *Arnold Bennett*, 201; Drabble, *Arnold Bennett*, 208.
31 *Riceyman Steps*, 227.
32 Wells, *Anticipations*, 110–111.
33 G. K. Chesterton, in *Daily News* (8 August 1903), cited in John D.
    Coates, *Chesterton and the Edwardian Cultural Crisis* (Hull: Hull University
    Press, 1984), 79.
34 Carey, *The Intellectuals and the Masses*, 54.
35 Margaret Canovan discusses Chesterton's support for land redistribution
    in G. K. *Chesterton, Radical Populist* (New York: Harcourt Brace Jovanich,
    1978).
36 G. K. Chesterton, [1904] *The Napoleon of Notting Hill* in *A G. K.
    Chesterton Omnibus* (London: Methuen, 1958), 3–200; G. K. Chesterton,
    (1908) *The Man Who Was Thursday: A nightmare*, with an introduction by
    Kingsley Amis (Harmondsworth: Penguin, 1986) 11, 16.
37 *The Napoleon of Notting Hill*, 54.
38 Coates, *Chesterton and the Edwardian Cultural Crisis* gives an excellent
    account of Chesterton's position on these issues in chapter 2, 20–44.
39 For an account of Wells's and Chesterton's differences over socialism see
    Foot, *H. G.*, 208–10, which includes a footnote that illuminates their
    mutual tolerance of each other's viewpoint.
40 Carey, *The Intellectuals and the Masses*, 152.
41 Terry Eagleton, 'Flight to the Real' in Sally Ledger and Scott
    McCracken (eds), *Cultural Politics at the Fin-de-Siècle*
    (Cambridge: Cambridge University Press, 1984), 11–21 (19).
42 *The Napoleon of Notting Hill*, 14.
43 The election in 2002 of Hartlepool Football Club's monkey pre-match
    mascot as Mayor of Hartlepool, on a platform of bananas for children,
    increased youth facilities and reduced crime, is an astonishing twenty-
    first-century realisation of Chesterton's joke.
44 *The Napoleon of Notting Hill*, 183.
45 See G. K. Chesterton, [1929] 'The Thing' in *G. K. Chesterton: A selection
    from his non-fictional prose*, selected by W. H. Auden (London: Faber and
    Faber, 1970), 147–149, where Chesterton takes Wells to task for his
    literalism over the myth of the Garden of Eden.
46 *The Napoleon of Notting Hill*, 70.
47 *The Napoleon of Notting*, 75.
48 *The Napoleon of Notting Hill*, 194.
49 *The Napoleon of Notting Hill*, preface.
50 *The Napoleon of Notting Hill*, 41.
51 Edmund Burke, [1790] *Reflections on the Revolution in France*
    (Harmondsworth: Penguin, 1986), 23.
52 See the introductory chapter of James W. Hulse, *Revolutionists in London:
    A study of five unorthodox socialists* (Oxford: Oxford University Press,
    1970).
53 Henry James, [1886] *The Princess Casamassima* and Conrad, [1901] *The
    Secret Agent* both wrote about anarchist cells in London. Fiction about
    the fear of foreign invasion was also popular; while Sherlock Holmes, in

Conan Doyle's detective stories, often tracked the source of crime down
to disaffected colonial subjects or masters. This suggests a high level of
insecurity about national safety.

54 *The Man Who Was Thursday*, 64.
55 *The Man Who Was Thursday*, 13.
56 Robert L. Caserio, 'G. K. Chesterton and the Terrorist God Outside
    Modernism' in Hapgood and Paxton (eds), *Outside Modernism*, 63–84.
    In his discussion, Caserio interrogates the supposed divide between
    modernism and non-modernism. In the context of early twentieth-century
    anarchism, he suggests that although the multiple meanings characteristic
    of a modernist text apparently act as a form of aesthetic terrorism in
    breaking up the possibility of knowledge and resolution in realist texts,
    modernist writers also came to reassert the value of tradition and
    continuity in response to undiscriminating and arbitrary violence.
57 *The Man Who Was Thursday*, 127.
58 *The Man Who Was Thursday*, 7.
59 *The Man Who Was Thursday*, 156, 161.
60 *The Man Who Was Thursday*, 147.
61 *The Man Who Was Thursday*, 184.
62 Carey, *The Intellectuals and the Masses*, 147.
63 Carey, *The Intellectuals and the Masses*, 163.
64 Dennis Hardy, *From Garden Cities to New Towns: Campaigning for town
    and country planning, 1899–1946*, (London: E. and F. N. Spon, 1991), 10,
    notes that after the First World War, 'For some, the suburbs were a land
    of opportunity' in a further wave of suburban development.
65 H. G. Wells, *Journalism and Prophecy, 1893–1946*, edited by W. Warren
    Waager (London: Bodley Head, 1964), 270.
66 *The New Survey*, 120.
67 See Arnold Bennett, 'Is the Novel Decaying?' *Cassell's Weekly* (28 March
    1923).
68 John Ruskin, letter from Venice (25 May 1846) in [1849] *The Seven
    Lamps of Architecture* (London: George Allen, 1903), vol. 8, xxiii.

SUBURBAN FICTION

A publication timeline

1879 Richard Jefferies, *Wild Life in a Southern County*
1883 Richard Jefferies, *The Story of My Heart*
      Arthur Conan Doyle, *Beyond the City*
1885 Richard Jefferies, *After London*
1889 Richard Jefferies, *Nature Near London*
      Jerome K. Jerome, *Three Men in a Boat*
1891 William Morris, *News from Nowhere*
      George Gissing, *New Grub Street*
1892 George and Weedon Grossmith, *The Diary of a Nobody*
1894 George Gissing, *The Odd Women*
      Alfred Austin, *The Garden that I Love*
1895 Edwin Pugh, *A Street in Suburbia*
      William Pett Ridge, *A Clever Wife*
      George Gissing, *In the Year of Jubilee*
1897 George Gissing, *The Whirlpool*
1898 Arnold Bennett, *A Man from the North*
      Elizabeth von Arnim, *Elizabeth and Her German Garden*
1899 Elizabeth von Arnim, *The Solitary Summer*
      William Pett Ridge, *Outside the Radius*
      Shan Bullock, *The Barrys*
      Arthur Conan Doyle, *A Duet*
1900 H. G. Wells, *Love and Mr Lewisham*
1901 Violet Purton Biddle, *Small Gardens and How to Make the Most of Them*
      Mrs Leslie Williams, *A Garden in the Suburbs*
      William Pett Ridge, *Mord Em'ly*
      Mary Hamilton, *Poor Elisabeth*
      Barbara Campbell, *The Garden of a Commuter's Wife*
1904 G. K. Chesterton, *The Napoleon of Notting Hill*
      George Gissing, *The Private Papers of Henry Ryecroft*
1905 [posthumous] Richard Jefferies, *The Open Air*
      H. G. Wells, *Kipps*
      H. G. Wells, *A Modern Utopia*

1906 Alice and Claude Askew, *Anna of the Plains*
        Barbara Campbell, *The Garden, You, and I*
        John Galsworthy, *The Man of Property*
        Keble Howard, *The Smiths of Surbiton*
1907 Shan Bullock, *Robert Thorne*
        Keble Howard, *The Bachelor Girls*
        Alice and Claude Askew, *The Baxter Family*
        E. M. Forster, *The Longest Journey*
        Edward Thomas, *The Pocket Book of Poems and Songs for the Open Air*
1908 G. K. Chesterton, *The Man Who Was Thursday*
        H. G. Wells, *Tono-Bungay*
        E. M. Forster, *A Room with a View*
        Edwin Pugh, *The Broken Honeymoon*
1909 H. G. Wells, *Ann Veronica*
        Keble Howard, *The Smiths of Valley View*
1910 Sophie Cole, *A Wardour Street Idyll*
        H. G. Wells, *The History of Mr Polly*
        Louise Gerard, *The Hyena of Kullu*
        E. M. Forster, *Howards End*
1911 Arnold Bennett, *Hilda Lessways*
        Louise Gerard, *A Tropical Tangle*
        H. G. Wells, *The New Machiavelli*
        Edward Thomas, *Light and Twilight*
1913 Mary Hamilton, *Mrs Brett*
        Edward Thomas, *The Happy-Go-Lucky Morgans*
1914 Louise Gerard, *Flower-of-the-Moon*
1917 Sophie Cole, *A London Posy*
        Keble Howard, *The Smiths at War*
1922 Elizabeth von Arnim, *The Enchanted April*
1923 Arnold Bennett, *Riceyman Steps*
1923 Louise Gerard, *A Wreath of Stars*
1926 Sophie Cole, *Daffodil Alley*

SELECT BIBLIOGRAPHY

Ackroyd, Peter, *London: The biography* (London: Chatto and Windus, 2000)

Altick, Richard D., [1957] *The English Common Reader: A social history of the mass reading public, 1800–1900* (Chicago: Chicago University Press, 1967)

Anderson, Linda, *Bennett, Wells and Conrad: Narrative in transition* (Basingstoke: Macmillan, 1988)

Anderson, Rachel, *The Purple Heart Throbs: The sub-literature of love* (Hodder and Stoughton, 1974)

Anstey, F., *Voces Populi* (London: Longman, Green and Co., 1890)

Ardis, Ann L., *New Woman, New Novels: Feminism and early modernism* (New Brunswick, NJ and London: Rutgers University Press, 1990)

Ardis, Ann L., *Modernism and Cultural Conflict, 1880–1922* (Cambridge: Cambridge University Press, 2002)

Askew, Alice and Claude, *Anna of the Plains* (London: F. V. White and Co., 1906)

Askew, Alice and Claude, *The Baxter Family* (London: F. V. White and Co., 1907)

Austin, Alfred, *The Garden that I Love* (London: Macmillan, 1894)

Ballaster, Ros, Margaret Beetham, Elizabeth Frazer and Sandra Hebron, *Women's Worlds: Ideology, femininity and the woman's magazine* (Basingstoke: Macmillan, 1991)

Beauman, Nicola, *A Very Great Profession* (London: Virago, 1989)

Beetham, Margaret, *A Magazine of Her Own? Domesticity and desire in the women's magazine, 1800–1914* (London: Routledge, 1996)

Bennett, Arnold, [1898] *A Man from the North* (London: Methuen, 1912)

Bennett, Arnold, [1911] *Hilda Lessways* (London: Methuen, 1961)

Bennett, Arnold, [1923] *Riceyman Steps* (London: Pan Books, 1964)

Bennett, Arnold, *The Journals*, selected and edited by Frank Swinnerton (Harmondsworth: Penguin, 1971)

Bennett, Sue, *Five Centuries of Women and Gardens* (London: National Portrait Gallery Publications, 2000)

Berneri, Marie-Louise, *Journey to Utopia* (London: Freedom Press, 1982)

Besant, Walter, *South London* (London: Chatto and Windus, 1899)

Biddle, Violet Purton, *Small Gardens and how to make the most of them* (London: C. Arthur Pearson, 1901)

Bodkin, Maud, 'Archetypes in "The Ancient Mariner"' in David Lodge (ed.), *Twentieth Century Literary Criticism* (London: Longman, 1972), 190–200

Bolsterli, M. J., *The Early Community at Bedford Park: 'corporate happiness' in the first garden suburb* (London: Routledge and Kegan Paul, 1977)

Booth, Charles, *Labour and Life of the People*, vols 1 and 2 (London: Williams and Norgate, 1891)

Booth, Charles, *Life and Labour of the People in London* (London: Macmillan, 1902)

Bradbury, Malcolm and James McFarlane, *Modernism 1890–1930* (Harmondsworth: Penguin, 1976)

Briggs, Asa, 'The Human Aggregate' in H. J. Dyos and Michael Wolff (eds), *The Victorian City: Images and realities*, vol. 1 (London: Routledge and Kegan Paul, 1973), 83–104

Brown, Jane, *The Pursuit of Paradise: A social history of gardens and gardening* (London: Harper Collins, 2000)

Bullock, Shan, *The Barrys* (London and New York: Harper and Bros., 1899)

Bullock, Shan, *Robert Thorne: The story of a London clerk* (London: T. Werner Laurie, 1907)

Burke, Peter, 'History of Events and the Revival of Narrative' in Peter Burke (ed.), *New Perspectives on Historical Writing* (Cambridge: Polity Press, 1991), 233–248

Buzard, James, 'Ethnography as Interruption: *News from Nowhere*, narrative, and the modern romance of authority', *Victorian Studies* (Spring 1997), 445–474

Calder, Jenni, *The Victorian House* (London: Batsford, 1977)

Campbell, Barbara, *The Garden of a Commuter's Wife* (New York and London: Macmillan, 1901)

Campbell, Barbara, *The Garden, You, and I* (New York and London: Macmillan, 1906)

Campbell, Barbara, *The Open Window: Tales of the months* (London and New York: Macmillan, 1908)

Carey, John, *The Intellectuals and the Masses: Pride and prejudice among the literary intelligentsia, 1880–1939* (London: Faber and Faber, 1992)

Carr, John Dickson, *The Life of Sir Arthur Conan Doyle* (London: John Murray, 1949)

Cavaliero, Glen, *The Rural Tradition in the English Novel 1900–1939* (Basingstoke: Macmillan, 1977)

Chesterton, G. K., [1904] *The Napoleon of Notting Hill* in *A G. K. Chesterton Omnibus* (London: Methuen, 1958)

Chesterton, G. K., [1908] *The Man Who Was Thursday*, with an introduction by Kingsley Amis (Harmondsworth: Penguin, 1986)

Chesterton, G. K., *G. K. Chesterton: A selection from his non-fictional prose*, selected by W. H. Auden (London: Faber and Faber, 1970)

Clark, Suzanne, *Sentimental Modernism: Women writers and the revolution of the word* (Bloomington: Indiana University Press, 1991)

Clarke, W. Spencer, *The Suburban Homes of London: A residential guide to favourite London localities, their society, celebrities and associations* (London: Chatto and Windus, 1881)

Coates, John, *Chesterton and the Edwardian Cultural Crisis* (Hull: Hull University Press, 1984)

Cockburn, Claud, *Bestseller: The books that everyone read 1900–1939* (London: Sidgwick and Jackson, 1972)

Cole, Sophie, *A Wardour Street Idyll* (London: Mills and Boon, 1910)

Cole, Sophie, *A London Posy* (London: Mills and Boon, 1917)

Cole, Sophie, *Daffodil Alley* (London: Mills and Boon, 1926)

Coleman, Stephen and Paddy Sullivan (eds), *William Morris and News from Nowhere: A vision for our time* (Bideford: Green Books, 1990)

Cooke, William, *Edward Thomas: A critical biography, 1878–1917* (London: Faber and Faber, 1970)

Creese, Walter L., 'Imagination in the Suburb' in Knoepflmacher and Tennyson (eds), *Nature and the Victorian Imagination*, 44–67

Cucullu, Lois, 'Shepherds in the Parlor: Forster's apostles, pagans and native sons', *Novel: A forum on fiction*, 32:1 (Fall 1998), 19–47

Daly, Nicholas, *Modernism, Romance and the Fin-de-Siècle: Popular fiction and British culture, 1880–1914* (Cambridge: Cambridge University Press, 2000)

Dawson, W. J., 'The Transformation of John Loxley' in *London Idylls* (London: Hodder and Stoughton, 1985), 145–178

Dixon, Jay, *The Romance Fiction of Mills & Boon, 1909–1990* (London: University College London Press, 1999)

Doyle, Arthur Conan, *The Great Shadow and Beyond the City* (London: Simpkin, Hamilton, Kent and Co., 1893)

Doyle, Arthur Conan, [1899] *A Duet, with an occasional chorus* (London: Smith, Elder and Co., 1903)

Drabble, Margaret, *Arnold Bennett: A biography* (London: Weidenfeld and Nicolson, 1974)

Dyos, H. J., *Victorian Suburb: A study of the growth of Camberwell* (Leicester: Leicester University Press, 1961)

Dyos, H. J. and D. D. Reeder, 'Slums and Suburbs' in H. J. Dyos and Michael Wolff (eds), *The Victorian City: Images and realities*, vol. 2 (London: Routledge and Kegan Paul, 1973), 359–388

Eagleton, Terry, 'Flight to the Real' in Sally Ledger and Scott McCracken (eds), *Cultural Politics at the Fin-de-Siècle* (Cambridge: Cambridge University Press, 1984)

Edwards, Arthur M., *The Design of Suburbia: A critical study in environmental history* (London: Pembridge Press, 1981)

Faulkner, Peter (ed.), *William Morris: The critical heritage* (London and Boston: Routledge and Kegan Paul, 1973)

Federico, Annette R., *Idol of Suburbia: Marie Corelli and the late-Victorian literary culture* (Charlottesville and London: Virginia University Press, 2000)

Fitzgerald, Percy, *London City Suburbs as they are Today* (London: Leadenhall Press, 1893)

Flint, Kate, 'Fictional Suburbia', *Literature and History*, 8:1 (Spring 1982), 67–81

Foot, Michael, *H. G.: The History of Mr Wells* (London: Doubleday, 1995)

Forster, E. M., [1907] *The Longest Journey* (London: Edward Arnold, 1964)

Forster, E. M., [1908] *A Room with a View* (Harmondsworth: Penguin, 2000)

Forster, E. M., [1910] *Howards End* (Harmondsworth: Penguin, 1989)

Forster, E. M., [1927] *Aspects of the Novel* (Harmondsworth: Penguin, 1990)

Forster, E. M., *Collected Short Stories* (Harmondsworth: Penguin, 1954)

Fussell, Paul, *The Great War and Modern Memory* (Oxford: Oxford University Press, 1977)

Galsworthy, John, [1906] *The Man of Property* (Harmondsworth: Penguin, 1967)

Gardner, Philip, *E. M. Forster: The critical heritage* (London: Routledge and Kegan Paul, 1973)

Gates, Barbara T., *Kindred Nature: Victorian and Edwardian women embrace the living world* (Chicago and London: Chicago University Press, 1998)

Geddes, Patrick, [1915] *Cities in Evolution: An introduction to the town planning movement and to the study of cities* (London: Ernest Benn, 1968)

Gerard, Louise, *The Hyena of Kullu* (London: Methuen, 1910)

Gerard, Louise, *A Tropical Tangle* (London: Mills and Boon, 1911)

Gerard, Louise, *Flower-of-the-Moon: A romance of the forest* (London: Mills and Boon, 1914)

Gerard, Louise, *A Wreath of Stars: A romance of Venice* (London: Mills and Boon, 1923)

Girouard, Mark, *The Return to Camelot: Chivalry and the English gentleman* (New Haven: Yale University Press, 1981)

Gissing, George, [1891] *New Grub Street* (Harmondsworth: Penguin, 1968)

Gissing, George, [1893] *The Odd Women* (London: A. H. Bullen, 1905)

Gissing, George, *In the Year of Jubilee* (London: Watergate Classics, 1895)

Gissing, George, [1897] *The Whirlpool*, edited by William Greenslade (London: J. M. Dent, 1997)

Gissing, George, *The Private Papers of Henry Ryecroft* (London: Constable, 1904)

Goode, John, *George Gissing: Ideology and fiction* (London: Vision Press, 1978)

Goode, John, 'William Morris's *News from Nowhere*: The figuration of desire' in *Wisps of Violence: Producing public and private politics in the turn-of-the-century British novel*, edited by Eileen Sypher (London: Verso, 1993), 87–103

Goode, John, *Collected Essays of John Goode*, edited by Charles Swann (Staffordshire: Keele University Press, 1995)

Greenslade, William, *Degeneration, Culture and the Novel, 1880–1949* (Cambridge: Cambridge University Press, 1994)

Greenwood, Frederick, 'What Has Become of the Middle Classes?', *Blackwood's Magazine*, 138 (August 1885), 175–189

Gregor, Ian, *Reading the Victorian Novel: Detail into form* (London: Vision Press, 1980)

Grossmith, George and Weedon, [1892] *The Diary of a Nobody*, edited by Kate Flint (New York and Oxford: Oxford University Press, 1995)

Hall, Mr and Mrs S. C. [1859] *The Book of the Thames from Its Rise to Its Fall* (London: Charlotte James, 1983)

Hall, Peter and Colin Wood, *Sociable Cities: The legacy of Ebenezer Howard* (Chichester: John Wiley and Sons, 1998)

Hamilton, Mary, *Poor Elisabeth* (London: Hurst and Blackett, 1901)

Hamilton, Mary, *Mrs Brett* (London: Stanley Paul and Co., 1913)

Hapgood, Lynne and Nancy L. Paxton (eds), *Outside Modernism: In pursuit of the British novel 1900–1930* (Basingstoke: Macmillan, 2000)

Hapgood, Lynne, '"The New Suburbanites" and Contested Class Identities in the London Suburbs, 1880–1900' in Roger Webster (ed.) *Expanding Suburbia: Reviewing suburban narratives* (New York and Oxford: Berghahn Books, 2000), 31–50

Hardy, Dennis, *From Garden Cities to New Towns: Campaigning for town and country planning, 1899–1946* (London: E. and F. N. Spon, 1991)

Hardy, Dennis and Colin Ward, *Arcadia for All: The legacy of a makeshift landscape* (London and New York: Mansell, 1984)

Harris, José, *Private Lives, Public Spirit: Britain 1870–1914* (Harmondsworth: Penguin, 1993)

Harrison, Frederic, *The Meaning of History and Other Historical Pieces* (London: Macmillan, 1984)

Harvey, David, *Consciousness and the Urban Experience* (Oxford: Basil Blackwell, 1985)

Hoggart, Richard, *The Uses of Literacy: Aspects of working-class life* (London: Chatto and Windus, 1957)

Howard, Ebenezer, *To-Morrow, A peaceful path to real reform* (London: Swan Sonnenschein and Co., 1898)

Howard, Keble, *The Smiths of Surbiton: A comedy without a plot* (London: Chapman Hall, 1906)

Howard, Keble, *The Bachelor Girls and their Adventures in Search of Independence* (London: Chapman and Hall, 1907)

Howard, Keble, *The Smiths of Valley View: Being further adventures of the Smiths of Surbiton*, 2nd impression (London: Cassell and Co., 1909)

Howard, Keble, *The Smiths at War* (London: John Lane, 1917)

Jackson, Alan A., *Semi-Detached London: Suburban development, life and transport, 1900–1939* (London: Allen and Unwin, 1973)

Jackson, Holbrook, [1913] *The Eighteen-Nineties: A review of art and ideas at the close of the nineteenth century* (London: The Cresset Library, 1988)

Jackson, Kate, *George Newnes and the New Journalism in Britain, 1880–1910: Culture and profit* (Aldershot, Burlington USA, Singapore and Sydney: Ashgate, 2001)

Jefferies, Richard, *Wild Life in a Southern County* (London: John Murray, 1879)

Jefferies, Richard, [1883] *The Story of My Heart* (London: Eyre and Spottiswoode, 1949)

Jefferies, Richard, [1885] *After London and Amaryllis at the Fair* (London: J. M. Dent, 1939)

Jefferies, Richard, *Nature Near London* (London: Chatto and Windus, 1889)

Jefferies, Richard, *The Open Air* (London: Chatto and Windus, 1905)

Jerome, Jerome K., [1889] *Three Men in a Boat (to say nothing of the dog)*, with an introduction by Humphrey Carpenter (Stroud: Alan Sutton, 1989)

Jerome, Jerome K., *My Life and Times* (New York and London: Harper Brothers, 1926)

Kaufman, M., [1907] *The Housing of the Working Classes and of the Poor* (London: E. P. Publishing, Rowan and Littlefield, 1975)

Keating, P. J., *The Working Classes in Victorian Fiction* (London: Routledge, 1971)

Keating, P. J., *Into Unknown England, 1866–1913: Selections from the social explorers* (Manchester: Manchester University Press, 1976)

Keating, P. J., *The Haunted Study: A social history of the English novel, 1875–1914* (London: Fontana, 1991)

Kellaway, Deborah (ed.), *The Virago Book of Women Gardeners* (London: Virago, 1997)

Kemp, Sandra, Charlotte Mitchell and David Trotter (eds), *Edwardian Fiction: An Oxford Companion* (Oxford: Oxford University Press, 1997)

King, Anthony D., *Urbanism, Colonialism and the World-Economy: Cultural and spatial foundations of the world urban system* (New York and London: Routledge, 1991)

Knoepflmacher, U. C. and G. B. Tennyson, *Nature and the Victorian Imagination* (Berkeley and Los Angeles: California University Press, 1977)

Krebs, Paula, *Gender, Race and the Writing of Empire: Public discourse and the Boer War* (Cambridge: Cambridge University Press, 1999)

Kumar, Krishan, 'A Pilgrimage of Hope: William Morris's journey to utopia', *Utopian Studies*, 5:1 (1994), 89–107

Leavis, Q. D., [1932] *Fiction and the Reading Public* (London: Pimlico, 2000)

Ledger, Sally, *The New Woman: Fiction and feminism at the fin-de-siècle* (Manchester: Manchester University Press, 1997)

Lewis, Roger C., 'News from Nowhere: Arcadia or utopia?', *Journal of the William Morris Society*, 7:2 (Spring 1987), 15–25

Lindsay, Jack, *William Morris: His life and work* (London: Constable, 1975)

Looker, Samuel J. and Crichton Porteous, *Richard Jefferies: Man of the fields: A biography and letters* (London: John Baker, 1964)

Low, Sidney J., 'The Rise of the Suburbs', *Contemporary Review*, 60 (October 1891), 545–558

Lucas, John, *Arnold Bennett: A study of his fiction* (London: Methuen, 1974)

MacCarthy, Fiona, *William Morris: A life for our time* (London: Faber and Faber, 1994)

Marrott, Harold V., *The Life and Letters of John Galsworthy* (New York: Scribner's Sons, 1936)

Martin, Robert K. and George Piggott (eds), *Queer Forster* (Chicago and London: Chicago University Press, 1997)

Masterman, C. F. G., [1901] *The Condition of England*, edited and with an introduction by J. T. Boulton (London: Methuen, 1960)

McAleer, Joseph, *Passion's Fortune: The story of Mills and Boon* (Oxford: Oxford University Press, 1999)

McClintock, Anne, *Imperial Leather: Race, gender and sexuality in the colonial contest* (New York and London: Routledge, 1995)

McLaughlin, Joseph, *Writing the Urban Jungle: Reading Empire in London from Doyle to Eliot* (Charlottesville and London: Virginia University Press, 2000)

Medalie, David, *E. M. Forster's Modernism* (Basingstoke: Palgrave, 2002)

Merivale, Patricia, *Pan, the Goat God: His myth in modern times* (Cambridge, MA: Harvard University Press, 1969)

Morris, William, [1891] *News from Nowhere, or, An epoch of rest: being some chapters from a utopian romance*, edited by James Redmond (London: Routledge and Kegan Paul, 1970)

Morris, William, *A Choice of William Morris's Verse*, selected and with an introduction by Geoffrey Grigson (London: Faber and Faber, 1969)

Morris, William, *The Political Writings of William Morris*, edited by A. L. Morton (London: Lawrence and Wishart, 1984)

Moss, Alfred, *Jerome K. Jerome: His life and work*, with an introduction by Coulson Kernahan (London: Selwyn and Blount, 1928)

Mumford, Lewis, *The Culture of Cities* (London: Secker and Warburg, 1940)

Murray, Kathleen L., *Letters from the Wilderness* (Calcutta and London: W. Thacker and Co., 1913)

Murray, Kathleen L., *My Garden in the Wilderness* (London, Calcutta and Sima: W. Thacker and Co., 1915)

Muthesius, Herman, [1904–05] *The English House* (London: Crosby, Lockwood and Staples, 1979)

The New Survey of London Life and Labour, vol. 1: Forty years of change (London: P. S. King and Son, 1930)

Nicholson, Virginia, *Among the Bohemians: Experiments in living, 1900–1939* (London: Viking, 2002)

Olsen, Donald J., *The Growth of Victorian London* (London: Batsford, 1976)

Parrinder, Patrick, 'News from Nowhere, The Time Machine and the Break-Up of Classical Realism', *Science Fiction Studies*, 3 (1976), 265–274

Partington, John S., 'The Death of the Static: H. G. Wells and the kinetic utopia', *Utopian Studies* (2000), 96–111

Paxton, Nancy L., *Writing under the Raj: Gender, race, and rape in the British colonial imagination, 1830–1947* (New Brunswick, NJ and London: Rutgers University Press, 1999)

Pearsall, Ronald, *Edwardian Life and Leisure* (Newton Abbot: David and Charles, 1973)

Poole, Adrian, *Gissing in Context* (London: Macmillan, 1975)

Potter, Jane, '"A Great Purifier": The Great War in women's romances and memoirs, 1914–1918', in Suzanne Raitt and Trudi Tait, *Women's Fiction in the Great War* (Oxford: Oxford University Press, 1997), 85–106

Pugh, Edwin, *A Street in Suburbia* (London: Heinemann, 1895)

Pugh, Edwin, *The Broken Honeymoon* (London: John Milne, 1908)

Pugh, Edwin, [1908] *The City of the World: A book about London and the Londoner* (London: Nelson and Sons, 1912)

Pykett, Lyn, *The Improper Feminine: The women's sensational novel and the New Women writing* (London: Routledge, 1992)

Pykett, Lyn, *Engendering Fictions: The English novel in the twentieth century* (London: Edward Arnold, 1995)

Randall, Don, *Kipling's Imperial Boy: Adolescence and cultural hybridity* (Basingstoke: Palgrave, 2000)

Reeder, D. D., 'A Theatre of Suburbs: Some patterns of development in West London, 1801–1911' in H. J. Dyos (ed.), *The Study of Urban History* (London: Edward Arnold, 1968), 253–271

Richards, J. M., [1946] *Castles on the Ground: The anatomy of suburbia* (London: John Murray, 1973)

Ridge, W. Pett, *A Clever Wife* (London: Richard Bentley and Son, 1895)

Ridge, W. Pett, *Outside the Radius: Stories of a London suburb* (London: Hodder and Stoughton, 1899)

Ridge, W. Pett, *Mord Em'ly* (London: C. Arthur Pearson, 1901)

Rose, Jacqueline, *The Case of Peter Pan, or, The impossibility of children's fiction* (Basingstoke: Macmillan, 1984)

Rose, Jonathan, *The Intellectual Life of the British Working Classes* (New Haven and London: Yale University Press, 2001)

Ruck, Bertha, *A Story-Teller Tells the Truth: Reminiscences and notes* (London, 1935)

Rutherford, Mark, [1881/85] *Autobiography and Deliverance* (Leicester: Leicester University Press, 1969)

Said, Edward, *Culture and Imperialism* (London: Vintage, 1994)

Scruton, Roger, *England: An elegy* (London: Chatto and Windus, 2000)

Silverstone, Roger (ed.), *Visions of Suburbia* (London and New York: Routledge, 1997)

Smith, David C. (ed.), *The Correspondence of H. G. Wells, vol. 1, 1880–1903* (London: Pickering and Chatto, 1998)

Smith, Stan, *Edward Thomas* (London: Faber and Faber, 1986)

Taunt, Henry, [1872] *The Thames of Henry Taunt*, facsimile of 5th edition (1886) edited by Sue Read (Gloucester and Wolfeborough Falls: Alan Sutton, 1989)

Taunt, Henry, *The England of Henry Taunt, Victorian Photographer*, edited by Bryan Brown (London: Routledge and Kegan Paul, 1980)

Thomas, Edward, [1906] *The Heart of England* (Oxford: Oxford University Press, 1982)

Thomas, Edward, [1907] *The Pocket Book of Poems and Songs for the Open Air*, (London: Jonathan Cape, 1928)

Thomas, Edward, *Richard Jefferies: His life and work* (London: Hutchinson, 1909)

Thomas, Edward, [1911] *Light and Twilight* (Holt: Laurel Books, 2000)

Thomas, Edward, [1913] *The Happy-Go-Lucky Morgans*, with an introduction by Glen Cavaliero (Suffolk: Boydell Press, 1983)

Thomas, Edward, *Cloud Castle and Other Papers* (London: Duckworth and Co., 1922)

Thomas, Helen, [1926] *As It Was and World Without End* (London: Faber and Faber, 1972)

Thompson, E. P., *William Morris: Romantic to revolutionary* (New York: Pantheon Books, 1976)

Thompson, F. M. L. (ed.), *The Rise of Suburbia* (Leicester: Leicester University Press, 1982)

Trotter, David, *The English Novel in History 1895–1920* (London: Routledge, 1993)

Unwin, Raymond, *Town Planning and Practice: An introduction to the art of designing cities and suburbs* (London: Fisher Unwin, 1909)

Von Arnim, Elizabeth, [1898] *Elizabeth and Her German Garden*, with an introduction by Jane Howard (London: Virago, 1985)

Von Arnim, Elizabeth, [1899] *The Solitary Summer* (London: Virago, 1993)

Von Arnim, Elizabeth, [1922] *The Enchanted April* (London: Virago, 1986)

Warden, Florence, *City and Suburban* (London: F. V. White and Co., 1890)

Waters, Michael, *The Garden in Victorian Literature* (Aldershot: Scholar Press, 1988)

Weinroth, Michelle, *Reclaiming William Morris: Englishness, sublimity, and the rhetoric of dissent* (Montreal and Kingston, London and Buffalo: McGill-Queen's University Press, 1996)

Wells, H. G., *A Quartette of Comedies* (London: Ernest Benn, 1928), including [1900] *Love and Mr Lewisham*, [1905] *Kipps: The story of a simple soul* and [1910] *The History of Mr Polly*

Wells, H. G., *Anticipations of the Reaction of Mechanical and Scientific Progress upon Human Life and Thought* (London: Methuen, 1902)

Wells, H. G., [1905] *A Modern Utopia* (London: Everyman, 1994)

Wells, H. G., [1909] *Tono-Bungay* (London: Pan Books, 1978)

Wells, H. G., [1909] *Ann Veronica* (London: Virago, 1980)

Wells, H. G., [1911] *The New Machiavelli* (Harmondsworth: Penguin, 1978)

Wells, H. G., *The Work, Wealth and Happiness of Mankind* (London: Heinemann, 1932)

Wells, H. G., *Journalism and Prophecy, 1893–1946*, edited by W. Warren Waagar (London: Bodley Head, 1964)

Wells, H. G., *H. G. Wells's Literary Criticism*, edited by Patrick Parrinder and Robert Philmus (Brighton: Harvester Press, 1980)

Wells, H. G., *The Correspondence of H. G. Wells: Volume 1, 1880–1903* edited by David C. Smith (London: Pickering and Chatto, 1998)

White, Cynthia, *Women's Magazines, 1693–1968* (London: Joseph, 1970)

Wilde, Oscar, [1891] 'The Decay of Lying' in *The Works of Oscar Wilde*, edited by G. F. Maine (London and Glasgow: Collins, 1948), 909–931

Wilding, Michael, *Social Visions* (Sydney: Sydney Studies, 1993)

Williams, Mrs Leslie, *A Garden in the Suburbs* (London and New York: John Lane: Bodley Head, 1901)

Williams, Raymond, *Culture and Society* (Harmondsworth: Penguin, 1961).

Williams, Raymond, *The Country and the City* (London: Chatto and Windus, 1973)

Williams, Raymond, *Marxism and Literature* (Oxford: Oxford University Press 1977)

Wilson, Elizabeth, *A Sphinx in the City* (London: Virago, 1991)

INDEX

Note: 'n.' after a page reference indicates the number of a note on that page.